ALSO BY GLORIA VANDERBILT

Once Upon a Time: A True Story

Black Knight, White Knight

Black Knight, White Knight

Gloria Vanderbilt

SIDGWICK & JACKSON
LONDON

First published in Great Britain in 1987
by Sidgwick & Jackson Limited
1 Tavistock Chambers, Bloomsbury Way
London WC1A 2SG

First published in the United States of America
in 1987 by Alfred A Knopf, Inc.

ISBN 0–283–99542–4

Printed in Great Britain by
Adlard & Son Ltd, The Garden City Press,
Dorking, Surrey

To
Wyatt Emory Cooper
Always

Foreword

My first book, *Once Upon a Time: A True Story*, covers the years from my birth in 1924 to the age of seventeen, and this foreword reviews some of what took place in those years.

Although I was born into a family that had come to America in 1650, when Jan Aertsen Vanderbilt arrived from Holland to settle on Staten Island, it is only now that I feel in some ways connected to my family. Other ways not. My great-great-great-grandfather was Cornelius Vanderbilt, who went from ferry boating between Staten Island and Manhattan, at which he earned an adequate profit, to commodore-owner of a fleet of steamships that plied the world and made millions; long after the age when most people retire, he built a railroad network and an even larger fortune. He and his wife, Sophia Johnson Vanderbilt, had thirteen children, and he provided for his descendants with money left in trust for each when they reached the age of twenty-one. (My father, Reginald Claypoole Vanderbilt, was third generation from this union.) I have heard it said that the Commodore thought highly of the boys that were born to him, for he wanted to found an empire and a dynasty, and in his time it was the men of the family who were expected to fulfill such ambitions. The Vanderbilt women were taken care of with dispatch and married off as soon as possible. In 1872, however, towards the end of his life, he must have had a change of heart, for he supported Victoria Claflin Woodhull in her campaign for President of the United States on a ticket "advocating equal rights for women, a single standard of morality, free love but campaigning against prostitution and abortion."

On my mother's side of the family there was Laura Kilpatrick

Morgan, my grandmother, who had been born in Santiago, Chile, where her father, General Judson Kilpatrick, had served as American minister and where he had married Louisa Valdivieso, my great-grandmother. My grandmother was passionately obsessive in her pride of ancestry, a pride which was handed down to all her children. My mother's father, Harry Hays Morgan, was American consul at Lucerne, Switzerland, when my mother and her twin sister, Thelma, were born. He came from a long line of diplomats who had served their government well. My great-grandfather Philip Hickey Morgan was a judge of the Supreme Court of the State of Louisiana and was later appointed the first judge of the International Court of Alexandria in Egypt, and after that he was American minister to Mexico. My grandfather Morgan was born at Baton Rouge, where his family owned a plantation called The Aurora.

At the time of my birth, Grandpa and Grandmother Morgan were separated, and she lived with my mother and father in their house in New York at 12 East Seventy-seventh Street and summered with them at Sandy Point Farm in Newport, Rhode Island. In New York my paternal grandmother, Alice Gwynne Vanderbilt, lived nearby in a house on Fifth Avenue and in the summer months at The Breakers in Newport, and at that time there were close family ties among all members of the family. But although I was fourth-generation Vanderbilt, I felt removed from the reality of this—an Impostor, one might say, even before the Custody Trial between my mother and my father's sister Aunt Gertrude Vanderbilt Whitney. Perhaps because I was seventeen months old when my father died, and, soon after, my twenty-year-old mother moved to Europe to live permanently with her mother, Laura Kilpatrick Morgan, and my nurse, Emma Keislich (Dodo), who had been with me since birth. In any event, my mother saw no reason to maintain ties with America—after all, her father had been a diplomat posted at various capitals in Europe, and her life had always been there. As for my father's life in Newport, that of horses, breeding and showing for championship, my mother had no interest in these pursuits after he died. Nor did the social life of New York have the appeal of the Continent. Although she did not inherit money from my father, whose trust had been spent (champion horses can be an expensive proposition), there was plenty to live well on from the income that came from a trust that I would inherit when I became of age. Perhaps my father's side of the family across the sea seemed remote and unreal to me because I knew of their existence only later through the tales I heard told to me by my Grandmother Morgan and Dodo and did not meet them until I was eight. By then it was too late to transplant roots which already had taken firm hold in the love I received from my Grandmother Morgan and Dodo, who were to me my *real* family.

My mother—so young, so beautiful—wanted to have a good time, and what better place than Paris in the twenties, in a house on the rue Alfred Roll. She went out a lot, but I was happy, for I had my Grandmother Morgan, whom I called Naney (but some-times the Little Countess, which was what Dodo called her), and of course Dodo herself, whom I loved more than anything and whom I called Big Elephant, because she was big and fat and put her arms around me like a big trunk when she rocked me back and forth. *They* didn't go out—they were there all the time. It was like having two mothers, really: Naney and Dodo. And as for my own mother, it got complicated. Not only did I not see much of her—there was her identical twin, Thelma, to con-tend with. She had married an English lord and was now Vis-countess Marmaduke Furness, but I called her Aunt Toto. When I did see the Twins together, it was quite perplexing trying to tell one from the other. But I got around it, more or less, as I got older, after going through my mother's closets on the top floor of our house on the rue Alfred Roll. There I would memorize her clothes, hats, and shoes, because although she and Aunt Toto looked exactly alike, they were grown-ups, and grown-ups don't dress alike.

Anyway—after my father died, there we all were, settled in

Europe. We moved around a good deal, though, living in rented houses in Paris, or traveling to hotels in Monte Carlo or Biarritz or London, sometimes elsewhere. As a child has nothing to which she can compare the situation, none of this seemed strange or unusual to me. It did not seem strange that I had no father, for in truth I didn't know what a father meant, nor did it seem strange that Naney Morgan and Dodo became surrogate mothers to me. As for my mother, she remained a figure of luminous beauty glimpsed fleetingly as I would see her disappearing, exquisitely gowned, down the long corridors of those many hotels we always seemed to be drifting to and from. Where was she going? And when would she return? But most frightening of all—would I ever see her again? How I longed to merge with her, into the beauty of her—for to understand the mystery of her would be to understand the secret of myself.

But I was always in pursuit, and she was forever in flight, and so instead a trio came to be: Naney, Dodo, and me—"You and I together, Love—Never mind the weather, Love" was the song we'd sing as we took off through the Champs-Elysées on an April afternoon. That was my family and I was happy, for no matter where we traveled we were safe and fast together in a Caravan. That was *real* (even though the Caravan was a place that existed only in my imagination), and no harm could come as long as we three remained together.

But one day everything started to change—it was as if some terrible nameless fear seeped into the Caravan. Until then, there had been no men around to consider seriously, for my mother had many friends. But one day she met a German prince—Prince Friedel Hohenlohe—and they fell in love. When this happened, Naney went quite crazed. Not only did she not like him at all, but if my mother married him as she intended to, it would mean that I would be taken to Germany to live and be raised as a German far from my own country, America, far from my father's people, where I rightly belonged. Naney's father had been the Civil War general Judson Kilpatrick. Ah, darling mine—if only

I'd been born a man! she'd say to me, and indeed there was much of the Napoleon in her nature. My mother, who had been relieved no doubt that Naney and Dodo were there to look after me, since it left her freer to do the things she wanted to do, was now faced with the force of Naney's opposition, but she let it slide by, or perhaps it never occurred to her that plots and subplots were gradually being set—unfolding, leading on slowly but relentlessly to that inevitable day of the Custody Trial when everything crashed around us.

What better person, who more powerful, than Aunt Gertrude, my father's older sister, to trigger these events, as Naney became more and more obsessed with the idea that it was with Aunt Gertrude I should live and so become part of the heritage that rightly belonged to me? She agitated and planned, until it came to be, when I was eight, that I did go to America to visit Aunt Gertrude. She was unknown to me until that summer when I stayed with her in Old Westbury on Long Island—a place I called her Kingdom, for her estate was a continent unto itself, requiring a retinue of over a hundred full-time employees to care for farm and stables. There were race horses, Angus and Guernsey dairy herds to tend, guinea hens, ducks, turkeys, chickens, and squabs. There were cooks, butlers, housemen, maids, stableboys, grooms, horse trainers, gardeners and greenhouse men, painters, carpenters, and electricians, and men to maintain the sewage system and roads. There were indoor and outdoor tennis courts and swimming pools, meadows and forests with curving roads and driveways leading to Aunt Gertrude's house and the other houses, where Aunt Gertrude's grown-up children lived with their families.

My mother didn't question (was relieved even, perhaps) when Naney and Dodo took me across the ocean for this visit. Could she have been so unaware that long before this Naney had been working with the energy of the fanatic towards goals she had set for me? Was my mother so out of touch that she was unaware that Naney kept telling me fearful things about Germany, stories about Prince Friedel and the German castle, Schloss Langenburg, where he and his family had lived for centuries? It was there I would be taken to live and never see her or Dodo again, ever. Then there were the days when I overheard things Naney whispered to Dodo, just loud enough for me to hear—things about her daughter, my mother, things I couldn't understand—seesawing me back and forth, torn apart by the longing to be close to my mother yet every day becoming more and more suspicious and afraid of her.

And soon after this visit to Aunt Gertrude I overheard Consuelo-Tamar, my mother's older sister, saying to my mother that Big Elephant should be sent away because I was becoming too attached to her and Prince Friedel would find a German Fräulein to take her place—the timing was perfect, so perfect Naney herself couldn't have planned it better. I pleaded in desperation with Naney not to let this terrible thing happen. She tried to calm me, told me that only if I continued to live with Aunt Gertrude would Dodo be permitted to stay with me, never leave me, but it was important that no one know this was the real reason I wanted to live with Aunt Gertrude. I would have done anything, said anything, to keep Dodo with me, so I went along with what my Aunt Gertrude's lawyers coached me to say, even though I didn't understand what was really going on. All I understood was that this was the key to keeping our trio together, our Caravan. I knew they couldn't send Naney Morgan away, because we were related, but Dodo—that was another matter.

There was no one to talk to about the things they said—that my mother was unfit, unfit to have me live with her. And so it led to a Custody Trial between Aunt Gertrude and my mother, and there were headlines in newspapers all over the country about what was happening. It was in the 1930s, during the Depression, and it captured people's imagination very much the way a television series like "Dynasty" does in this present day—although to us it was not a story about people we didn't know; it was about us. I begged the Judge to let me stay with my Aunt

Gertrude, not daring to tell him the real reason I wanted to, which was to keep the one security I had—Big Elephant. Letters Naney had coached me to write against my mother were brought into the testimony and the trial went on and on—it seemed to me forever.

But the day did come, the day the Judge handed down his decision. Yes, I was to remain with Aunt Gertrude, but Dodo was to be sent away. I was never to see her again, never be in touch with her again. My mother's lawyer had told the Judge it was she who had influenced me against my mother (no mention of Naney Morgan's part in the matter). It was like being part of some terrible accident boomeranging me into a tidal wave of churning sand and seaweed, and I thought death had come to me. But I had the will to live, to survive, and I knew I wouldn't give up—ever—and I wouldn't die, because I knew without having the words for it then, I knew that finally I was alone, as we all are alone, and that it was up to me to find within my own spirit the determination, the energy, but most of all the trust and belief in myself to put things right, even if it would take me forever.

So there it was, the Judge's decision that we all had to live with, each in his own way. But still it went on and on, for my mother kept appealing the case, failing every time to win. The Court allowed me to see my mother on weekends at her rented house in New York and for the month of July at one rented house or another in the country. (Why was she good weekends and not good between?) I was torn apart, not knowing what to feel, becoming more wary and frightened of her, yet longing to love her and be close to her. I also longed to be close to Auntie Ger, and I know by letters she wrote to me, letters expressing her love, that she loved me, and I now realize how hard it must have been on her (that most private of persons) to go through the Custody Trial. Yet, if in letters her words were those of love, in person she remained aloof, a different woman. I felt that she wanted to be close to me as much as I wanted to be close to her, and perhaps to her way of thinking we were. After all, she was of the Edwardian period, when children were "seen and not heard," and she extended herself to me as much as it was possible within her nature to do. But it was difficult to talk to her about things, unthinkable to ever mention my mother or the Custody Trial, for it was made clear from the beginning that any questions I had should be relayed to her through her lawyer, Mr. Crocker, or through my legal guardian, Mr. Gilchrist.

It has been said that as the twig is bent, so grows the tree—and when we are born, it is from those around us that we learn not only who we are but what we *can* be. They are our mirror—and if the mirror is distorted, it is as if we are looking into one of those curved mirrors in a fun fair. Unbalanced, we totter away (is *that* what we really look like?), for without the supportive image reflected back to us from the beginning, it takes us longer to find the truth of ourselves.

And so I come to Winter Austin Smith III, the young man I fell in love with when I was fifteen and whose love gave me a mirror reflection of myself that gave me self-esteem. He was a most important person in my life, a junior at Yale when we met, and we had high hopes and dreams of someday making our future together. But Naney would have none of this, for she had her own plans for me—that I would make a marriage of richness that would lead to more power. It was her belief that love existed only with one's own "flesh and blood," and that marriage was a serious matter of convenience only—love didn't enter into it. Aunt Gertrude wasn't too encouraging either, but Winter and I held fast to each other until things happened between us: things changed.

Yet it was through him that I started to have some sense of myself, but even before this, within myself, I had found courage to speak up, asking the lawyers if they thought Aunt Gertrude and the Court would agree to permit my mother and me to be more spontaneous regarding the times we saw each other and not on the rigid dates the Court decreed. I felt a great surge of hope when this new arrangement was granted—perhaps now my mother and I would get to know each other, become closer.

Then in June 1941 I went for a few weeks to visit my mother and Aunt Toto in Beverly Hills, California, where they lived in a rented house on North Maple Drive with Aunt Toto's twelve-year-old son, Tony. From the day I arrived I felt very much like a bird let out of a cage—for at Aunt Gertrude's, life was framed by chaperones (especially the po-faced Constance) who accompanied me on dates to parties—everywhere—quite unshakable! But after all, what could Aunt Gertrude do? The Court was my legal guardian until I was twenty-one, and Aunt Gertrude had to be most circumspect so as not to be criticized in her care of me, criticized as my mother had been. And although The Constonce had accompanied me on this visit to my mother, she left soon after we arrived, finding no place in the easy ways of the household on North Maple Drive.

Black Knight, White Knight starts in June of 1941, where *Once Upon a Time* ended. In it you'll meet a girl of seventeen, with the things I have just described already behind her. Yet not behind her—for there was not a day that passed in which they were forgotten, not a day when these events did not in some way infiltrate her mind as she struggled to be free. . . .

But now it's time to let her speak for herself.

Black Knight, White Knight

The House on Maple Drive, July 1941

Every morning when I wake up the first thing I do is pinch myself, because I can't believe that I'm really here living with my mother in this house on Maple Drive in Beverly Hills, California. I don't have to go to school and I don't have to have The Constonce chaperoning me and I don't have to abide by Aunt Gertrude's rules and regulations. I don't have to do anything except what I want to do, because my mother lets me come and go as I please with never a question, so you can see why I hate the thought of going back to Aunt Gertrude. I try not to think about that inescapable day and pretend that this heaven will never end. My mother thinks I'm really grown-up (at least I think she does), so if she thinks I am I must be. It's silly anyway, isn't it? How most people think you aren't grown-up until you're twenty-one when it can happen earlier, much earlier, like it has to me right now at seventeen. And so fast, the minute I got away from Aunt Ger—overnight, as they say, or like a bird let out of a cage. And soon I'll feel really at home here and not like an Impostor. Not that I do—after all, she is my mother, so I have every right to be here visiting her, but it's all so incredible that I keep worrying I won't be beautiful enough, or something enough, to be deemed worthy: to belong.

In some ways this house is not unlike Burrough Court, the house in England near Melton Mowbray in Leicestershire where Aunt Toto lived when she was married to Lord Furness. It's gone now, that house, burned accidentally while the Canadian Air Force was billeted there. Everything's gone: the Waterford chandeliers, the festive gatherings in the great hall . . . the room where I sat when I was six, listening to Big Elephant dictating a letter, that fatal letter planned by Naney Morgan but written in my own hand, later to be used against my mother in the Custody Trial. In it I was told to say my mother was "a rare beast," spelled out for me as "bease" so it would have the ring of a child's truth . . . gone that room, burned to the ground as if it had never existed. But it does . . . in the maze of my brain somewhere, just as it was reflected that day in the mirror over the mantel.

My mother and Aunt Toto don't seem to mind, though, that the house is gone. After all, they have each other, or maybe it's because they never stay in any one place too long, that way they don't get attached to things—perhaps that's why it doesn't upset them, for they talk about this and the war in the most singsong way. They don't seem to have the knack of holding on to a home. They discard houses as sea creatures abandon inhabited shells, taking with them what they will: the pear-shaped diamond engagement ring, pearls from Grandma Vanderbilt strung into a necklace—the one my mother used to dip in seawater when sojourning in Monte Carlo, to refresh, she said. Then there are the huge silver trophy cups won by my father's champion horses, engraved with names like "Tiger Lillie," "White Oak Maid," and "Fortitude," and other silver enjoyed every day, tea sets and flat silver, china too. But what of Aunt Toto's black pearls the size of plover's eggs? I haven't seen her wear them since I got here.

Of course, the house we are in now isn't really like Burrough at all, it's just built in the style of an English Tudor house to convey, no doubt, an air of the past and give some sort of permanence to the present. But all the houses around us are like that, so take your pick—there are Spanish haciendas, New England farmhouses, and Moorish pagodas, even a replica two blocks away of the gingerbread house of Hansel and Gretel. (Who lives

inside is another story.) In a ranch-style house across the street from us live George Burns and Gracie Allen, but I've never seen them or any of our other neighbors, even though the houses are all so close together. There are also endless varieties of trees— tropical palms side by side with northern pines, other trees I don't know the names of—and around each house all manner of flowers planted in varying patterns, and behind each house there are more trees and more flowers, with a swimming pool set in each garden. Yes, it is paradise—sort of.

Maple Manor, although it's a rented house, doesn't appear to be once inside. For even if Mummy and Aunt Toto haven't permanent roots, there are things here and there, everywhere I look, that have at one time or another been in a house they have lived in somewhere, so the effect is very much theirs. There are photographs around on tables in chased silver frames, and my father's goblets of silver for cocktails, with his usual stylized monogram, an acorn engraved above it. This acorn is on all of the family appointments, not only silver, but linens, crystal, and china. It was worked long ago into a crest when Commodore Vanderbilt took it upon himself to invent one for the family inspired by the motto "From little acorns mighty oaks do grow." In my mother's bedroom on the bureau (as always), the picture of my father in its silver frame, again with monogram and crest. And in the living room, as always: the portrait by Dana Pond painted of my mother when she and my father were in Paris at the Ritz Hotel on their honeymoon. There she stands, tall so tall and thin so thin, in a sleeveless Madeleine Vionnet dress of black velvet with silver bands circled low around her waist, holding an ostrich fan of cadmium green, just so, that almost touches the floor. Aunt Toto, I'm told, had an identical dress but in white velvet, and fan of what color, I wonder? She was eighteen when it was painted, and this image has been part of me ever since I can remember. She was just a year older than I am right this minute, so I better hurry up, hadn't I? I've only one year left to grow up to be as beautiful as she is.

The Garden Party

Since the party yesterday the phone hasn't stopped ringing, so I guess I did the right thing changing at the last minute into the pink instead of wearing the black with the V neck. It looked babyish beyond belief hanging there in my closet, sort of a pink thing with ruffles and tea roses, but once I put it on there was a certain "je ne sais quoi" about it, as The Constonce would say, a rosy freshness that impressed even my mother and Aunt Toto (at least I think it did). Anyway, I was sure they were going to wear black, and who wants to be a copycat, which is really why I decided on the pink at the last minute just as the guests were starting to arrive. I was frantic, because Mummy wanted me to be in the receiving line with her and it was so late I knew I'd never make it and it was something, I can tell you, getting down those stairs to the front hall, because I had these *impossible* shoes to cope with. They were bought especially for the occasion and have the tallest, spikiest heels ever, so it's like walking on stilts. Then as I maneuvered myself on down I could see my mother wasn't in black at all but in frothy white, in a dress that looked as if it had been made of flowers strung together, those flowers called Queen Anne's lace, and standing there beside her was Aunt Toto in something yellow, all petally like a jonquil. Their skins shone so pale and the crimson of their lips so red and they stood there like queens in a fairy tale with guests fluttering around them in hues bright as flowers, but none so beautiful as the Queen Anne of Lace and the Queen Jonquil. Bedazzled, I just stood there gazing at them when suddenly my mother looked up and saw me.

Oh, there you are, darling! she called gaily. Come down and join us, come meet Louella Parsons. And she introduced me to a fat short person next to her who peered up at me rather like a walrus at the zoo.

So this is Little Gloria, it said.

Oh, Lolly! the Queen Anne protested. Soon it will be Young Gloria and Old Gloria, which they both thought most amusing.

Of course I didn't. Mummy had taken to saying this quite often lately, and I shook Miss Parsons' hand pretending I hadn't heard. Then the Lolly person said to a man beside her, Dockie, Dockie, this is Little Gloria. My mother patted Dockie's arm and said to me, Gloria, may I present Doctor Martin.

He shook my hand in a cross-eyed, confused way, muttering something. But nobody paid attention and he faded away. Guests were now drifting out into the garden, but even the men didn't look out of place among the flower faces of the women as they came from the house onto the lawn. Everyone talked and moved about as mortals do, but surely they were not: they were lords and ladies and knights in shining armor, and the Queen Anne of Lace kept bringing one or another up to meet me, and it was all I could do to keep my head about me and speak up when spoken to.

The plump porpoise spooking around the fringes of the flower beds was Aunt Toto's son, Cousin Tony. He was twelve years old and had come from England when the war started to live at Maple Manor for the duration. He occupied himself inspecting the empty glasses here and there to see if bits of cocktails had been left, taking sips and making toasts to no one in particular. Next day he was flat out. Must be the heat, Aunt Toto said, and it was left at that.

Suddenly a purple mouth pushed its way towards me with urgent news. It was a woman, but her face was close to me, too close, so that it was only her mouth I saw, and it was as if frost had touched me.

I'm Agnes—Agnes! she said, trying to make herself heard above the other voices. Purple lipstick had bled onto her teeth, and her mouth opened and closed like a carnivorous flower. I have to talk to you, talk to you, things to tell you—school, school! School with the twins, convent school, Sacred Heart Convent School.

And I remembered. Paris . . . it was Agnes Horter, who had been at the convent school with my mother and Aunt Toto in New York, and later she had come to Paris hoping to be a chanteuse and sometimes she came to the house where we lived on the rue Alfred Roll to manicure my mother's and Aunt Toto's nails. I hadn't known she was here, hadn't thought of her since then. There was something about her that frightened me. I pulled away from her, but someone took my arm: it was Phil Kellogg and behind him coming towards us I saw Errol Flynn. Make her stop, the purple mouth stop, I wanted to say to Phil, but she had gone and Errol Flynn was introducing himself. I couldn't take my eyes off his emerald green tie—it couldn't be the same one he had worn years ago at the *Wizard of Oz* party—or could it? And could it be really true that it was me, standing in my mother's house on Maple Drive among flowers here in her garden, just as though I belonged? And not only that—my mother, the Queen Anne of Lace, had arranged this party especially for me!

How would *they* be in this garden? Big Elephant, the Little Countess, Winter Austin Smith? But their faces wouldn't come to me. All that came to me about them were things I couldn't see—the sweet softness of Big Elephant as her arms held me, the scent of Naney Morgan's handkerchief, things like that, and as for Winter it was only the sound of the rain on the roof of the Cottage that I heard. And Aunt Gertrude? That hat she always wore was the only thing I could remember. And what of places? Old Westbury Capital—the Caravan—they too had disappeared, and the only place that was real was this garden, and the only face I saw full plain was that of my mother as she stood far away across the lawn waving to someone . . . me? I raised my hand in answer, and as I did a rainbow arched between us high above the garden, plunging me in light.

Next day, not only Cousin Tony was exhausted. Ditto the Queens—they didn't even make it down to the porch for the usual lunch at two o'clock.

As for me, I'd been too excited to sleep and spent a good part of the night on the edge of the bathtub, soaking feet in hot water, dreaming about the party and looking at Winter Smith's photograph. His picture had been with me on my bureau at Wheeler next to photographs of Big Elephant, Naney Morgan, Aunt Ger, and my mother, and my little gallery of loved ones had accompanied me on this journey to Hollywood. But now, as my feet eased into the blessed heat, I looked at the stranger who smiled out from the burgundy leather frame, amazed that I hadn't noticed until now how young he was—yes, babyish even.

Later, when I padded down the stairs to survey the scene of last evening's triumphs, there were still traces here and there of the party: furniture pulled into unaccustomed groupings, pillows squashed, and on a coffee table a bit-into canapé pushed under an ashtray. Trusty Wannsie, who'd been with my mother for ages and ages, was cheerily tidying up, directing with gusto the helpers who had come to assist her, for it was only Wannsie who knew where this and that went, and everything had to be put back in its right place, just so. Still, there had been no major mishaps—no cigarette burns on the rug or that sort of thing. I looked over at the piano. It was still there, and I went and stood next to it, on the very spot I'd been last night when Agnes had followed me in from the garden trying to tell me something. . . .

Then I went on into the kitchen to get yogurt from the icebox. Cook Katya made bowls fresh every day for breakfast, and I dribbled honey over it and went outside to sit on the grass under the mulberry tree. Far away, a water sprinkler twirled over the begonias at the edge of the garden. It circled around and around, and after a while I looked up at my mother's window on the second floor. The shades were pulled down, and I knew that inside, the curtains would be drawn against the light. Mummy couldn't sleep unless the room was as dark as dark could be, and I closed my eyes imagining myself there with her in the room. Her radio would be turned on, because Mummy never could rest without the sound of it playing in the background, softly, all through the night. What song would be on at this moment? Perhaps that jingle for the new drive-in on La Ciencga: "Good morning, Friends! we recommend Blue Plate Number Two. Our food is the best in the whole wide West—what can we do for you?" What indeed!

Although I couldn't see Aunt Toto's window from where I sat, I sauntered, in my fancy, on across the hall from my mother's room, past my door, which I'd left open, on into her room. It was all chintzy yellow and English country, this room, whereas my mother's room was more of the Vieux Paris genre. If these rooms happened to be in the sky, Aunt Toto's room would be a

Sun Room and my mother's would be a Moon Room. I liked Aunt Toto's room a lot—not that I got to see it that often, because most of the time she and her movie star friend Edmund Lowe were closeted there and didn't want to be disturbed. I wondered if he was there now. He was shooting a picture and would have left at dawn to go to the studio. Had he absent-mindedly forgotten his pipe on the night table as he gazed lovingly for a moment at Aunt Toto while she slept, before hurrying on down the stairs? Her hair would be spread out on the pillow, and so would my mother's, for she had grown it long again: it would be tangled on sheets of palest blue crêpe de Chine that I knew were on her bed. Did she lie on her side, face half-hidden, makeup still on from the party, a robe thrown carelessly on the floor? . . . Was she alone?

A phone kept ringing and ringing from the house next door, but then it stopped and Wannsie came towards me across the lawn calling, It's Mr. Flynn, Miss Gloria, for you on the telephone.

Tell him Maid Marian has gone out somewhere, I called back to her. On the lawn I could see the foot marks of yesterday, from the party. So it had been real: the knights in shining armor standing here, and the flower ladies fair . . . the Jonquil Queen . . . and my mother in her gown of Queen Anne's lace . . . and the rainbow? Yes—the rainbow was the *realest* of all those unreal things. I mustn't hesitate, and I leaned over to trace a footprint in the grass beside me. Why, of course! My palm fitted, exactly.

Tony has wandered out to where I'm sitting by the pool. He is wearing that ridiculous cap Aunt Toto insists on. His hair is taffy-colored, and Aunt Toto often remarks, as if she just thought of it, Why, look at his little face, it's like the map of England! The cap over the map is made of hair net, and it's to make his hair grow back off his forehead instead of flopping over the way it wants to naturally. He loathes it, of course, but every time he goes in swimming without it Aunt Toto spots it and it's got to go back on again. Then, times he does have it on, she's away somewhere and doesn't show up at all. I feel sorry for him, not only because of that cap but because he's going through the same fatness stage I did at twelve. From time to time Aunt Toto remarks to my mother it might not be a bad idea to send him to that military school in San Fernando Valley, the one Melsing Meredith goes to. Meanwhile, the plump porpoise smarts from too much sun as he buoys around alone in the pool. He's acquired quite a stammer too, quite like I used to have. I'd like to talk to him more, but it's uneasy, and anyway I can't think of a thing except that soon this time will be over, soon I'll have to go back to Aunt Gertrude's. That's all I think about: Do I dare? Do I dare say to her—Mummy, please, do I have to go back?

The phone rings all day long, mostly with calls for me inviting me out to dinners and dances. But Phil Kellogg is the person I most want to see. He's got problems with a girl called Sue Barrow who's crazy about him, and he was seeing a lot of her until I appeared on the scene. Phil hadn't set eyes on me since that summer when I was thirteen visiting with my mother out here in Hollywood, although we have written to each other since then, and now here I am back again, only it's all different, because I'm seventeen and grown-up and he's fallen in love with me. I am grown-up, aren't I? I do everything possible to appear so, and Big Elephant always did comment on what she calls my "poise."

Anyway, Phil and I see a lot of each other, and I try not to think about Auntie Ger. Or Winter Smith and the letters that keep arriving from him, letters which so far I haven't answered. It gives me a twinge when I see them, on that stationery of his, grey with the faint lines patterned in checks over the page, engraved at the top in red: Winter Austin Smith III. Every time I caught sight of that familiar handwriting in my mailbox at Wheeler, my heart was like a singing bird, but that seems a

hundred years ago and now it only fills me with panic. I hide
them in odd places unopened, hoping I'll forget where I put
them. But no such luck. It only postpones the fateful moment
when I'll have to read them. Lately, however, even when I'm not
looking at his photograph, his face pops up here and there. It's
spooky but I can't stop it. Like yesterday on the beach with Phil
I was doodling a silly face in the sand and suddenly it started
looking like a portrait of Winter! A sand portrait, you might
say—but I scrambled it away before the resemblance really caught
on. He's called long distance more than eight times, but I keep
telling Wannsie to say I'm out. He's spoiling all the fun, he

really is, and I wish he'd stop stop stop, because even if I did go back to Old Westbury Capital, even without Aunt Gertrude's rules and regulations, even if things there were different, it wouldn't matter, for I'll never get closer to Paradise than I am right now, here at Maple Manor, in the presence of the Queen Anne of Lace, in a garden of flowers who turn out to be grown-ups, and bells tinkling through the livelong day with messages from knights in shining armor just for me.

Conundrum

And now that I am here in the garden of the Queen Anne of Lace, where is the Caravan? Does it exist even without Big Elephant and the Little Countess? Without the three of us—You and I together, Love—Never mind the weather, Love?

Right this minute I believe the Caravan does exist and that I am alone in it here in this garden. But will that suffice? I think not. I tremble for the knock on the door that will come, but from whom or what I cannot say; a longing fills me, a yearning and searching for something I have no name for. From somewhere the tinny sound of a barrel organ comes and around it goes in my head and oh! so faintly in the background a muffled song:

> *Lady Moon, Lady Moon, where are you roving?*
> *Over the sea.*
> *Lady Moon, Lady Moon, whom are you loving?*
> *All that love me!*

Lady Moon must be my mother. But she's not here with me in the Caravan, of that I am certain. No, I am alone here, but outside, in the garden, someone is waiting for me. Who is it? I have to know. Soon I won't be able to wait a minute longer to find out.

Family Gatherings

Uncle Harry lives on Walden Drive in a house near my mother's. The Angustias person he used to be with is no longer around because he has married someone called Mrs. Arnold, Edith. No one's actually said it, but hovering about somewhere in the air is money money money, and this Edith person has heaps of it. She also has a daughter, Virginia Arnold, who lives with them. So does Edith's and Uncle Harry's child, who has been named after Aunt Toto and is known as Little Thelma (God help her) and she's six years old. I haven't met them yet, but later today my mother and Aunt Thelma are taking Tony and me to their house for drinks and a swim in their pool. I haven't seen Uncle Harry since the beach at Monte Carlo and I keep wondering if he still looks as much like his mother, my Naney Morgan, as he did then. Of course, he doesn't speak to the Little Countess since the Custody Trial. My mother and Aunt Thelma don't, either. Nobody speaks to anybody. Maybe he won't speak to me, either, maybe he'll be like Aunt Consuelo-Tamar who blames me for all of it and cuts me dead.

Well, we all got there in my mother's car. She and Aunt Thelma don't know how to drive and have no interest in it whatsoever because they know there'll always be someone or other around to drive for them. Right now it's a car and a part-time chauffeur. Not that Mummy goes out that often during the day except for a lunch now and again with Doris Stein or Cobina Wright. Aunt Thelma goes out more—to the Wally Westmore hairdressers mainly, with someone between times coming to Maple Drive to tend hands and feet.

There was quite a crowd at Uncle Harry's—more like a cocktail party than the family gathering I expected. Uncle Harry said hello to me but quite coolly, as if something had happened, and then I was introduced to Mrs. Arnold—I mean Mrs. Morgan, whom I was to call Aunt Edith. Aunt Edith Aunt Edith Aunt, it's an odd sound on my lips, but I'll get used to it when I see more of her. She was in a black dress, oh so quiet, with dark hair curving around her face in soft waves, and I didn't once see her smile.

As for Uncle Harry, he looks more like Naney Morgan than ever. It's quite startling. All he needs is a henna wig and a dress and at a distance you couldn't tell one from the other. I'd forgotten he's even the same height as the Little Countess.

Virginia Arnold is about my age and very pretty. Friendly too, and we are going to go on a double date together tomorrow night: me with Phil Kellogg, and Virginia with a boy she's got a crush on called Wayne something or other.

Little Thelma darted about wearing a two-piece bathing suit over the sliver of her body. She has hair like Mother Edith's but has escaped inheriting the Morgan nose which is centered so prominently on the faces of Uncle Harry and Aunt Consuelo-Tamar. She sang quite loudly to herself as she jumped in and out of the pool, over and over again—"Mares Eat Oats and Does Eat Oats and Little Lambs eat ivy, kid'll eat ivy too wouldn't you?" That was her favorite, and some of the grown-ups thought it cute for a minute, but it got rather trying after a while, and it wasn't long before someone bustled out of the house and took her away.

Tony changed into his bathing suit the minute we got there and dove in sans the hated cap. He was betting on Aunt Toto being chitchatty elsewhere so it would go unnoticed. And for a while it did. Then, just as he thought he was home free, Aunt Toto spotted him and without putting her drink down strode right up to the edge of the pool, leaning so far over I thought she was going to fall right on top of him.

Tony—where's your cap?

Mumm-mmmum-mum-mmmmy, he sputtered, I lef-ft it—h-h-ho-home.

This information didn't please her one bit, and just when I was sure she was going to insist he march straight back to Maple Drive and get it, a waiter sallied by with a tray of drinks, and without saying another word Aunt Thelma put her drink on it and took another one and moved over to where my mother stood talking to one of the Dolly Sisters. Tony kept looking over at his mother even though her back was turned towards him, and if his face hadn't already been wet from swimming I would have thought it was covered with tears.

What are you going to wear tomorrow night? I asked Virginia. And for the rest of the time we occupied ourselves over these pressing questions. Come up to my room, she said, and I'll show you my eyelash curler. I had never seen one before. She clamped it over her lashes and said, I hold it like this and count to forty, slowly—but if it's a really important date count to sixty—after that, give it a few squeezes just to make sure. It was an astonishing piece of information, and I couldn't wait to get one. Her array of makeup is an amazement, with the pinky tones separated from the corally shades because, she said, of course no one would wear pinky makeup with an orange dress. Oh, perish the thought! I said quickly, although it was news to me. No wonder she was so beguiling. Maybe later she'll show me how to use the sponges and sticks of color—there wasn't time then, because Tony bounded into her room panting from running up the stairs with an important message: his mother and my mother wanted to leave and to hurry hurry up so they wouldn't be kept waiting. We rushed down, which turned out to be for naught, because both mothers had drifted into conversations with a group of new arrivals, and it was ages and ages before we finally did pile in the car to go home.

It was dark by then, and Wannsie had spread out an impromptu cold supper in the dining room. Tony and I sat around the oval mahogany table listening to my mother and Aunt Thelma gossiping in a fuzzy way about who was at Uncle Harry's and so on, but they weren't making much sense out of it, and after a while it got very boring and I went up to my room and sprawled out on the bed.

Oh well, this was as good a moment as any, and all around me on the coverlet I spread a fan of all the letters Winter had written to me since I'd last seen him. It was quite a guilty array . . . but nothing like the guilt after I had opened and read them. Time passed and after a while I took gobs of my GLMV stationery and with all the flourish I could muster wrote on an envelope Mr. Winter Austin Smith III, and his address, neat as could be. I stuck an airmail stamp in the upper-right-hand corner, but it landed askew, too near the top. Redo it? No, best press on; July 6, 1941, I wrote on the blank stationery, and under it:

Darling Darling Winter,
    It's hard but I'm going to try and tell you exactly how I really feel

But that's as far as I got. The words wouldn't come, and I sat looking at the page not knowing how I felt, not knowing anything about anything, only that I had to tell someone, and if not him—who?

    I don't know what Phil said to Sue Barrow, but whatever it was she's out of the picture and now I'll be seeing Phil more and more (I hope!). This Saturday he's taking me to the Beverly Hills Hotel to have lunch by the pool. *What* am I going to wear? He's seen me in just about everything. Best not to ask what he said to Sue. Phil's so kindhearted, and if you can believe Veneta Oakey, Sue is the type who wouldn't let go ("twenty-eight and itching to be married," according to catty Mrs. Oakey), plus she says Sue's mother drinks like a fish and lives in Pasadena. What Pasadena has to do with it I don't know, but that's the gist of her opinion on the Sue-Phil situation, which comes up if I run into her when she drifts by Maple Manor for gossip and cocktails,

as is her wont, around five most afternoons. Sometimes Melba Meredith drops by too, but no sign of Agnes Orchid since the party. Queen Anne and Queen Jonquil don't seem to be too keen on seeing her again, and for the moment she's out of the picture along with Sue and Errol. He's the one *I* have no interest in (although he keeps on calling)—after all, who needs Robin Hood with Phil Kellogg close by? But the one I am curious about is Agnes. Tell me about Agnes Horter, I said.

What about her? Mummy said.

Well, you know—what does she do all day?

What does *that* mean? Aunt Toto said, looking over at Mummy.

Oh, poor Agnes, Mummy murmured hazily as Aunt Toto made a little moue of her mouth without commenting.

The queens looked at each other and gave little sighs both at the same time before going back to their royal knitting.

Ketti Keven lives in an apartment somewhere on Sunset Strip, the same one she lived in when I met her that summer I was thirteen. I haven't seen it since then, but my mother goes there a lot. Sometimes she stays overnight, but when she does she never takes a suitcase with her. I guess it's because when she goes there it's just for dinner, but then it gets later and later, and even though Ketti knows how to drive and has her own car, well, I guess it just gets too late to risk the roads, so my mother stays over. Sometimes she doesn't get back until long after lunch the next day. When she does get home, usually she's so exhausted she takes to her bed and Wannsie brings dinner up to her on a tray. Today she came back just as Phil and I were on our way out. Oh, good morning, darling, she said, as though it was dawn instead of eight o'clock in the evening and starting to get dark. Maybe it's a strain on her, my being here. What with Aunt Thelma, who has Tony on her hands, and now my mother with me underfoot as well, maybe—maybe, she wants me to leave, maybe it's time for me to go back to Old Westbury Capital. Is it is it is it is it . . . time for me to go back to Aunt Gertrude?

Veronica Lake

The night Phil was having the final heart-to-heart with Sue, I found myself at the strangest place. How I happened to end up there is a long story, and considering everything it's surprising that when I found myself there I still had the floppy white picture hat on my head just as it had been when I'd gone with Aunt Toto and Edmund to Mr. and Mrs. Jules Stein's for cocktails. Not that I drink cocktails, except for this one time when I had quite a few something or others. They tasted like yukky poison but were passed around in frosty silver goblets, each engraved with a curlicued *DS*, set appealingly row upon row on a tray, so when I saw them I thought, why not? After a while someone offered me a cigarette, and I thought why not? about that too. Soon I was juggling both with great savoir faire, including keeping up my end of witty repartee as I sallied from one group to another around the Steins' enormous living room. At least I think it was witty—actually now I'm not all that sure. I mingled right in with the grown-ups. But after that, things happened which I only recall vaguely—and when I came back into it again, as it turned out, I wasn't at Mr. and Mrs. Stein's at all, but somewhere else.

It was some sort of nightclub, somewhere underground. Aunt Toto and Edmund weren't there, and I had no idea what time it was. My mother hadn't been up to going to the Steins', so of course I didn't expect to see her in this place, but it made me panicky, and nauseated, definitely nauseated, when I looked around and there wasn't one single person I recognized among the couples dancing together, much less the people at the table I was sitting at. Who was the man sitting next to me? And who was the woman on the other side who looked disturbingly like Agnes, only she was blond?

Would you like to dance? the man said.

Good grief! It was Georges Metaxa, an actor I'd had a crush on as a child when I'd seen him in the Broadway show *Revenge with Music*. How did *he* get here? He hadn't been at the Steins', had he? But more to the point, how did I get here? He led me onto the dance floor, but all I could think of was how I had sat in the theatre, all those years back, looking up at the stage, where in smoldering arms he held Libby Holman, singing

You and the night and the music
Fill me with—flaming
Dee-sire!

And now here I was grown-up and it was me he was holding.
Well, at least I had on a black dress somewhat like the one Libby
had worn—that plus the picture hat and, as luck would have it,
the Alice Faye "Rose of Washington Square" fishnet black stockings: altogether a fetching combination that might attract his
favorable attention.

What holds your pretty black stockings up? he asked me as
he dipped and eased me past the noisy band.

What? I must not have heard him—What? I said.

Now that we were face to face, I thought he'd be much taller,
like he'd looked onstage, but he wasn't as tall as I was, shorter
in fact, much shorter, and he tilted his head back roguishly. My
mouth twisted up at the corners, but it must have come out
funny, because it wasn't pleasing to him, and he held me in front
of him as far as his stubby arms would reach. Staring down at
my legs, he said sternly, A garter belt, no? Yes, a black garter
belt, he went on, looking at my legs as he swayed me back and
forth to the music. A willowy someone wearing a turquoise cum-
merbund had materialized in front of a microphone and was
singing—

You stepped out of a dream
You are tooo won-der-fullll
To beee what you seemmm . . .

Quite suddenly Mr. Metaxa pulled me back to him and put
his mouth close to my ear—

Yes yes yes without your pretty little black dress on, eh?
Without anything on, nothing on at all, nothing nothing nothing
except your big white hat and your little black garter belt and
your naughty black stockings—*salope!*

I pushed at him and ran past the band as the Agnes woman called out something to me, but I ran on past her, past the bar where two men in velvet smoking jackets sat holding hands, up up the steps and out onto the street.

Where was I?

In front of me a bald-headed man with a monocle was assisting Veronica Lake into an enormous cream-colored Rolls-Royce. He turned to me and said, Can we drop you somewhere, Gloria?

Please take me home, I said.

I sat between them on the backseat. Up close it wasn't Veronica Lake after all but a girl-baby clone that looked like her.

I'm Edgar Auschnic, the bald man said. Remember? We met at the party. I didn't ask him what party, and we were all silent, staring at the back of the chauffeur's head as he drove smoothly along the deserted roads, past palm trees and dark houses. The car rocked back and forth, back and forth, like being rocked in a huge pram, and soon the girl-baby Veronica fell asleep.

Thank you, I said, when the car stopped outside the house on Maple Drive.

Gute Nacht, Kindchen, said Mr. Auschnic as he put his face close to mine to whisper something, but I pulled away. See you tomorrow, he said, raising his eyebrows.

Tomorrow? What did that mean?

I walked up the stone pathway towards the front door. Somewhere along the way I'd lost my keys—maybe Wannsie would be up by now, for it was starting to get light. Behind me Mr. Auschnic called out *Auf Wiedersehen!* but I didn't turn around, and the big cream-colored car rolled away, leaving me on the empty street.

Wasn't it a lovely party, Aunt Toto said. Did you have a good time? But it wasn't really a question.

Oh, yes yes yes, I did.

Mummy and Aunt Toto don't encourage confidences that are too complicated, and this one was, so I didn't elaborate. I needn't have worried, because she had become quite preoccupied with her pinkie. Oh, damn, damn, she said, examining the chipped nail polish. Wannsie, Wannsie, she called out, get Miss Rita to come over right away today instead of tomorrow, something has to be done about this.

It's hot, hot and muggy, she said, picking up her silk fan from the seat beside her, fluttering it back and forth, back and forth. We were sitting out on the porch recovering from the night before, but so far Mummy hadn't made an appearance.

Where is Wannsie—*Wannsie*, she called louder, tapping a little foot impatiently on the flagstone.

Yes, it sure is hot, I agreed.

She glanced out distractedly over the lawn, but nothing caught her attention. Apparently neither had my departure from the Stein soirée the night before. Somehow maybe (since she'd been there) I could talk to her about it, even if I couldn't to my mother. But that's not such a hot idea—Phil would be better. I have to talk to somebody or I'll faint. But Phil might not understand. Why would he when I don't understand myself how I got into such a mess? That *place* and all those icky people. And Mr. Metaxa. I still can't believe he's really like that, but he was and he is. It's not meant to be this way at all, what happened last night—that's not the way it's meant to be. I just want to die. . . .

When I set eyes on Phil, it was as if none of it had happened. Well, almost. Because just when I think it's in the past, I'll get a whiff of that brilliantine Mr. Metaxa had on his hair and it gets right in my nose and I can't blow it out. I'll never be able to bring myself to open my mouth to Phil or anybody about any of it. Dear God, if he knew he'd turn away from me, never wanting to see me again. I'm so afraid he's going to find out about it—but how could he, when no one knows except me, and of course Mr. Metaxa? But what is there to know anyway, when you come right down to it? It's not as if anything happened really. I mean, it was Mr. Metaxa who said all those things, wasn't it? So if it's anyone's fault it's his—so why does it hover around somewhere that it's my fault? There are other things too . . . like that time when Mummy said "Good morning" to me as if the light in the sky were the day breaking when it was really twilight descending and night coming on . . . things like that.

The first thing Phil said when he saw me was, My, you look pretty today! (*Pretty!* Oh God, if he only knew!) We were on our way out the door to the Beverly Hills Hotel for lunch, and when he said that I stopped by the mirror to look at myself. It was true—I did look pretty. How could that be? How could I how could I how could I when inside . . . inside . . . Please, God, I'll go without desserts for a year, *forever*, if only, please, dear God, I'll never ever as long as I live ask you for another thing, please, dear Father God, don't let Phil find out ever, ever, ever.

Most of the people gathering around the pool at the Beverly Hills seemed to know one another, and there was much hand waving back and forth greeting new arrivals. It was more like going to a party at someone's house instead of to a hotel.

There were gorgeous girls, and the men were gorgeous too—some of them, that is, others were fat and not all that gorgeous. But gorgeous or not, they all looked like actors on location somewhere. So it was rather like being part of a scene in a movie, but I couldn't decide what part I was playing. The day was fine as could be, the sun lighting things evenly so that not one palm tree cast a shadow, nor was there shade at the tables around the pool, where couples sat under umbrellas lunching on leafy green things and pineapples stuffed with fruits. Ice melted in glasses and sprigs of mint floated on top of pastel-colored drinks. On some of the round tables were black telephones with long extension cords and serious conversations going on. Other guests lay spread out on chaises doing nothing, eyes closed up at the sun. They all had tans as if milk chocolate had been melted over them, and once in a while a girl would rouse herself to sit up and rub oil over the shoulders of the man beside her, then she would hand him the bottle and he would do the same for her. It was quite a ritual.

Looking around at the scene, I knew that my getup was too much, but maybe it wasn't. I still didn't have the knack of knowing what to wear to what around here. It was confusing, because some got really gussied up, and then there were others who didn't. You could go either way. I had thrown myself together in rather a rush, what with Mr. Metaxa on my mind and all, but luckily Phil had suggested taking along a bathing suit, and I hot-footed it into a cabana and changed into this quickly as I could, the strapless one, shocking pink, and the one I looked best in even if I never seemed to be able to get thin enough. Without heels I was five feet eight inches and weighed one hundred twenty pounds, but no one, least of all my mother, could say that I came anywhere near close to being thin-as-thin as Her Thinness Connie Bennett. Well, that would all change now that I had given up desserts forever (please, God, please don't let Phil find out). After deliberating over things in the full-length cabana mirror, I decided not to wear the matching shocking-pink terry jacket. Instead, I carried it over my arm and sauntered back on out to the pool as if I hadn't a care in the world. Heads glanced up as I passed, and I knew outside I looked OK—it was inside that I couldn't get at. Phil was already waiting for me, having changed into bathing trunks. My, he's handsome, and along with it just so really nice and so sweet to me (please, God, don't let him find out).

Are you getting hungry? he said.

Just starving, I said. Thank God he didn't know the gory details of the whys and wherefores: Wannsie letting me in at the crack of dawn, me falling dead asleep on the bed without taking clothes off much less makeup, waking up so late, no time for breakfast or anything except getting myself together to see Phil. It was then I'd noticed the picture hat wasn't around anywhere (in Mr. Auschnic's car, no doubt)—anyway, it didn't matter because I never wanted to see it again.

As we made our way around the bathing-suited bodies, lots of people smiled up at Phil to say hello. Our table was right by the pool, and soon a waiter handed us menus, pages and pages with elaborate descriptions under each selection (so there'd be no surprises, I guess). It took a lot of study, but finally Phil decided on the "Whahini Salad Aloha" with iced tea, and I said I'd have that too. If only my tummy would settle down. Everything was jittery, and I reached around in my beach bag for the compact Carol had given me for my birthday—it was like the one she had, an exact replica, with flowers painted on it that resembled poached pansies. It was always soothing to look at these flowers, and I traced my finger over them and opened the lid. There was something I wanted to check—the mirror, actually, to see if I was still there. Well, whoever was there, she needed lipstick. I must have chewed it off. At least I'd had the wit to put the shocking-pink shade of lipstick in the bag along with my swimming paraphernalia—it matched the color of the strapless bathing suit to a tee, so at least, at least, I got *something* right. So what was I worrying about? Why did I feel an ax was about to fall! Any moment it was sure to happen, any second now: a voice would speak up, Phil's voice, and he would be saying—

How was the party last night? The party at the Steins'?

But instead it was someone else's voice calling, Phil—hi, Phil!

A big man was coming towards us, and with him were two other men waving to us. They were dressed in varying shades of vanilla on vanilla and cut quite a swath as they bounded on down the steps in their cocoa-butter shoes, nimbly, as if the soles were lined with foam rubber. In another minute they were standing by our table, behaving as though Phil Kellogg was the one person in the world they had been looking for. They were saying "Hi, Phil" again, but they were all looking at me.

Were they movie stars? As it turned out, the one who looked most like a movie star wasn't a movie star at all. His name is Pat, or rather Pasquale, De Cicco, but everyone calls him Pat. He had a crumpled pack of Picayune cigarettes in one hand and with the other shook hands with me as Phil introduced us. Next came the sandy-haired one, the least movie-starrish of the trio. His name is Van Heflin. Later I found out he was the actor in a play Mummy took me to see in New York ages ago, called *The Philadelphia Story*. Katharine Hepburn was in it, and we had seats in the third row, but I had been so goggle-eyed to be close to her that I didn't notice much else, and even now I can't remember Van Heflin in the play (except that there must have been men in the play too, so one of them could have been him). Then Phil introduced me to a very movie-starrish-looking man with quite a gleam in his eye. He was Bruce Cabot, and I had seen him in a few movies—*King Kong* and another with Marlene Dietrich. But I kept seeing him on a stage more, maybe in the uniform of a hussar in a Victor Herbert operetta, singing something. None of them had changed into swimming trunks yet, and they kept standing around our table like they were waiting for something. And they were—they were waiting for Phil to invite them to sit down, which is finally what he did.

They all said it was too early for lunch and ordered rum-and-Cokes with lime. I hadn't said a word except the three hellos when we'd been introduced. They were all so grown-up, much more grown-up than Phil even, and I didn't want to risk it. I didn't want to utter something that might be misconstrued as babyish—or worse still, impostorish. When you get right down to it, the tall-dark-and-handsome Pat-Pasquale one is really the most movie-starrish of them all, and I am very curious about him. He sure is sure of himself, but in a much too conceited way. Still, Van Hepburn is intriguing too, mainly because of the Katharine connection. Bruce Hussar also draws the attention, but I'm not crazy about the mustache. He and the Pat-Pasquale must pal around together, because there was a lot of banter going on between them and inside jokes, but they always wheedled their way back one way or another to the gin rummy games which apparently go on all the time, mainly at Joe Schenck's house, it seems (whoever he is). Well, whoever he is, they were on their way there now, which is why they hadn't changed into bathing trunks. Yes, Van Hepburn was going too, all on their merry way to Joe's for a continuation of last night's gin rummy game, which has been interrupted by an unfortunate incident. Someone called Cubby—some vegetable name or other—along with another man called Rosey Rosenberg, had also been there, and it sounds like it's a club, and whoever this Joe person is owns the club or runs it or something. But whatever, one thing is for sure: their main interest is getting together as often as possible to play gin, and the only reason last night's game wasn't still going on was because one of the members, called Charlie Feldman (I think that's his name), had one of his girlfriends sitting around waiting (for what?), but the game went on and on and on until dawn, when she started acting up. They tried to pacify her by taking her into one of the guest rooms, but she would have none of it, and finally it all got out of hand and she had to be removed bodily by ambulance in a straitjacket. They all thought it hilarious, but I didn't get it at all. Phil didn't think it was so funny either. But I didn't want to be impolite, so I made my demeanor quite pleasant (at least I think I did).

After more rum-and-Cokes things went along more or less like this for quite a while until Pat-Pasquale (clearly the leader) stood up.

Well, Cousin Brucie, he yoohooed, guess time's a-wastin', guess we'd better mosey on over to Uncle Joe's ole corral.

Cousin Brucie thought that the funniest thing ever, and he stood up smartly to attention, clicking his heels together and saluting. Then he bent over my hand (just like Prince Friedel used to do to kiss Mummy's), catching my eye, as he did, in a most devilish way.

Enchanté, Mademoiselle, enchanté.

Moi aussi, I said, sort of laughing.

Nice to see you, Phil, Pat-Pasquale said. Gloria—and he shook my hand quite solemnly.

Think I've had enough gin rummy for one weekend, Van Hepburn said. I'm going to stick around and have a swim.

More iced tea? Phil asked me.

No thanks, Phil, I think I'll go in the pool.

My tummy was starting to act up again. Pat-Pasquale and Cousin Brucie walked away from us, springing up the steps. From the back, in their vanilla-on-vanilla suits, they looked almost alike. Would I recognize one from the other if I didn't know which back was which? Would I ever see them again?

I jumped up and ran towards the pool, but just before I plunged in, coming down the steps towards me—there they were! Veronica Lake and Mr. Auschnic!

Well, I could always drown myself, couldn't I, dive in and never come up? But if I did I'd never see a flower again, or Pat-

Pasquale or my mother, or anyone, and I wasn't ready for that—
yet. Was I?

Dear Diary

Van Hepburn confided to me he is really thirty-six, but
Metro-Goldwyn-Mayer puts out that he's thirty-one because that's
what they want the "great American public" to believe. Why,
thirty-six, that's my mother's age! And I think he likes me and
thinks I'm grown-up even though I'm seventeen. So if it's true,
and I am grown-up, why am I still an Impostor? When you're
grown-up it's all supposed to change. Aunt Gertrude said I am
"seventeen whole years old." That "whole" is what I've been
counting on. What I need now is more time around grown-ups,
so the more of them I can be friends with, the sooner I'll learn
their secrets and get the knack of it. Apropos of secrets, there
are heaps of whispers going around Maple Manor, doors closing
and so forth. But I don't get to hear any of it, because I'm much
too grown-up to play Invisible anymore. But something's going
to happen, I can feel it, and I don't just mean my having to leave
here. It makes me mad, these secrets, and not only at Aunt
Gertrude—even Tony with his "little map of England" face under
that idiot cap makes me mad, not to mention Ketti Keven and
a lot of others. But the one I get most angry at is myself. One
week from today, I'll be getting on a plane with The Constonce,
a plane that will land me back at Old Westbury Capital, and I
don't want to go, I don't I don't.

Van Hepburn keeps asking me out, so does Brucie Hussar,
and well, there's a long list. It's exciting hearing the ting-a-ling
of the phone so often and have it always for me, or so it seems.
Even Pat-Pasquale called once, but when I said I had a date (Phil
and I were going dancing at Ciro's) he hasn't called again, and
now he's all around town with a girl called Bettye Avery. Phil

and I even ran into them at Ciro's the night Pat had invited me (well, he had asked me first). What a dippy way to spell Betty. I mean, how affected can you get? She's going to be a movie star someday—meantime being a starlet and seeing a lot of Pat keeps her busy. She is pretty, I'll have to say, but can she tap dance like me? Of course, I don't know how to tap dance, ha, ha, but I could learn. Mummy and Aunt Thelma say (jokingly?) that if I stay on any longer I'll have to get my own phone, one that would ring only in my bedroom, because Wannsie's out of breath all the time what with running to answer the phone and at the same time doorbells ringing with flowers arriving, all for me. Do they really mean it about the phone? I like the idea a lot. It's the most grown-up thing I've heard of. Anyway, I do feel like Miss Popular, and if I wasn't seeing Phil all the time—well, lately every time the phone rings I've started to feel maybe I'm missing something by saying no no no to Van and the others when what I'm really dying to do is say yes.

A Dream

Aunt Thelma was away with Edmund somewhere.

Can I sleep in your room tonight, Mummy?

Of course, darling, she said.

So I put on my best nightgown and went into the Moon Room and got under the covers, way way at the other side of the huge bed. She was already ensconced there, Cucumber Night Cream on her face.

There was no music playing, and I said—

Mummy, I'll be able to sleep with the radio on, don't leave it off because of me.

Oh, I won't need music, darling, with you here beside me.

What did you say, Mummy?

And she said it again—yes, she did!

She turned off the light and we both lay in the dark, but no conversation came to mind and soon I could tell by her breathing that she had fallen asleep. Could it be she's glad I'm here after all?

My hands were cold and over me a longing came, a longing most terrible, to roll across an ocean, seize her in my arms, clasp her to me, tight so tight, so close we would merge into each other, no longer separated by the space between us. . . .

But as this longing possessed me I became frightened, and it took all my will to lie still, unmoving.

But suddenly I let go into sleep, and as I did I fell into a dream . . . and when I came to the end of the dream, I woke up—so sweetly, as if a gentle wave had lifted me up onto warm sands of an endless beach.

What time was it . . . dawn?

In the half-light I could see my mother's hand thrown out towards me on the pillow, for in sleep she had reached out for me.

But I feared waking her and lay there without moving, going over the dream. It had been a dream about finding something, something that had been lost to me for a long time . . . and in the dream I had found it again.

But what? What had I found?

Round and round this went as I tried to remember. But the more I tried, the more it slipped away. And soon, the only thing I knew for certain was that if I was to know what I had found, I would first have to remember what it was that I had lost. If I could do that, everything would be all right . . . yes, everything.

Airmail Special Delivery, July 1941

Dearest Auntie Ger,

There hasn't been much to write about since the first letter to tell you I'd arrived safely, which is why I haven't written since then. But I think about you a lot and wonder if the

weather's been as hot in Westbury as it is here? It sure is true
what they say about Sunny California, but at night it gets so
cool you have to wear a sweater. I've also been wondering
if it would be OK if maybe I stayed on here for a few weeks
longer? Maybe if I got back in time to go with everybody to
the Adirondacks—that's only a few weeks off. Do you think
that would be a good idea? It's just a thought but as long as
I'm out here already I might as well stay a few more days—

   Please give my love to everybody and loads and loads
of love to you.

Gloria

P.S. My mother says it's OK with her if I stay on a bit longer.
I mean nobody else needs the room I'm in or anything like that.

Return Airmail Special Delivery, July 1941

Dearest Gloria,

   By this time you will know I have sent word to your
mother, through Mr. Crocker, that I expect you to be on the
plane with Constonce, as agreed to before you took this trip
to visit your mother in California. We will be leaving for the
Adirondacks the day after you get back. They tell me the
weather has been delightful this year, so what with fishing,
hiking, and what-not, there will be lots of things to do.

Lovingly,
Aunt Gertrude

A Red Yo-Yo

   Mummy, do I *have* to go back?

   Well, I don't know, Pooks, my mother said, glancing over
at Aunt Thelma.

I mean, can they *make* me go back?

You're a big grown-up girl, darling. Aunt Thelma sounded peevish. What do you think they can do, chloroform you and *carry* you on?!

We were all silent for a while, mulling this over, each in her own way, but then we all got quite caught up by Tony, who stood far away at the end of the garden playing with a red yo-yo. Up and down, up and down it went—he was quite expert.

I wish he'd stop with that damn thing, Aunt Thelma said. To-nee, To-nee, she called out.

He trotted over the grass to us in bare feet. Yes, Mummy? Yes, Mummy?

Tony darling, don't you have something else to do? You've been playing with that thing all day.

He put the yo-yo down on the grass tenderly as an egg and we all considered it.

How about a nice swim? Aunt Toto said brightly.

What a good idea, echoed my mother.

But Tony didn't hear, and he sat down on the grass cross-legged, next to the yo-yo. He gave it a little pat and said, I'll just rest a bit.

So, Mummy . . . about my going back, I mean . . . if I could just stay on a bit longer, maybe?

Pooks, darling—now my mother was edgy—all that's already settled.

But *how* is it settled? Who'll tell Auntie Ger?

Crocker, of course, Aunt Thelma said.

Yes, of course. Why hadn't I thought of it before? Hadn't he always been the messenger to carry communications to and from Aunt Gertrude?

I'll call him later sometime, my mother sighed and closed her eyes.

Why not now? I said.

Aunt Toto looked at Mummy and said, We might as well get it over with.

My mother stood up and followed Aunt Toto on into the house. As the screen door slammed behind them, Tony got up and started again with the yo-yo. Up and down, up and down, the red ball of it went. Aunt Toto was right, there was something irritating about it. I felt sick to my stomach. Maybe I'd better go in and lie down for a while.

Is That You?

The next day it was Wannsie who brought the breakfast tray up to my room.

Where's Constance? I said.

She's gone, Miss Gloria. Yes, this morning. Mrs. Whitney arranged for her flight back to New York.

You mean—for good?

I'm quite sure of that, Wannsie said.

This riveting bit of news would have made me jump for joy, but I had other things on my mind.

Wannsie, tell me—did my mother come back yet?

I'm not certain, Miss Gloria, but Her Ladyship is wide awake and having breakfast in her room.

The phone next to my bed started ringing. I took a deep breath and held it long as I could, but it didn't stop. Maybe it was my mother, so I picked it up quickly.

Hi, sweetie, Pat said. Did my orchids arrive?

Did orchids arrive, Wannsie? She was on her way out into the hall.

Some flowers did arrive for you, Miss Gloria, but I don't think they're orchids. I'll bring them up as soon as I get Her Ladyship dressed for her luncheon.

No, they didn't, Pat, they didn't—

Well, sweetie, they will, they will. Fun last night, wasn't it?

Was it? The getting ready for the date had been fun: the

long soak in Ardena Fluffy Milk Bath, deciding what shoes to wear with what dress, taking hours to make up (quite expert I had become, thanks to Virginia)—that had been fun. So was the looking forward to the dancing at Mocambo. But then it happened again (it's the third time now): just as it's fun, Pat-Pasquale opens his mouth and out comes something which turns out not to be fun at all. Last night it was after one of his old girlfriends danced by, a very grown-up sort of movie star, Margaret Lindsay.

Now there's an attractive girl, he said as we left the dance floor and went back to our ringside table. Not beautiful but, well—attractive—there's nothing *wrong* with her face.

Is there anything wrong with mine?

No, sweetie, no. You're not beautiful, but you're attractive, almost as attractive as that one—

He waved across the dance floor to that one, but she didn't wave back.

Maggie always was nearsighted, he said, dismissing her and gesturing to the waiter for the check. On we go to Uncle Joe's, he said. See how the game's going.

No, I said, it's time for me to go home, Mummy doesn't like me to be out too late. (What a fib.) But he didn't seem to care one way or the other, and when we got back to Maple Drive he came up to the front door with me and stood there while I got the key out of my bag. I thought he might be expecting to kiss me, but I needn't have worried because he didn't, so I thanked him for the lovely time and went on into the house.

Call you tomorrow, sweetie, he said. You be good now.

Inside the house it was quiet, so quiet. As I got to the top of the stairs my mother's door was open but the room was empty. Aunt Toto's was closed but there was no light under the door and I knew that she and Edmund must be asleep.

Well, it was late. In New York right now it would be six in the morning. Aunt Gertrude would be asleep still; Big Elephant already up taking Smokey for his morning stroll . . . Naney Morgan lifting the window at the Hotel Fourteen to get lemons from the sill to squeeze into a glass of water, hot from the tap. . . .

Suddenly my phone started ringing. Who? At this hour? It must be a wrong number, but when I picked it up a voice said—

Hello? Hello? Little Gloria? Is that you?

Murder

It was Ketti Keven.

Listen to me, listen, Big Gloria and I are here having breakfast.

Breakfast? It was three in the morning.

Do you hear me? Are you there, Little Gloria?

Yes, yes, yes, it's me it's me, I'm here.

Well, if it is you listen to me, it's important very very important.

Ketti must have put her hand over the receiver because there were muffled sounds and then there was a crash.

Mummy, Mummy, I called out.

Sorry 'bout tat, Ketti said, something happened to phone.

Let me talk to Mummy, please?

Noot noo, Ketti said, she busy, very busy—soo you listen me.

What's wrong, what's wrong? Is Mummy all right?

Sure she right—never better.

Then came a long pause and giggling in the background.

Only one little ole thing botherin' her—you.

Me?

Yes, *you*, honey—she very worried about *you*.

Why? Why? Why?

She heard all about you and Virginia and those marijuana parties.

Marijuana? Marijuana? What is marijuana? Ketti, Ketti, I

don't know what you're talking about. What's marijuana? Please let me speak to Mummy—please please please.

Something terrible was going on, but I didn't know what it was.

Ketti, please listen to me, *please*—I haven't seen Virginia since we went out on a double date with Phil and Wayne. What's marijuana?

Honey—you're too much of a kid to be puffing on that stuff—get you in mucho trouble, mucho mucho—then there's this Pasquale you're seeing so mucho mucho of—we know all about him.

What what what—*what* about him?

Honey, come on—everybody knows he was the one who killed Thelma.

Thelma! I screamed.

Hot Todd, Toddy Thelma Todd—and you listen here to me, I was better friend of hers than Patsy Kelly ever was, if she'd been with me that night 'stead fair weather friends, wouldn't have happened.

What happened, what wouldn't have happened?

Wouldn't gotten murdered, that's what wouldn't happened.

Murdered, murdered?

Damn right, baby. Murdered. Pasquale's ex-wifey—now ya gettin' it straight?

Please, God, please, God—God?

You listen to me, honey, listen to me 'cause everything's gonna be rosy from now on, just hunky-dory, don't you worry about a thing, jus' some things we gotta set straight.

There was scuffling in the background and arguing like maybe my mother was trying to get the phone away from Ketti. Then a bang and the drone of a dial tone . . . it went on and on and on and I held the phone calling Mummy Mummy Mummy, but then a frantic clicking came on and a strange voice saying—Hang up, please—your line has been disconnected—disconnected—disconnected—discon—

Dearest Cathleen

August 1941

Dearest Cathleen,

There is so much to tell you I don't know where to begin. That's why I haven't written until now. How are you and Ramón? Have you moved into the new apartment yet? I'm having the best time out here. You should see my new hairdo. It's called a Pompadour and it's five inches high above my forehead!!! To get it that high, Miss Loretta (she's the hairdresser at Wally Westmore where all the Stars go) has to stuff it with lots of rats and then comb it over. It's all held in place by tons of bobby pins and hairspray, but it's worth it because it really looks—as Mummy would say—divine! Only she hasn't noticed it yet. Last week—before the Pompadour— George Hoyningen-Huene took my photograph for *Harper's Bazaar*. I wore a white blouse, *very* décolleté, with slinky black satin trousers. Tomorrow I'm going to try a grey streak on the Pompadour to make me look older, Miss Loretta says she can paint it right on with a brush. Wish I'd had it like that for the *Harper's Bazaar* picture, still I'm keeping my fingers and toes (ha ha) crossed hoping the pictures will come out OK. But what I'm really writing to tell you is—and it's a BIG SECRET—no one knows it yet except *You*. And for God's sake DON'T TELL AUNTIE GER. Well—here it is—I'm getting married!!! To Van Heflin!!!! You've probably heard about him because he's a famous actor and he's going to be a Big Movie Star as soon as the movie he's doing now comes out. It's called *Johnny Eager* and Lana Turner's in it too. We haven't set a date yet but we have been around looking at houses, so far haven't seen any particular one that we'd like to move into. He's really divine and I think he had a romance with Katharine Hepburn

when they were in the play *The Philadelphia Story*. But it's *me* he's going to marry. I can't wait for you to meet him. Well, that's all for now—got to rush—Van's picking me up to go to Sherman Oaks to look at another house.

I miss you so much. Please write soon.

Tons of love and hugs and kisses,

Gloria

P.S. Wore the dress you gave me (I call it my Sister Dress because it's exactly like yours) the navy with white polka dots. Anyway, wore it on the set when I visited Van and even Lana noticed it. Also found the cutest hat at John Frederics, white with the floppiest peonies ever (goes perfectly with the dress)—wanted to get one for you too, but didn't 'cause you only wear turbans.

P.P.S. *Swear* not to tell Aunt Gertrude. I haven't even told my mother about it yet.

Home

What is this about you and Van Heflin?

Aunt Toto had come into my room without knocking, my mother following close at hand.

How could you *do* this to your mother, Gloria?

I was speechless. So was Mummy.

I'm livid, Aunt Toto sputtered. Livid, do you hear me! How *could* you put your mother in this terrible position? Is it true? Is it? Is it?

Is what true? My voice came out funny.

Crocker just called to say Mrs. Whitney knows all about it, yes, all about it, that you're going to marry this—actor! Yes, *she* knows all about it, but your mother knows *nothing* about it. How do you think that makes *her* look to Mrs. Whitney—not to mention the Courts?

My mother kept looking at Aunt Toto, waiting to hear what she'd say next.

Speak up, Little Gloria, don't just sit there! Speak up—speak up—

My mother turned away from me and looked out the window. She didn't say anything.

Cathleen had betrayed me—why? I had never said anything to Aunt Gertrude or anyone about Havana and Ramón: How *could* she?

I don't know, I don't know if we'll get married or not. . . . Why all the fuss—?

Fuss, fuss, Aunt Toto repeated. Are you such a nitwit? I don't give a damn who you marry—it's your mother I'm thinking about, can't you see how this makes your mother look? She's *suffered* enough already! I won't have it, do you hear me, I won't have it!

As Aunt Toto raised her voice, my mother looked towards the door, worried the servants might hear. But she needn't have, for now Aunt Toto was so angry her voice had lowered and the words came from her as though a clamp had tightened around her throat. Do—you—hear—me?

I hear you I hear I hear I hear you, I wanted to scream back, but instead I walked out the door and down the stairs onto the street, as if I were late for an appointment. I could never go back now after what had been said, never, never, and if Aunt Toto didn't give a damn, it was sure to follow that my mother didn't either.

But I did go back, and now I've stopped seeing Van and instead I go out on dates with lots of different people, but I'm jumbled up about everything. Some of those things Ketti Keven said that night on the phone, I found out they're true. Pat-Pasquale was married to a movie star called Thelma Todd, and it's true that she was murdered and that no one has ever found out who killed her. Pat says he works for Howard Hughes, but what does that mean? What does he do exactly? Play gin rummy and win loads of money—that's all I've ever seen him do. Yes, he really does love to play cards, and when he's not seeing me, it's Bettye Avery he takes dancing. And when he does I keep wishing it was me.

Today I took my paints and walked up in the hills. Around me everything was beauty and I painted all that I could see— hibiscus flowers, the fig trees, and way below me, a kite held by a child running with it along the beach, ocean beyond and sky above. I'd forgotten how it is when I'm painting—that feeling, alone, working in the studio at Wheeler—today, it came back to me and I was happy.

The Mysterious Stranger, August 1941

Mummy is dieting and floating around the house the way she did the summer of The Second Unfortunate July (when Mr. Roberto Mendoza appeared), the summer she cut her hair in a pageboy. Maybe it's being cut in the same style right this minute at Wally Westmore's, where she's having her hair done, a makeup too, by Mr. Westmore himself no less. She's most secretive about who this date is, so I bet it's someone she's just met, but where? I wonder where he'll take her for dinner . . . and what she's going to wear . . . I'm dying to know all these things, but what I'm dying to know most of all is *who* is he?? Maybe they'll get married, hot diggity! Then I'll have a father, and even though it won't be my real father, it certainly would be better, much better, than having no father at all.

As I was on my way out to meet Pat at Romanoff's, the door of the Moon Room opened.

It was my mother.

Her hair hadn't been cut, but it was fluffed up somehow, and the wavy beauty of it flounced around her shoulders as she walked past me, and the silk of her pearly dress flounced, up and down, around her ankles, while around her neck garlands of beads, opaline colors of the inside of seashells, swung, back and forth, reflecting onto her face so that it was pale and luminous.

Oh, Mummy, I said, you look beautiful! And she turned to me and smiled. But the smile went past me as if to an unseen audience out there somewhere.

Wannsie, she called out.

Yes, Modom, Wannsie said, coming out of the Moon Room into the hall.

Wannsie, I'm not taking any calls, unless, of course, it's Mr. Hughes.

So *that's* who it was!

I followed her down the stairs, and she went on into the living room just as the front doorbell rang. I opened the door, for I was on my way out, and a man was standing there. He wore a hat tilted back on his head and he was tall, really tall, as his jacket swung over one shoulder in a most appealing way. He couldn't think of anything to say and I couldn't either. But Wannsie, who had come in answer to the ring, did, and she said—

Come this way, Mr. Hughes—Mrs. Vanderbilt is expecting you. . . .

Your mother's awake, Wannsie said, and would like to talk to you. She's waiting for you in the living room.

I ran ran down the stairs. It was the morning after Mummy's date with Mr. Hughes.

She was sitting on the sofa, very serious, when I went in. I sat down solemnly beside her.

As you know, she said, taking a deep pull of her cigarette, Howard Hughes was here yesterday, and it seems the reason for this visit

Visit? But I thought he was—

Don't interrupt, she said. He—he had phoned me out of the blue asking if we could meet and—and although we had never been introduced I, of course, knew of him, so naturally I suggested he drop by for a drink. Well, it seems that what he wanted to meet about was you.

Me!

So it seems, yes. It seems he's going to do some movie or other and he's looking around hither and yon for a new face and he'd seen you somewhere or other and wanted to ask my permission about doing a screen test of you.

A screen test?

Yes, she said flatly, mashing out her cigarette. Of course I told him it was up to you, so no doubt you'll be getting a phone call from him at any moment.

And just as she said this the phone did indeed start to ring.

Well, that's probably him right now, and she stood up.

Mummy, what'll I do?

What do you mean, what'll you do? Do whatever you want to do, it's up to you. And now I'm going to lie down for a bit, I have a headache. Where *is* Wannsie with that aspirin—aspirin—aspirin. And she went on up the stairs to her room and I went on out into the front hall and picked up the phone.

He drives a car that no one would notice, and the first time we went out together it was raining. We drove over the hills far away down into the valley. Neither of us said a word, and the rain fell, hitting the car with a spattering sound. Inside we were safe as could be, gypsies in a caravan on our way to some unknown destination to set up camp for the night. I would have been content to keep driving on and on, but it was getting dark and he stopped the car. How about some dinner? he said. And soon we were sitting in a restaurant looking at each other across candles and velvety white petunias. Around us piney-wood walls, and a tablecloth—black-and-white check, like the raincoat I was wearing. We looked over the menu and he said, What would you like? And I said, What are you going to have? Oh, I always have steak, peas, and baked potato. Always? Yep, always. That would be fine for me too, I said, and then he started telling me about a movie he was going to make and that he had seen photographs taken of me the weekend I'd visited Shearen Daniel Elebash at Choate. A photographer representing Howard Hughes had been there that weekend, taking photographs, hoping to discover a girl to play the lead in a movie, and he had taken pictures of me. I'd been thrilled, but after a while, when I didn't hear from him, I forgot about it. But it turns out Howard had seen the photographs and that's why he called my mother. The movie's called *The Outlaw* and it's about Billy the Kid. Another movie of his is *Hell's Angels* and when I said I hadn't seen it he said he'd screen it for me sometime. *Then* he said "next time it isn't raining" he'd fly me to Catalina in his plane and we'd spend the day there. The "next time" is full of signs and portents, for it *must* mean he wants to see me again. I like that raincoat, he said. And now I keep looking at it hanging here in my closet and wondering if I'll ever see him again.

My mother isn't what you'd call burning with curiosity that Howard and I are seeing so much of each other. It's as if she doesn't even want to know about it. But she does bring Pat-Pasquale into the conversation whenever I see her (which isn't much these days)—how handsome he is, how funny, how charming, how blah blah blah. Every time I try to talk about Howard, she changes the subject, so I've taken the hint and don't bring his name up anymore. As for Aunt Toto, she isn't interested in either one of them, but I'm sure she and Mummy talk about things when I'm not around, for there's a lot going on behind closed doors—the serious talk, that is. When I'm around it's just blah, blah, blah. . . .

Very early in the morning he picked me up in his car and we drove to the airport. There, waiting for us, all shiny, was his plane, and I jumped in beside him. Then as he started the motor I sang loud so he could hear through the sound of the propellers, "Come, Josephine, in my fly-ing ma-chine." It came out sort of off-key, but it made us laugh as the propellers whirled and whirled around, and soon he was skimming us along the runway, on up up into the sky. Higher in the sunlight, fair blinding, as we topped the clouds . . . Yes! faster, faster! I called out, as we went higher still. I wasn't frightened of anything anymore, I was

free, and turning to him, I called out again (but did I?), and later was it my hand that reached out to him as he looked down far below, curving the plane around in slow descent before touching lightly upon a strip of land close to the sea? We walked along, over a hill, no other human being in sight, on down a steep path to a cove below, towards a rock beach, secret as could be. As we came closer, I had an impulse to hunt for pebbles, stones of unusual shapes and colors, but instead we settled under a tree, sheltered from the sun. It didn't matter that the feeling wasn't there anymore, because in its place contentment had come.

After a while he opened a paper bag and took out meat loaf and two baked potatoes. There was a pepper mill, too, and ketchup, a thermos of icy spring water, and cheese—Crema Danica, he said. No kidding? I said. It's good with cherries, he said, and put a handful of plump red-black ones in a neat pile on the rock next to the cheese. Far in the distance a pinpoint was coming closer—a sailboat perhaps? We sat there looking out over the ocean not saying anything at all. After a while I tried to tell him about my mother and Aunt Gertrude, but it came out confused, so I said, I guess I haven't figured it all out yet, but someday maybe I will, and when that day comes you'll be the first to know. Ha ha. But he didn't laugh, instead he took me in his arms and kissed me. I think I'm in love with him.

Now that I'm seeing so much of Howard, Pat-Pasquale keeps calling and calling to ask me out. I make excuses, but I've run out of them. Why can't I just say I don't want to see him anymore (because I don't—at least I don't think I do). Howard's the only person I want to be with, but then I'll run into Pat somewhere and everything gets mixed up. Mummy goes on and on about him, which helps a lot, ha ha, Pat's divine, darling, she'll say. Maybe that's why I can't stop thinking about him. Then yesterday she said, You know, Pooks, you did string him along and now you're dropping him like a hot potato, don't you think you should at least talk to him when he calls on the phone? Then I feel guilty, because maybe I have been stringing him along, because when I do happen to run into him I'm very friendly, but then I avoid his calls, never picking up my private phone unless it rings once, stops, and after a moment rings again (Howard's secret signal). Even when Pat calls on the main house number I usually tell Wannsie to say I'm out. Mummy, I said, Mummy—but that's as far as I got, as far as I'll ever get—she just has other things on her mind, I guess.

I was desperate, and so I finally talked to Howard about it, because I had to talk to someone.

I'll send him away for a while, he said.

Send him—away—what do you mean *away*?

Well, there's a catering project I have going on in Kansas City for my TWA flights which needs attention—let him do some work for a change, go and attend to that.

Oh, yes yes yes yes, I said, without even thinking what I was saying. Yes, yes, away away away.

And now Pat-Pasquale is indeed on his way away, to Kansas City for an indefinite time. God, what have I done? He hasn't a clue why he's being sent on this sudden mission. He told Mummy that he's very put out and may quit his job with Hughes (that's how Mummy refers to Howard). I got so guilty about it I found myself saying distraught good-byes to him. Good-bye, good-bye, Pat-Pasquale, I said as though bereft that he was leaving. You be good now, he said in final parting. And now I feel more guilty than ever.

Well, Pat didn't quit his job with Howard, and there he is in Kansas City. When he calls, since he's so far away I do speak to him, but now I wish I hadn't. The last time he was in a fierce temper and it erupted through the phone like a volcano. He's heard I'm seeing a lot of Howard and has no doubt put two and two together and come up with Kansas City and his reason for being there. Well, it wouldn't take a genius to figure it out—

he went on and on about Howard and the dozens of girls he has every day of the week, and none of them mean anything to him, least of all me.

And you can tell him what I said, Fatsy Roo—Yoo-hoo-hoo! and he laughed that hoot of his that you can hear through walls of cement.

Fatsy, do yourself a favor, hear me? You just sit there until I get back and you won't have to hold your breath long because believe you me, it'll be sooner than you think, much sooner. . . .

Phil

Ever since I'd started seeing so much of Van there has been a big hole in my heart—Phil. He keeps calling and calling asking to see me, but I keep putting him off with one flimsy excuse or another. Not that I ever actually told him that Van and I were engaged (much less looking around at houses to live in), and he knew I'd gone dancing with Pat at Mocambo—but so what? Why shouldn't I have lots of dates? Still, I feel awful about it, because I do love him—Phil, I mean—but how can that be true when all I think about is Howard? As for Van—what a relief! He's drifted off somewhere in an easygoing way—our engagement broke off (after the scene with Mummy and Aunt Toto) without our having to go into any big scene about it. I don't know why they all made such a fuss about it when it was only the *idea* of it that was real. Neither one of us really believed it would ever happen. But Phil—that's different. Oh yes, very different, because I want to belong to someone more than anything—but Oh misery! now Phil's stopped calling! If only he'd—what? Fight for me—is that what I want? And Howard? Maybe I'm not worthy of him? As for Pat-Pasquale, why do I keep listening to him when he makes me feel so awful! Hammering on about Howard, how I mean nothing to him because he "pulls the same old line on all the girls." He's got lots of stories to point this up, like the one about Ginger Rogers, who was all set to be flown to a secret wedding place, but at the last minute Howard never even showed up. Well, Howard hasn't asked me to marry him, only to *be* with him all the time. Is that a good sign or not? Big Elephant always says, Don't be so impatient, so impulsive. But I am, no matter how hard I try not to be, because I have no sense of time, of tomorrow, only of what's happening right now. And right now, all I know is that I don't know how I feel about anything.

Darling Dodo

Darling Dodo,

I've met the most wonderful man. You told me long ago that someday I'd meet someone who would cherish me—and that's the way he makes me feel. He hasn't asked me to marry him yet, but if he does—I will I will I will—oh yes, it's what I'm praying for more than anything, and if he does I just hope I'll be worthy of him. It's so funny, but I feel safe with him—like nothing terrible could ever happen as long as he's there. We have so much fun together—he flies his own plane (don't worry, he's a great pilot!) and next weekend we're flying to Santa Barbara for the Fiesta—it's a weekend of dancing and celebration. I'm going to put my hair in a chignon and use Naney's Spanish tortoiseshell comb to hold her black mantilla—you know, the black lace one she gave me that used to belong to Great-Grandma Valdivieso. I'll write you all about it. How is Smokey? Is he still so growly and unfriendly? I miss you and think about you all the time. Wish me luck. I love you.

Gloria

Garbo

I've never seen my mother so excited. A casting director has asked her if she would let me be in a movie that Greta Garbo is about to start shooting at MGM. The movie's called *Two Faced Woman*, and from what I can make out (Mummy is so beside herself she gets quite incoherent on the subject) they need a debutante to stand in front of the mirror in a ladies' room restaurant shot and comb her hair. It would all flash by in a second, and I wouldn't have to *say* anything—*but*—and this is why she's so unhinged—

Think of it, darling, you'd get to meet Garbo! And I'd have to be on the set with you, naturally. They'd *have* to let me— even though Garbo always works on closed sets. I mean, after all, I am your mother.

Mummy, I don't want to do it—

What do you mean, don't want to do it? You *must* do it.

If I'm in a movie I don't want to be a debutante and I want at least to have some kind of scene—

Scene, what do you mean, scene?

I mean say something, not just stand there looking at myself in the mirror and combing my hair.

She was silent, quite baffled, but only for a minute.

You know how I feel about Garbo, she pressed on. You know she's the *one* person in the world I've always wanted to meet.

Wanted to meet wanted to meet wanted to meet. That's what she said, and it went around and around in my head.

Listen, Mummy—I—don't—want—to—do—it.

And I turned from her, but as I ran away, blood surged through me. It was so unexpected that I felt good about things all of a sudden, as if I was connected to her, as if maybe there was hope after all.

The Visitor

She appeared at Maple Manor uninvited—without warning.
The queens were out somewhere—Romanoff's, I think—having
lunch with the Baroness Kuffner. But when she was told they
weren't here, she asked to see me. I panicked and told Wannsie
to say I wasn't in, then I changed my mind and found myself
standing with her in my mother's room. Why Wannsie put her
there I'll never know. Maybe she had pushed past her, forced
Wannsie aside, running up the stairs into the Moon Room to
see if maybe Wannsie had lied to her and my mother was really
there after all. But of course she wasn't. As usual, the curtains
were drawn against the light, it could have been dawn or twilight
instead of two in the afternoon, and at first I didn't see her, red
on red, you might say, for she sunk thin and small in her red
dress into the puffy red pillows of the chair by my mother's bed:
her face a white sliver of chalk, the petaled mouth erased, for
without makeup it was only her eyes, sooty and enormous, that
shone, luminous, unblinking. Red elbows resting on the sides
of the chair, hands together . . . in prayer?

Miss Horter, I said, Mummy's not here, and I went over and
sat on the edge of the bed facing her.

She put the flat whites of her hands over her face, but she
didn't cry, and we sat there not moving or saying anything until,
sudden-like, her hands flew apart and she looked full at me and
smiled . . . she was trying to tell me something. . . .

Your mother, I must talk to you about your mother, she
said, her manner changed now, quite conversational, but then
she leaned forward and her voice got low, talking fast fast. Mother,
Mother Dammen, at the convent, the Sacred Heart Convent—
Mother Dammen was the Mother Superior, we loved her—oh
yes, we loved her very much.

My head nodded up and down, up and down. As her mouth

pulled me, I felt sucked into her, but then she fell back against the chair and her face got all funny. Oh God, she's going to reach out to take my hand, but she didn't—instead she tapped my knee smartly with a long fingernail.

Pay attention! she said severely. It's beautiful there, you understand? Many halls, many rooms, the chapel, places we knew well—it was *home* to us, a serene place. Listen to me, do you know—what—that—means? She leaned close, and as she did her face blurred in front of mine, her dilated eyes devouring me.

I couldn't breathe.

Understand what? what? I moved quickly, but her hand sprawled out to me and she called out in a sudden flutey voice, unexpected—

Don't—don't—please don't leave me—

It was a great good place for us—do you understand what a great good place means?—do you? do you? Our whole lives ahead of us—I was beautiful too, yes, in my way just as much a beauty as the twins, but I was different, she said proudly, different because I had my gift, the gift of my voice. . . .

She scrunched a fist into her face and her body shook but no sound came. It was grim to see, for until that moment, no matter what, I'd felt somehow protected because there had been something actressy about all of it: the dawn-twilight room, the red of her melting into the red chair, face of chalk, hands floating in the shadowy light. But there was nothing stagey about it now as she threw herself on my mother's bed, clutching at the beads around her neck, reaching out to me, beads big as grapes they were, green and purple, scattering over the spread as the string broke, rolling onto the floor like marbles hitting at each other with a clicking sound.

I couldn't bear it and I ran to the door—

And there they were, standing one behind the other in their luncheon-lady hats, veiled and feathered. What's going on? What's going on? Aunt Toto was angry.

I don't know I don't know. But already they had pushed past

me into the room and closed the door. All through the house it was silent, quiet, as if no one was there, as if nothing had happened.

But it had, it had, and I keep feeling there's something I should have done or should be doing, something I could have done and didn't. But whatever it is, now it's too late.

Magritte

A car driven by a silent man in a dark suit was taking me somewhere. He was faceless as I sat behind him looking at the back of his neck where the hair had been shaved up high, almost to the edge of a cap pulled down straight on his head. He concentrated on the task at hand and we drove along the road with rhythmic speed, curving by the ocean past Malibu, on and on. He reminded me of something, but what? Later, it occurred to me, as we pulled up to a big house set in a garden by the sea— Magritte. A Magritte painting I had seen once in a book, yes, it was that.

A door opened and I entered the cool hallway. An Aunt Gertrude butler said, Miss Gloria, follow me, please, and he took my suitcase from Magritte and smoothly led me along halls, past rooms of plump sofas, past hallways of other rooms with doors closed . . . on up the stairs we glided, fleetingly as shadows, the only two people left in the world. At the end of a hall, a door opened suddenly . . . a figure in black received me. My suitcase opened and the ruffled gauze of my white dress carefully shaken, tissue paper drifting onto the rose-patterned carpet with the rustle of dry leaves . . . the lace of Great-Grandmother Valdivieso's mantilla spread on the chaise, tenderly.

I went over to the window and looked out at the sea. The sun had shifted and below, the gardens in half-light reminded me again of something. Miss Gloria, would you like some tea?

No thank you, I said, perhaps later, after a nap, before dressing. The black figure nodded, drawing soft curtains across tall windows. Please ring if you require anything, Mr. Hughes is expected at eight. On the table by the bed, a pink quartz circle to press twice, beside this a clock with diamond arrows pointing . . . five o'clock precisely. I slipped out of my dress and lay on the bed. The spread had been taken away and the sheets were silky and cool. Through a half-open door I glimpsed my dress, cloud-like, floating. Whose house is this? I closed my eyes. . . . Who lives here? And where are they? But the more I puzzled, the drowsier I became, and soon . . .

Suddenly I was sitting up—what had awakened me? For I had been dreaming a long, complicated dream, the kind of dream that when you wake up seems more real than the so-called real life. In it I had driven to a place—a great good place—a place in a garden by the sea, but now that I was awake I came to realize that it was not a dream at all, for a door had opened and a figure brought a tray with tea, little sandwiches and cakes, and soon I looked out onto the gardens at the sea, for the curtains had been pulled back and everything was as it was before I had fallen asleep.

In the bathroom, water plunged into a scented tub. Everything happening became more and more like the dream as I poured tea into a cup—jasmine tea with blossoms floating . . . What time was it? Only six—two hours to prepare for the Fiesta. I closed my eyes, but when I opened them again, everything was still there exactly as it had been in the dream . . .

It was past eight—I better hurry. I looked in the mirror once more, a long view and then closer, up closer. Yes, there was no question about it. No matter how I tried to find fault with myself, there was no mistaking it—

I was beautiful . . . if only Mummy could see me. And Naney and Dodo and Aunt Gertrude.

Well, Howard would. I gave one last look and walked out along the halls until I came to the staircase. On the floor below—there he stood, by the banister, looking up . . . waiting.

It was crazy but I pulled back. . . .

All at once I wasn't sure about anything. I'd lost myself somewhere in the dream, in the long mirror, back in that unknown room. I wanted to run back, find it, for surely my image would still be reflected there proud and serene. I'd forgotten what I looked like, for now the frothy white of my dress felt all wrong, and the lace floating around my face, which before had caressed me, now scratched and seemed about to topple off onto the floor.

Then he saw me . . . his eyes pulled me forward, down each step, slowly, slowly until we were close, so close, but there was nothing to say, for he was speechless with wonder.

And I looked into his eyes, and as I did: I came back into myself, because I knew, I knew for certain—

Yes, I was sure—he loved me.

The Day After

On the way to the airport, the day after the Fiesta, we were going to stop somewhere for lunch but instead found ourselves sitting in a park on a bench, munching through crisp chocolate—Good Humors—into cool vanilla ice cream, and speculating about a couple sitting on another bench. They were bickering at their Chihuahua, who pulled on its polka-dotted leash most tediously, in some kind of argument. After a while we got down to the wooden sticks on the Good Humors and it was time to move on. Now I know what "lovely time" means. It turns the smallest everyday occurrence into an event of immense importance. So I'm going to save these Good Humor sticks forever and ever, like people save a cork from a bottle of champagne, only this is better.

.   .   .

But after Howard left me at Maple Manor and I walked through the silent house, up the stairs into my room, it all started slipping away. Because there, on the table by my bed, were orchids in a vase. How long had they been there? And where was he? For the flower arrangement had a Pat-Pasquale look about it, and, as I approached, there it was tied to a flowering spray, a neat white envelope with my name floundering across in that scrawl I knew so well. I made a fist and shut my eyes tight. One, two, three, I started counting, wishing, wishing, that when I came to ten the vase would have disappeared. It was a dippy game I used to play as a child, and it never worked then and it didn't work now. I took the Good Humor sticks out of my pocket, pressing my fingers across the satiny flatness. But they only felt like two stupid pieces of wood I should have thrown away instead of holding on to them like this.

> Gloria
>   Call me soon as you get back—don't plan
> anything for the next few days.
>
> > > Pat

I tore the card up and dialed. It rang and rang—maybe there wasn't time for him to have gotten home yet—after all, he'd just left me at Maple Manor. I called the other number, a message-leaving number, picked up always on the second ring by one of the Magritte persons who could always get my messages to Howard if I couldn't reach him.

Oh, he said, sounding surprised. Didn't Mr. Hughes tell you? He had to go out of town. Of course, I'll tell him as soon as I hear from him, yes, yes of course, I understand. I have no idea when I'll hear from him, but you can be certain he'll get your message the moment I do. Yes, of course.

At the very instant I put down the receiver, my private phone started ringing and ringing and ringing, but I didn't want to talk to Pat-Pasquale and I put pillows on top to make it stop. But I could still hear it, on and on it rang, following me into the bathroom, even through the sound of the water as it ran into the tub, and the more it rang the surer I was that I never wanted to see Pat-Pasquale again.

Suddenly it stopped ringing. But instead of taking a bath I called for a taxi, quickly, quickly I wanted to get out of here. Soon, Pat-Pasquale would be calling the other number, the Maple Manor number, sooner or later there would be no escape.

The hall was as before, empty and silent. Mummy out or resting, the door of her room closed. Aunt Toto's room had also been closed, but as I ran past the door was partly ajar and sunlight spattered across the carpet onto the dressing table and over the yellow roses rambling around on the chintz of the skirt. Maybe I could hide there, underneath the skirt, safe in the dark. Somewhere in the room a voice started talking to someone, Aunt Toto, so she and Edmund must be home, and I ran on out into the street.

To Saks, quickly, I told the taxi driver.

Not that I had anything particular in mind. For one thing, my monthly allowance was almost gone. It was just someplace to go. But when I got to Saks, it was quite a surprise.

Something was going on there. At the portals of the main entrance, a miniature village had been set up: houses with roofs painted to resemble thatch, organdy-curtained windows, and, frolicking around each little house, a puppy tied to a plaid leash, each sporting a tinkling bell on the collar. People were crowding around, oohing and aahing, and in the center of the hubbub there was someone rigged up to look like W. C. Fields. A woman? But you couldn't be sure, no. Whatever *it* was, the dogs were all cocker spaniels, and one of them looked exactly like Lolly, Big Elephant's caramel-colored new favorite. Its ears flopped around phlegmatically as Lolly's did—even the cringe was Lolly-like, not to mention a sidestepping kind of bow that Big Elephant finds so endearing and that I find mildly annoying. Nevertheless, I cooed and oohed along with the others and found myself shelling out the last of my allowance to buy the dog.

Now, my little Miss Chickadee, what will you be naming this fine specimen of puppyhood?

Puppyhood indeed. Now that W. C. Fields was closer, he was either a woman or a very corseted man.

Lolly-pop, I said, that's what I'll be naming her. It is a her, isn't it?

Pedigreed, pedigreed, he said, untying the leash from the wee Irish cottage, pedigreed, Miss Chickadee, right down to the fur on her little manicured paw. He gave the leash a yank and handed it to me. The puppy simpered up at me, waiting.

Okay, I said, let's go.

And off we went. She flopped along beside me, cringing and sniffing until after a while I picked her up. She nestled into me and closed her eyes. I closed my eyes too and pretended I was Big Elephant. It was uncanny: everything about Lolly-pop was as Lolly-like as could possibly be.

Gloria!

A voice shouted and a car, big and white, stopped short beside me. Other cars honked and screeched and there were other shouts and brakes shifting and there was almost an accident. I wanted to run and run, but instead I was sitting on a white leather seat holding on to Lolly, pat-pat-patting her. But she kept on shaking. Behind the wheel sat Pat-Pasquale, big and straight, white on white, for on his feet were white shoes, and he was wearing white pants, white shirt, white jacket, everything white, so around us all was white as white could be. He must have gotten lots of sun in Kansas City, for he was tanner than I remembered, the black of his hair curling around his forehead like wire, and his face, pirate-like, so fierce to see that the white of him and the white around us became thunderous and dark, and it was as if we hurled through seas of night instead of clouds of day. Without a look or a word he drove on and on, and I was sore afraid with the not knowing where we were going or why I found myself beside him in a car with this trembling dog in my lap. I wanted to open the car door, fling out onto the pavement—holding Lolly tight, we would roll and roll until nothing would be left of us but a tiny ball hurling through space. But we sped on, past Maple Manor, past the Beverly Hills Hotel, up, up, into the hills, until finally Lolly stopped her shaking and I closed my eyes and tried to pretend it was a terrible dream and soon I'd wake up.

Mornings

Some mornings I awake gently, lifted onto the shore by the tenderest of waves. It comes to me, the daylight, as natural as it is to breathe. And I open my eyes to gaze around the room, wondering where I am, what place I have come to after the long journey. For on these days when I awake, if I have dreamed during the night, I cannot remember. Nor do I desire to remember. For all memory of the journey has been obliterated, hazardous conditions, if indeed there were any, put to rest, and here I am, safely on the shore. Best not to question. I'll turn over, luxuriating, thinking of other mornings, forever ago it seems, when I'd wake at Wheeler by the earthquaking sound of the bell, and the first thing I'd tell myself was Soon soon I'll be grown-up and wake up every morning with the day before me, a day in which I'll be able to do anything I want. Then come the other mornings, dawns when I crash awake, thrown up on the shore by a wave, discarded by the night but still bound by its terrors, the journey and peril remembered, and I cry out, and wish with all my heart that I was back at Wheeler, the day ahead progressing in perfect order, each hour accounted for. Yes, because then . . . I wouldn't have to be grown-up at all.

Tiger, Tiger Burning Bright

The first day I arrived at Maple Manor Wannsie presented me with a key ring. On it, a heart-shaped charm, big as a red doughnut, and dangling alongside, the key to the front door—simple as could be and difficult to misplace. So why do I keep forgetting to take it in my bag along with compact, comb, and lipstick when I go out? To make certain someone will be here when I get back, is that why? My mother and Aunt Toto say from time to time (in jest?) that if I stay on here they'll have an outdoor staircase built onto the back of the house. It would be easy to do, building it down from the porch off my bedroom on down to the lawn below. Then I'd have my own entrance, so to speak. Wouldn't that be something! Somedays I think it would, other days not. But I don't know why I keep changing my mind, because if it's great one day why isn't it great another day?

Since The Constonce left, there has been silence from Old Westbury Capital. Aunt Gertrude must be really furious at me. Sometimes I wish I could talk to her if only by telephone, but this is only a vague hope floating around somewhere, because how could I talk to her long distance if I couldn't talk to her short distance? Not much from Naney Morgan these days either. Maybe she's given up on me too now that I'm staying on with my mother. And Cathleen—well, I don't expect to hear from *her*, but it doesn't matter, no it doesn't matter at all at all because how can I ever trust her again after the Van Heflin rumpus that was all for naught anyway? But about this key situation, Wannsie is a good sport about it and when you come right down to it, it's as much a nuisance to me as it is to her, this habit of leaving it in my dressing table drawer every time I go out, not grown-up at all! This is a firm resolution right this minute to take the key with me every time I set foot out of the house. It will make me independent and I'll stop worrying about things—Ketti Keven, things like that. I'll be going and coming as I please, free as a bird, and everything will be swell.

That is, until the summer is over. It won't be so swell then, because inevitably I'll have to go back to Old Westbury Capital, back to Aunt Gertrude, to the rules and regulations with chaperone Constance in attendance until September and the big escape to Wheeler. But when I get there what have I escaped to! Geometry. I almost flunked Algebra last year. You just don't get it, Gloria, Miss Tooker, our math teacher, kept saying. And it's true, I don't. It's like Chinese to me and I kept begging her to explain it to me and she tried, oh how she tried, but it was hopeless hopeless and made me feel so unsuccessful. This sounds idiotic, but maybe it's a solution—getting married no matter to whom so I won't have to go through that again, much less go back to Aunt Gertrude. But aside from all that, how can I ever go back to Wheeler after this taste of grown-up territory? Half of me longs to return, the other half knows I'd rather die than go back. If only Aunt Gertrude would let me skip school and go to the Art Students League in New York. That's what I really want to do. There is an eeriness about this silence, as if Old Westbury Capital existed only in my imagination, or maybe they've all died and nobody's thought to tell me.

Of course I know they haven't. Aunt Gertrude, I'm sure, is very much alive, because she could never die. I bet there's a lot of back-and-forth with the Tiger, Foley. He's my legal guardian and whatever happens happens because he decrees it. He's a tiny man but he makes up for it in other ways. That room of his in the courthouse, walls high as trees, and that desk of granite he presides behind when he's not pacing and roaring around the jungle. Aunt Gertrude sitting opposite him in grey silk wearing a summery version of the well-known hat. Her pearls warmed by skin from the day hot with summer, arms resting on the leather of the big brown chair, gloved hands clasped coolly together as she observes Tiger Foley pressing a handkerchief over the drips of sweat on his forehead. After a while Aunt Gertrude will be ready to speak about my future and Surrogate Foley will put his hands on the desk and lean towards her. He listens to Auntie Ger. When I'm there, the only listening that's done is me to him, as he prowls around, pontificating. What a lecture that last time—the evils of Hollywood and so on. He had long debates with himself while I sat there listening: should he permit my mother to take me across the state line to California, or would it be more in my best interests to remain in New York? Long days went by before the decision was handed down—yes, I could go, but only for these few weeks. Well, it's August now and way past curfew and here I still am. But I'm only fooling myself. It's only a matter of time before the summer's over. Such power he has in that jungle of his, but what is scariest of all is that this power reaches out into the world. My world anyway. But there must be other worlds that he doesn't have power over, and soon when I'm older I'll find out what they are—I'll get out of this jungle and never have to think about him again.

Limbo

/ One of the Magritte persons called. He said Howard's been phoning and phoning but I'm never here. Of course I'm never here, stupid, because most of the time I'm with Pat-Pasquale. Then Magritte dropped, quite casually, that Howard had been trying to reach me that day we came back from the Fiesta, right after he let me off at Maple Manor, to tell me that he had to go out of town unexpectedly. So it wasn't Pat calling that day as I stuffed pillows over the phone—it was Howard. Oh God, and now I'm enmeshed with Pat-Pasquale and Howard will never forgive me, never never and I'll never see him again ever. O misery! How could I have lost faith so quickly, but I did, and with it the belief that he loved me. Where is he? Where can I reach him? Where? Where? But Magritte said there was no way of knowing, we'd just have to wait for Howard to call in. Oh, tell him, tell him, tell him I'll be waiting waiting waiting. And I will. I won't move or go anywhere or set foot out of the house until I hear from him. All day I sit in limbo by the phone waiting for it to ring. And it does, only it's not Howard Howard it's Pat-Pasquale—oh God, what'll I do?

Please Do Not Disturb

It was early in the morning. Like eight o'clock. That's the crack of dawn from Mummy and Aunt Toto's point of view. The doors between their rooms were open out onto the hall and Wannsie ran back and forth between them trying to keep her wits about her—for it was clear to see that the twins had lost theirs. They were throwing themselves together any which way—and in the confusion Mummy had a brown shoe on one foot and a black shoe on the other, even the heel heights were different, but only Wannsie noticed this and she kept trying to get my mother's attention, waving the misplaced black shoe back and forth while Aunt Toto kept saying, Taxi, Wannsie, taxi, taxi! and Wannsie kept saying, Soon, Your Ladyship, soon soon. And sure enough, almost immediately there was a honk-honk-honking outside and there was a scramble while Mummy pulled a turban over her head so that none of her hair showed, and Aunt Toto said, Give me the other one, and she snatched a turban just like the black one Mummy had on, only it was white, and she yanked it down over her head without even looking at herself in the mirror. Then without putting lipstick on they both scurried down the stairs, calling back to Wannsie, who was following after fast as could be, Hurry, hurry, hurry, quickly quickly, hurry before they get there, the press, the press, and the three of them piled into the taxi and it backed out of the driveway and drove away.

. . .

Mesmerized by details of the disarray, I wandered back and forth between the two rooms. It was something to see, because Wannsie usually kept everything so neat and tidy but this morning the hasty departure left no time for such fripperies. Even the jars and bottles of mysterious lotions on my mother's dressing table were strewn about all higgledy-piggledy, and in Aunt Toto's room her nightgown lay in a heap on the floor beside her bed like a gauzy shadow. Dresses with hooks too complicated for the quick getaway had been discarded here and there, for the Queen Anne and Queen Jonquil had finally donned sporty slacks to speed out of the house in. On the chaise was the dress my mother had worn that evening she had said, Good morning, darling. It lay there scrunched up in a heap among the other dresses, so small it looked like the dress of a child. Should I tidy up a bit? This idea appealed to me enormously, but I hesitated because I wasn't sure where my mother's and Aunt Toto's things went and it would be a nuisance for Wannsie to sort them out again if I mixed them up.

Suddenly a ringing started and I lickety-split it to my room, terrified it would stop before I got there—

Hello hello?

When can I see you?

Oh darling darling darling—

I'll pick you up at seven—

Seven, seven, oh darling—seven!

Yes, it was him and I'm in heaven, but my hair looks hopeless and what'll I wear? I looked through my clothes and threw them on the bed. Soon my room was even messier than my mother's and Aunt Toto's. But he'd seen me in this dress, but not in that, so maybe the one he'd seen me in was—luckier? If only it would rain I could wear the black-and-white checked coat—he really liked that coat. Hours passed taken up by these absorbing problems. Then, just as I was about to come to a decision, they arrived in another taxi, and out they piled, rather noisily—my mother and Aunt Toto with Wannsie close behind carrying something, a big box which loaded her down, making her appear a short person and not her usual self at all.

Take it away, Wannsie—away away— Aunt Toto waved at it impatiently.

Yes, Wannsie, away away—my mother echoed, dismissing the box in the same manner. They were both sorely vexed by its presence, and Wannsie hesitated as if she wasn't sure what to do, but she slipped discreetly out of sight, holding the box as if it might be a coffin with a dead baby inside.

Mummy sank into the sofa, quite depleted, calling out, most feebly—

Scotch and soda, please, Wannsie.

For both of us, Aunt Toto said, please, and she sank down on the sofa next to Mummy and took her hand, murmuring to no one in particular, Can you imagine what would have happened if . . . if we hadn't gotten there before—before . . .

Before what?

But no one answered, and they lapsed into silence. Mummy closed her eyes, shaking her head back and forth, the revelations too horrendous to contemplate. Aunt Toto closed her eyes too, shaking her head back and forth in the same speechless way until finally the Scotch-and-sodas arrived which revived them a little. But not much.

I sat there, silently pondering over what terrible thing could have happened, but at the same time another part of me pondered over what I would be wearing when Howard picked me up at heaven—I mean seven. Finally I couldn't stand it another minute.

What happened, Mummy—what happened?

Aunt Toto and my mother looked at each other, but I'd be hard put to say what kind of look it was—inscrutable, but at the same time—questioning, as if maybe I was too young to hear about it.

Agnes! they both said.

Agnes?

Yes, poor Agnes. Something unforeseen. My mother's voice faded out, and she looked at Aunt Toto as if *she* could tell us both what had happened.

Dead. Aunt Toto spoke quickly.

Dead?

Yes—unfortunately—she killed herself.

How, why? I couldn't believe it, but then the more I thought about it the more I could believe it.

Who knows how or why these things happen? Aunt Toto said testily, and she shrugged her shoulders and made that little moue, not choosing to elaborate. She glanced over at Wannsie puttering around a table in the background with ice cubes, refreshing their drinks. Wannsie? Our lotto game? Where did you hide it?

Try not to think about all this, darling, my mother said to the room in general and she leaned towards me, vaguely patting my arm.

Wannsie fiddled around in a drawer and moved forward with chips and cards which Aunt Toto spread out in front of her on the coffee table.

Well, Aunt Toto smiled comfortingly, at least the press will have nothing to pounce on. Nothing to connect us with any of it—any of this—unpleasantness.

Mummy and I sat back and dwelt on this while Aunt Toto ruffled the cards.

Thank God we got there before the press did, Aunt Toto said, optimistically repeating herself as she stacked chips, chatting away. You know, she went on confidingly, Agnes had photographs of your mother and me all over the place—not now, of course, because we got there in time and took them all away—all away—there's nothing of your mother and me left there in that tiny place of hers—nothing at all to connect her with us.

So it wasn't a dead baby in the box after all, only photographs.

But I didn't want to think about it—about the room of tininess and the shades pulled down, the photographs of my mother and Aunt Toto going back over the years, to Paris no doubt, or the Please Do Not Disturb sign on the door—or know where Wannsie would bury them, or be part of any of it. But I kept seeing Agnes as she had been in my mother's room that day, reaching towards me, the grape beads scattering across the bed like marbles. If I had gone towards her instead of away, said something that would have made a difference, perhaps none of this would have happened—but it has, and even if I don't understand Mummy and Aunt Toto, or understand how it happened, somewhere mixed in with the idiotic pondering over what I'm going to wear tonight is the loneliness of the way it happened. And I do understand that.

Saying Things Like

Driving along Santa Monica switching the radio dial around, suddenly someone strumming a guitar, singing—a man—

> *There's a long, long trail a-windin'*
> *Into the land o' my dreams*
> *Where a nightingale is singin'*
> *And a white moon beams. . . .*

Then the singing stops and he goes on in a dippy voice saying things, things like—

Yes, it can happen to you, you're going along for years and years down the long, long trail a-winding into the land of loneliness, when suddenly, yes-sir-ee, that well-worn path leads straight through a tunnel, straight through to the lane o' my heart as it comes to you—

Howard looked over at me and smiled just as if the voice were talking about us.

Yes-sir-ee, and the vines of love and the flowers of cheer grow there all seasons of the year, and on every day they will bloom anew with my heart's love all for you-oo. And ya ain't lonely no more, 'cause—

And then he started up again, strumming and singing away—

There's a long, long night a-waitin'
Until my dreams all come true
Till the day when I'll be going
Down that long, long trail with you. . . .

I got so scared because then Howard said, Corny but it's true, isn't it?—and he stated it, it wasn't a question. He's serious about me, he is he is he is. Oh God, help me to really believe it.

No matter how much Howard tells me he loves me, somehow I can't believe it—why this wonderful man would love me, be in love with me and want to marry me, because he does he does. I look at myself in the mirror and I can't quite grasp that he could have any girl in the world but he wants— chooses—me. That picture he has in his room of Katharine Hepburn taken on his boat. She's laughing as if he said something funny just as he clicked the picture. Her eyes are so full of love for him, and he loves her, I know, because in his room that's the only thing that has to do with him. The room itself is like a room someone would rent just for a short time, it could belong to anyone or to no one. Like a room that someone has just moved out of, hurriedly perhaps, so that by some mistake a most precious possession is forgotten, left behind—this photograph of the person he loved. How can I ever come up to that? Why, if I can't even please my own mother, how can I possibly ever please him?

Castles

Aunt Gertrude has summoned me to New York. And Mummy is lying in bed doing nothing while Wannsie is bustling about packing. In my own way I'm packing too, if you can call throwing things into one suitcase packing. It's been weeks now since The Constance withdrew. Withdrew is hardly the word, however, because Auntie Ger didn't withdraw her—she just plain quit. Dropped off the face of the earth with ne'er a toodle-oo. I'm very scared. Scared that Aunt Gertrude is going to make me go back to where I was before I flew the coop. But even more than that, I'm scared that things are going to go on the way they have been here at Maple Manor.

A few days ago Aunt Toto came to me all askew, wringing her hands together. I'd never seen her this way before. Even when what happened to Agnes happened, she held herself in command throughout.

I don't know what I'm going to do about your mother. The words came out of her stunned face in a monotonous hum over and over, while her hands kept wringing themselves together as if they had a life all their own.

I tried to think of something to do, something to say, but no words came, and after a while she looked right at me and put her arms around me and started to cry . . . almost. Almost, because instead she pulled away and went over to the sofa and sat down and lit a cigarette calm as could be.

Of course, I knew what was on her mind. Because it was true, my mother was like someone I'd never seen before, much less met. Most of the time she was away, and when she wasn't away she'd be at Maple Manor and Ketti Keven would be here too. But even when Mummy was at Maple Manor, she was— away—impossible to reach. She'd fade in and out of things, and while she was drifting, sometimes she'd come across an idea and she'd come back again to tell us about it because it was an important idea, a *very* important idea.

I'm going to dye my hair blond, she confided challengingly as if we were all going to stop her, and over she hurried to the dressing table, leaning too close into the mirror, examining her face like it belonged to a stranger.

Over and over again she'd say it, and Ketti would follow her and sit in a chair beside her to listen. After a while even Ketti got bored and would try to snap her out of it by giving a definitive answer to the blond question, only it came out like an answer to an entirely different question, one that hadn't been asked. And although no one else knew what Ketti's answer meant, my mother did, and it would divert her for a moment, make her laugh, and off they'd go into that land of secret jokes where none could follow. Forget about me following—even Aunt Toto was left behind. That's what made it scary. That is what makes Aunt Toto desperate, why as a last resort she came into my room expecting me to have the answer, when she knows I don't have the answer to anything, much less my mother. Mummy, where are you where are you where are you . . . ?

Well, right now it's in bed with no decisions to make about the blond situation or anything else, because Wannsie is making all the decisions about what to pack for this little jaunt to New York. How long we are to stay has not been mentioned. What has been mentioned is that Ketti Keven is going with us. And Aunt Toto is to remain at Maple Manor. So it is these things that bat around us in the silent night, holy night, and make everything scarier as the minutes pass. For pass they do, and it's as if I am on a rushing train going faster and faster—

Away, away from Aunt Toto—for try as I will, I find no answer to give her, and now it's Aunt Gertrude I rush towards.

But as I do, there is something I fear even more, because as

I rush towards, I am also rushing away, further and further away from what I want most of all, and that's my mother.

We almost didn't make the plane. There was a fight before we left, a terrible terrible fight, more terrible than any I could imagine, even in a movie. It was between Aunt Toto and my mother. Yes. It's almost impossible for me to believe they fought with each other, even now as having seen it I think back on it. It started out quietly with Aunt Toto explaining to my mother that *she* would go with us to New York and there was no need for Ketti to tag along, no need at all at all. Now, Aunt Toto can be powerfully strong once she puts her mind to something, and she sure had put her mind to this, although she put it to my mother calmly enough. But my mother came forward with a power I never could have foreseen and the battle was fearsome to see, and even when the doors closed their fury could be heard resounding through the house, and in the midst of it all who should arrive but herself—Ketti Keven, suitcases packed, ready to go, and up she went straight into my mother's room, her voice slicing through Aunt Toto and my mother as they sat there talking and all over everywhere all over the house there was no place to go, no place to hide, and no doubt in my mind as to who would win.

No surprise that here we are, the three of us on a TWA plane—my mother traveling as Mrs. Vane with moi as her daughter, Miss Grace Vane (incognito), to avoid the press finding out about this impromptu trip. The "Vane" was selected to coincide with the initials on our luggage. Yes, Mummy and Ketti are pretty foxy. Oh well, even though Aunt Toto is left behind, she has Edmund to console her. We are in an area with seats facing each other, Mummy and Ketti sitting opposite me, and as the plane drones on there is much giggling which I disassociate myself from, but I can't help feeling irritated by the dingle-dangle of charms they wear, identical charms on ditto bracelets. Ketti had them made up, quite large as charms go, cut out of gold in the shape of a castle with numerals and initials here and there, their significance enigmatic to all save my mother and Ketti. She wears hers all the time, she says, and my mother never takes hers off either. You know it's true you really can see red (or should I say green?), for that's what I see when I look at those dippy bracelets. Sometimes I have to stop myself from tearing my mother's off her wrist. Of course, they don't know this, because I ooh and aah over how cute they are, hoping maybe to curry favor and wangle the secret out of one of them. But so far no such luck. Oh well, who cares! As Ketti gets noisier, so does my mother. I'd like to change seats, but the plane is full. Katharine Hepburn is on the plane too. Any other time this would have sent me into a tizzy, but those castles really get to me and I can't think about anything else—not even the sneakers K.H. is traveling in.

Later: An hour ago someone came and said to me, Miss Vane, the pilot would like to see you, please follow me. And I did, right through a door no one but those qualified are permitted to enter, right through into the cockpit of the plane. Mr. Hughes wanted you to see everything, the pilot said, and he proceeded to show me just that. It was like being inside of some gigantic watch, seeing how it ticked. It took my mind off things. But now we're about to land and I'm right back in them again. I'm worried my mother and Ketti won't make it all right to the Elysée Hotel. Anyway, I'll be able to drop them off first so I'll see they get in OK before I go on to 60 Washington Mews to meet Aunt Gertrude. I wish I was somewhere else. But where?

A Short Trip

Well, they refused to set foot in Aunt Gertrude's car, so there was nothing for me to do but get them in a taxi and hope they'd make it to the hotel one way or another. After that I tried to stop worrying and it was like old times, just me and Freddy in Aunt Gertrude's grey Rolls wending our way through the New York traffic towards Washington Mews.

But instead of Hortense opening the door it was Butler Edward. And he took a long time doing it, so as I stood outside, sticky and hot, waiting for the door to open, I had quite some time to gather my thoughts, such as they were. About Auntie Ger, mainly—wondering what she'd say, but most of all what she'd do about the overextended stay with my mother in California. Through all this Winter Austin Smith floated in and out, here and there—because at some point I'd *have* to see him. Wouldn't I? Maybe not. But more like maybe yes. The Mews was quiet, separated from the city, nestling into the hazy heat which shimmered fair around the wisteria twining on up from the cobblestones to the balcony of what had once been my room. But why did I think of it as *once*? After all, it was still my room.

Inside, although everything was in place forever so, the room felt empty, inhabitants away somewhere for the summer, no one except Butler Edward and me as I followed his swallow-tailed self into the shadowy living room. The balloon curtains had been lowered against the August heat and through the glass wall only part of the garden was visible, with light filtering through the trees, making patterned shadows on the Persian rug. I almost stooped down to touch the spot where I had spilt the tea that afternoon so long ago, when snow had swirled outside and Winter and Aunt Gertrude and I had sat talking to each other, but I didn't because a border of begonias planted along the pathway leading to the fountain at garden's end drew me to the window. Through the ballooning curtains of yellow silk I could see the nymph Psyche, as the water splashed around her, still I kept seeing her coronet of stone flowers as it had been that December transformed in the snow to a crown of crystals . . . only seven months had passed since then.

Butler Edward carried my suitcase on up the stairs, but as I

started to follow him, quite unexpectedly the door leading from
the living room to Aunt Gertrude's room opened. A shadowy
Hortense in her usual black looked at me coldly and said briefly,
Mrs. Whitney will see you now. Stepping aside, without looking
at me, she held aside the door and I went past her into Aunt
Gertrude's presence.

How tall and thin she was (I'd forgotten that) as she stood
with her back to me rather like an elegant flamingo, poised in
front of a full-length three-way mirror. Kneeling in front of her
was a small person who did not look up when I entered but
continued inching her way on her knees around Aunt Gertrude,
taking pins from pursed mouth, respectfully weaving them in
and out around the hem of Aunt Gertrude's skirt. It was tweedy
as tweedy could be, this skirt, and resting on a chair close by
was its own matching tweedy jacket, along with other things,
most untweedy, like a dress made of georgette, and a long satin
something—what had happened to the pants outfits I knew so
well? My arrival had interrupted a fitting séance of some sort,
for the autumn season was almost upon us. But I didn't disturb
anything, since Aunt Gertrude needed not turn around as she
saw me reflected behind her in the mirror. She remained concentrated on the task at hand, and I hesitated before moving
forward to embrace her, because something about her manner
made me sense she preferred I restrain myself.

How was your trip, Gloria? she said, without turning around.
She was quite taken by the performance of the lowly person
kneeling at her feet, for the pins held in her teeth kept falling
onto the floor and disappearing in the Aubusson.

Gee, it was fine, Auntie Ger, just fine.

I kept staring at her hat. It was one I hadn't seen before, but
I couldn't figure out why. It was the same, but different—
something about the crumple of it maybe? Rather like a velvety
version of an Edwardian chimney sweep. Or the absence of the
feather perhaps . . . no matter.

I like your hat, I said, hopefully.

Flattery never had appealed to her, and anyway she was about to say something to the person now groping around her feet, for the pin situation had gotten quite out of hand, and Aunt Gertrude was losing patience as the creeping figure ferreted around in the carpet to retrieve them. But she sighed and let it pass, turned her head away towards the garden. So there we stood for quite a while as time passed, as it does, until finally she turned around and looked at me.

Why don't you unpack and get settled and after that we can talk.

Talk talk talk—oh yes, talk!—and I bounded up the stairs and into the silvery lavender room and threw myself on the bed. I was going to cry but instead fell dead asleep.

Tap tap tap, then a voice. Miss Gloria, Miss Gloria, it called, loud, right through the door, right into the death of my sleep, Miss Gloria, Mr. Smith is on the telephone for you.

Hello, Winter, I said.

How's it been in sunny California? he said.

Then there was a lot of talk about oranges and the good orange juice out there, so much better than in New York.

Lots of good fresh grapefruit juice out there too, I bet.

You better believe it, I said.

Well . . . he said.

Well . . . I said.

Well, I'll be seeing you soon, he said.

Soon soon—what do you mean soon?

This weekend, dummy—it'll be nice having the weekend together, give us a chance to catch up on things.

Catch up on things? What things? What things could Winter and I possibly have to catch up on? It was much too late for anything like that.

What do you mean weekend? I said.

Mrs. Whitney invited me to Old Westbury for the weekend, isn't that nice, Pookie?

It's the first I've heard of it! It made me furious and I slammed down the receiver.

But now Winter will be arriving any second and we'll be driving out with Freddy for the weekend to Old Westbury Capital. Not only that: Aunt Gertrude is driving out with us. Yes, she is—isn't that great?

I just tried to call my mother at the Elysée Hotel but was informed they have a Do Not Disturb on the phone. Say it's her daughter, I said. But no no no no—the operator was quite put out, and when I started screaming at her she hung up on me.

I took a bath, and after I was all dry, I took an enormous puff and dusted my limbs with powder (Chanel Numéro Cinq, what else), and the only thing on my mind right now is selecting a dress to wear for the meeting with Winter. I don't have all that much choice due to the hasty packing, so it comes down to the black linen or the black cotton. Both are sophisticated beyond words, real eye-catchers. Especially when teamed up with the ankle-strap shoes, spiky! (tamed and brought to heel with masterly perfection). No more teetering-around episodes to broadcast my former babyishness. This time it's grown-up all the way.

Just as I was about to sally downstairs all ready for anything, Hortense brought in the most enormous vase of yellow roses. Of course I knew right away they were from Howard. He always sends yellow roses. But Pat-Pasquale's voice popped into my brain about Brenda Frazier and roses, saying that Howard sent Brenda *red* ones always when he was taking her out, as though yellow roses were second best. Well, they certainly don't look second best to me. Hortense put the vase on top of the Venetian bureau gilded with the winged creatures and switched on the lights.

Thinking of you.

That's what the card said (no name necessary). Nothing necessary for me but to know he's thinking of me, missing me. Yes, that's where I'd like to be right now. With Howard somewhere, high up in a plane, on our way to nowhere in particular, with twinkly lights below and nothing on our minds but each other.

The weekend at Old Westbury Capital was cut short, very short. From the beginning, Winter was impossible, but what really did me in was Aunt Gertrude's saying that Winter and I could get married right away, immediately. Yes, a big wedding or a small wedding, whatever we wanted. This plan unfolded as we were in the car on our way to Old Westbury Capital, and I was speechless. Winter was too, I think, although I guess he's always thought someday we'd get back together again and be married. But how can I ever go back to where I was before Watertown, before I went to visit my mother in California? They think I'm the same. But I'm not, I'm not. Things have happened. I've seen things now that I didn't even know existed before. I'm grown-up, aren't I? And because I am, everything has changed, forever . . . everything.

All night long I lay in my room at Old Westbury Capital unable to sleep . . . wondering what Aunt Gertrude had said to Howard on the phone. Because he called right after we arrived, right after we got out of the car, just after I had asked if I could speak with her alone. Winter went back to the Cottage to unpack before dinner, to the room under the eaves where he always stays, and I went into the living room with Aunt Gertrude and closed the door and said that Howard wanted to marry me. She was taken aback, I could see, and she sat down by the fire and there was silence between us, until she said, Why haven't I heard about any of this? How old is he? Thirty-six, I answered quickly, trying to make out what she was thinking. You're *only* seventeen, she said, but I felt three years old as I listened to her. I'm seventeen *whole* years old, you said so yourself, Auntie Ger, on the postcard you sent me for my birthday. Well, she said, I must talk to him. He's in California, I said. We can call him now, she said. I will speak to him by phone, and right on cue in came Winter, and behind him Butler Edward with something to say to me. Mr. Hughes is on the phone for you, Miss Gloria, is what he had to say, and I went across the hall into the phone room with Aunt Gertrude close beside me as I picked up the receiver. I half expected Winter to come along too, but he didn't. All flustered up and scared and in a panic I said, Howard, Auntie Ger's here and wants to speak to you, speak to you, and I handed the phone to her as though it were hot, red hot, and I ran out of the room, up the stairs, away away, away from Winter and Aunt Gertrude and Howard, for I wanted to be away from everything and never have to buffet back and forth between people ever again. Hundreds of years went by and my door opened and it was Auntie Ger. She said what a nice talk she and Mr. Hughes had and that she was certain everything would work out one way or another for the best and that I'd best go back downstairs as Winter was waiting for me. What did that mean, one way or another? But try as I would to find out, that is *all* she would reveal, and the only thing I can do now is wait until I can find out from Howard exactly what she did say. So that's why I didn't sleep all night, because there was no way of reaching Howard back by phone . . . he's who-knows-where. And I lay there all night until light came into my room through a crack in the curtains, like a long icicle it was, even though it's summer, and the sun had risen and the new day begun . . . Saturday with its hours and hours ahead, hours to be with Winter, hours of Auntie Ger, as if everything were fine and dandy sugar candy, if only I could sleep. . . .

Hortense brought my breakfast tray in and said that Mrs. Whitney was already up and in the living room. "Mr. Smith is also there and lunch will be at one o'clock promptly." She glanced at the clock on the night table—it was noon. There was only one thing for me to do. I had to get back to Howard, find out what had happened. Mummy would understand, wouldn't she,

and let me go back with her to California? Freddy couldn't help
me even if he wanted to. I did the only thing possible. I called
a taxi. I threw clothes on; my suitcase I'd leave—too cumbersome
in trying to slip out of the house unnoticed. I'd walk down the
stairs, out the front door, just as if I were going out for a walk
before joining Aunt Gertrude and Winter for lunch. Should I
try getting my mother on the telephone? No—best just get on
the train and show up at the Elysée Hotel. She'd have to see me
then, wouldn't she? Yes, that's what I'd do. All I needed now
was luck—luck as I went down the stairs, past the dining room,
nodding good morning to Butler Edward as he put finishing
touches on the lunch table—four more steps now to reach the
front door . . . soon soon soon—

Good morning, Gloria—my, what a good sleep you got! It
was Aunt Gertrude. I listened to the crunch on the driveway as
a car drove around the circle and stopped outside the front door
between the standing Dalmatian dogs. They were painted white,
these statues, with black spots, and I'd called them domino dogs
ever since I could remember. They had always been there, as they
would always be there, forever guarding the portico. But why
did that seem important now? Aunt Gertrude heard the car too
and said—

Who could that be? No one is expected.

Auntie Ger, someone is expected, I said. A taxi someone—

A taxi someone? What do you mean by that? She seemed
really puzzled.

Look, Auntie Ger, I said, I've got to go now·

What do you mean you've got to go now? It's almost time
for lunch.

Somewhere far off in the nether regions of Old Westbury
Capital the front doorbell had sounded and Butler Edward was
purposefully moving forward to answer it.

Look, I said, look, Auntie Ger. It's my fault the taxi is
arriving—I called it because—

Taxi, she said smoothly, and without a shadow she moved

away. Edward, take care of the taxi, will you please, and tell the driver it's not necessary to wait. Then she said, Come with me, Gloria, and I found myself following her into the phone room. Sit down, she said, closing the door. *Why* did you call a taxi? Now that Butler Edward was no longer present, her voice had changed and she sounded put out, yes, most put out and quite annoyed.

I don't know why, Auntie Ger, I don't I don't—

I must say, Gloria, your behavior these days is most—well, difficult to understand—to say the least. She looked at me as if I had the answer to this. But it was a long wait, because I didn't have an answer to this or to anything. Then suddenly she said—

You just *love* publicity, don't you!

What do you mean, Auntie Ger, what do you mean?

All the publicity you get in Hollywood—you just *love* all that, don't you!

She was really angry. Her words numbed me and I felt my body all over go cold, so cold, and I started to tremble. I'd never heard her like that before, and although her words paralyzed me, someplace within me there was a surge, small though it might be, of something almost like hope—because at last she was talking to me, face to face, as never before. No Tweedles present, no messengers—just Auntie Ger and me, here in this tiny room, having what was almost turning into a fight, and there was something about it that was almost—thrilling. Yes! But then she pulled back.

Look, you better leave, if that's what you want—go! I'll not keep you here—go! she said disdainfully. Go! wherever it is you want to go, and do whatever it is you want to do!

But I don't know I don't know, and I took a deep breath, determined not to cry.

Already the bell had been pressed in the wood-paneled wall, and I opened the door and ran past her, past Butler Edward who stood there as Aunt Gertrude gave him instructions about Freddy, that he was to drive around immediately, for Miss Gloria wished to be driven to the city. Up the stairs I ran and put my things into the suitcase, and after that I walked down the stairs and out of the house into the car. Take me to the Elysée Hotel, Freddy, please, I said, and I looked at the domino dog statues standing there as they always did, looked back at the front door, somewhere hoping—but already I knew it had closed behind me.

"God's Perfect Child"

Mrs. Vane and daughter Grace, accompanied by Miss Keven, did go back to California, on the same day that Freddy drove me from Aunt Gertrude's and left me off at the Elysée Hotel. It was quite a feat getting Ketti and my mother packed and so forth, but anyway I won't go into that, and there we were back on Maple Drive much sooner than any of us expected. Still, what my mother and Ketti expect is anyone's guess. When I did get back, Howard had dropped off the face of the earth, and the only person waiting for me was someone dark, someone dark and unkind. And he said he had to see me about something. And because it's impossible to go back to living with Aunt Gertrude and impossible to continue on here as things are with my mother, I am trapped, and because I am frightened and there's no one to talk to about it I find I have said—Yes. And here it is only a few weeks later and plans are underway for a wedding. Not only a wedding but a big church wedding (the kind of wedding Aunt Gertrude would have given me), a Roman Catholic church wedding in the Old Mission in Santa Barbara—that'll show her. It is to be High Mass that will go on for three serious hours with lots of bridesmaids all in a row, ushers in penguin suits, and tons of movie-star guests in all the pews, and after the ceremony we will all drive back along the coast in limousines to a reception in Beverly Hills at 719 North Maple Drive.

Yes, it seems I am to become Mrs. Pasquale John De Cicco, and I am happy as happy could be. Yes, I go skipping around happy as a bird, singing all the livelong day, and between all this skipping and singing I am making important decisions, deciding this and that and what to wear or what not to wear. During the day I sport an engagement ring. Pernod green it is, a square-cut chrysoberyl with a V-shaped ruby on either side, twinkly as can be, and I am so in love I never take it off except at night when I place it in a little demitasse cup by my bed to give it a rest until morning. Last night my mother left a note on my pillow with a message just for me . . . *"Que tu siempre seos feliz como te ves esta noche,"* that's what it said, written in that extravagant up-and-down daddy-longlegs spidery writing I've imitated for years (with some success). What does it mean, Mummy? I asked her next day. "May you always be as happy as you are tonight," that's what it means, Pooks. Pooks indeed. I even pretend to Dodo and Naney Morgan. Letters to them, going on and on about how happy happy happy I am. I got up courage to beg Mummy to let them come out here for the wedding, but all the agonizing I went through could have been avoided because she said yes without a moment's thought. (What *does* she think of these days?) But because they *are* coming, Uncle Harry, Aunt Edith, Virginia, and little Thelma will all be conspicuous by their absence—as for Aunt Consuelo, forget it, although it might interest you to know (then again it might not) that she's dropped the Tamar because it didn't bring the luck the wizard predicted. No, none of them will be there because of the way their mother, my Naney Morgan, behaved at the Custody Trial towards my mother. As for Dodo Big Elephant—well, that's another reason they won't attend, because she's also to be a member of the wedding. Yes, a very important-to-me member, and she is to accompany Naney Morgan from New York on the Silver Chief train, arriving a few days before the wedding. Strung up is how I feel, right in the middle, but most of the time I try not to think about it.

After all, there is a lot on my mind. Aunt Gertrude, for example—not that I expect it, but not a word has come to me from her. I keep hoping that she'll get so furious at me she'll send a bolt of lightning to prevent the wedding. Sometimes I dream about her, dream I'm banished forever, that she is lost to me and I'll never see her ever again. Oh well, if it comes to that—how can I be banished when I never really belonged there anyway, so what's the diff? Right? Right. Still, I wake up in the middle of the night with a pain in my chest, like there's a clamp right in the center, squeezing. After a while I put my mind on other things and in the morning it's gone—sometimes. Other times not. Howard's in the back of my mind all the time. I keep hoping I'll just run into him somewhere by chance, but out here it's not like New York where you always run into people on the street when you least expect it. I don't phone him because he might hang up on me. And if Pat-Pasquale ever found out about it he'd have a fit, and I'm terrified of his temper. He gets all—dark—and a terrible storm ravishes his face, and when it happens I'd do everything to distract him. Once I thought he was going to hit me, but he came out of it, saying to me over and over again, What is it with you, what is it with you! And I went to find my mother to ask her if maybe it's not such a good idea, this wedding. But I guess I didn't explain it right, because all she said was, You're overtired, Pooks, why don't you take a nap? Come see me when you feel better. Better better better, yes, that's what I feel every day. What was it Dodo Elephant used to say? Sometimes it goes around, around in my head like music on a merry-go-round . . . Every day in every way you're getting better and better because you're God's perfect child. So even if Pat-Pasquale says to me, What is it with you! Look at yourself, look at that pimple on your face, it's the *badness* coming out of you, all I have to do is look in the mirror and try to find the pimple, and say to myself that I'm Big Elephant's— I mean, "*God's* perfect child," and the pimple will go away and everything will come out all right.

A Letter to Carol Marcus in New York

Darling Angel,

Guess what?! I just saw the sketches for the dresses—not only mine, but the bridesmaids' too! They're really gorgeous. I'd asked Howard Greer to make them as Rita Hayworth as possible and boy—did he! (She's coming to the Wedding by the way.) *Very* sophisticated and I can't wait to see the pale ice blue of your bridesmaid dress with the color of your hair. The other bridesmaids are going to be Shirley Cowan, Valerie Cole (Val's from England visiting an aunt in Westwood for the summer), Betsy Newling (she just had a big coming-out party in Beverly Hills), and Frances Savino (Pat's niece, who I haven't met yet). You'll love them all. Everyone thinks Shirley and I look like sisters—I wonder if you'll think so? Sometimes I think I do, other times, I don't. Anyway, you'll see. She's very pretty and just gave up her job teaching dancing at Arthur Murray's Dance Studio in Burbank. Charley Wrightsman is just nuts about her, really crazy, and she goes out with him, but only when she can't go out with—guess who? Errol Flynn!!! 'cause that's who she's *really* in love with! She sees him every chance she gets, but it's not much 'cause he sees a lot of other girls betweentimes and it makes her feel just awful and we talk about it all the time. Errol's going to be one of the ushers along with Rosey Rosenberg (he's an actor's agent), Bruce Cabot, and Cubby Broccoli (he's Pat's cousin and is married to Gloria Blondell, Joan Blondell's sister). The other usher was going to be Prince Mike Romanoff—that is, until Mummy had a fit. Seems he is not really a Prince at all even though he calls himself one, and Mummy's friends with the real Romanoffs and says they wouldn't take to it one bit. He tried to crash a party Mummy and my father gave in Newport hundreds of years ago and the very mention of his

name makes her have apoplexy! He has a restaurant on Rodeo
Drive that we all practically live in, and I don't get what all
the fuss is about. Anyway—fuss there is, so Pat is going to
have to ask someone else to replace him. Who? I wonder.

Other fusses go on too about bridesmaids. The Deenie
Hutton situation, for example. Errol met her on a train going
somewhere and went coo-coo over her, and so he and Pat
cooked up the coo-coo idea that I should invite her out here to
be a bridesmaid!!! It's the worst idea he's ever come up with.
She just had her coming-out party on Long Island which I
wasn't invited to. So I was *mortified*, because even though
Deenie and I were at Green Vale together, we only saw each
other now and again walking through the halls, and it's too
weird to suddenly out of the blue ask her to be one of my
bridesmaids if you know what I mean. Plus the fact that

Shirley is in love with Errol and she's my friend so I feel terrible doing that to her. Well, Pat and Errol went on and on about it, saying that Deenie would *know* the reason behind my asking her to be a bridesmaid and would jump through hoops for the chance to see Errol again. Her mother is even more of a terror than Auntie Ger when it comes to chaperones, on and on they went, blah blah blah—so I got just plain worn down and said OK OK OK do anything you want. So between them they cooked up a telegram and sent it off in my name. God knows what it said but by then I didn't care. Pronto the answer came back—*NO*. Well, it was no surprise to me, but I'm so embarrassed. Anyway, I just wanted to dash this off quickly 'cause I got so excited when I saw the sketches for the dresses—

Tons of love, darling, and try to get your mother to let you come out at least a week before the Wedding. Lots of parties and every day is such fun and I'm so happy.

XXXX OOOO

Gloria

P.S. Have you seen Winter at all? He must be back at Yale now. I haven't heard a word from him since I saw him in August.

P.P.S. Pat just called. Charlie Feldman is going to be Prince Romanoff's replacement. Oh, well.

Rhapsody in Blue

Over and over again I play *Rhapsody in Blue* on my portable Victrola, the sound up high as it will go, lying on the floor I close my eyes and turn loose, letting go into the soaring, soaring music, soon nothing is left of me, only—only—

Banging banging on the door. Wannsie stands there saying, Mr. Smith is here.

What!

Yes, Mr. Smith, on the porch. Modom has been advised and is on her way down to see him, but it's you he's waiting for, yes, he flew out on a plane all the way from New York.

Creeping to the window, bending low, I peer out over the edge. There he stands, hands behind his back, surveying the sprinklers twirling monotonously around on the grass, taking it all in as if Maple Manor were the most natural place in the world for him to be. If he hears the deafening sound of music from my open window he gives no sign, nor does he turn when I lift the needle off the record, mid-crescendo, as the screen door opens and out comes my mother in one of her robes, hastily donned, mules clacking on flagstones.

Why, Winter, she says, what a surprise! What are you doing here?

Oh, he says, casual-like, just came out for the weekend, for a little sunshine. And on and on they go chatty-chitting about this until finally my mother says—

Well, let me see if Gloria's in.

Well, Gloria isn't in, and I run and hide, but there is no place to hide so I sit and wait, and soon Mummy is clack-clacking up the stairs into my room, most persistent that I come down to see him, but I can't I can't, I'm afraid, afraid of being torn in still another direction and ending up nowhere.

Look, Gloria, she said, you can't just leave him standing down there—after all, he has come three thousand miles to see you.

Please, please, I can't, I just can't see him!

What do you mean—*can't*—after all, he knows you're going to marry De Cicco. The name makes me shrink whenever I hear it on my mother's lips, for she pronounces it "De Chee-co," in the correct Italian manner, of course, but it comes out strange each time, a name I've never heard before, because Pat and all his friends pronounce it "De Sic-co." But when my mother says it (it's one word she never stammers over), out it comes: cheeky, somehow dubious, a made-up name, not a real name at all. Each time it comes out I hold my breath, hoping it's going to be different, a prelude perhaps to confidences between us? But maybe it's not like that at all, for despite the cheeky-De-Cheeco she really seems to favor Pat-Pasquale, even as she sing-songs along with Aunt Toto, casually gossiping that someone said "De Chee-co's" job with Hughes was really nothing more than that of "procurer." What's that mean? I'd asked. Oh, you know, getting girls for him, they had answered with a discreet little giggle, before fussing on with their knitting.

Mummy Mummy, I can't see Winter I can't I can't, there's nothing to say, nothing to do, it's all hopeless hopeless.

Well, what am *I* supposed to do about it? she said as she click-clacked aimlessly around the room. There seemed to be some difficulty about the mules, keeping them on, like maybe they were a size too big for her.

Really, Gloria! And she stopped by the table next to my bed, looking around vaguely for something.

Here, Mummy, I said, and emptying a dish of candy, I handed it to her. As she used it to snuff out her cigarette, she noticed the turtle on my night table. Quite taken aback, she stared at it, but as it came into focus she realized that it was only a lump of spinach jade carved to resemble a turtle and fashioned into a bell, and she pressed up and down against the scratchy shell, careful not to break the long oval of her nail. Restlessly she lighted another cigarette and circled back around the room while I sat on the sofa wondering if Winter still stood on the same spot on the porch—or had he wandered down to the pool to stand gazing up at my window?

Silently, around and around in my head the *Rhapsody in Blue* had started up again. If only I dared put the record back on, loud, loud, as loud as it would go—but all I did was to stare at

my trusty portable, the black, round disc lying there, dead as a
charred pancake, while its roar thundered silently inside my brain.·
But then a knocking on the door made my mother jump and the
sound in my head stopped.

Come in, come in, Wannsie, she said.

Yes, Modom? Wannsie said expectantly.

Wannsie, Her Ladyship is out, isn't she, so someone will
have to tell Mr. Smith that Miss Gloria is not at home, which
he already knows, doesn't he? Anyway I think he does as that's
what he's been told, hasn't he? So I suppose the best thing,
well—is for you, Wannsie, to say to him—to simply tell him
that—that Miss Gloria is not at home and does not wish to see
him. Yes, of course—she glanced sideways at me, quite pleased
with herself at this solution—that's the thing to say, the very
thing.

Oh Mummy, oh Mummy—I screamed, but no sound came
out of me, and Wannsie said, Very good, Modom, and turned
around and went out the door on down the stairs.

My mother said, Well, that takes care of that, and out she
went, only she didn't go on down the stairs but across the hall
into her room. I could hear the door close and I knew she wasn't
going to see Winter again. Wannsie would take care of that, and
I wondered how long it would be before I saw my mother again.
Or Winter, for that matter—that is, if I ever did see him again.
For surely this was it—Winter would be lost to me forever along
with all the other losts . . . unless, unless he stormed up the
stairs, hurled furiously through tunnels of night at incredible
speed to find me. I held my breath . . . muffled sounds downstairs,
talking, doors opening, car door slamming—no, these were not
hurling-through-tunnel sounds, these were driving-away sounds
. . . and now the only sounds are those of silence, yes, all around
me . . . silence! and the sounds inside my head? I stand still
. . . still, waiting, but after a time I give up, because now there's
no sound outside or inside or anywhere at all.

Preparations

My mother and Aunt Thelma skip through the days with their frothy plans for the wedding, gay as can be, when at the same time there float around—in and out, over and under everything—innuendoes that seep into little things—like the cheeky "De Chee-co" and a raised eyebrow going up simultaneously on their ditto faces. Not so ditto these days, as something has happened to my mother's skin, to her smooth, beautiful skin, but what it is I cannot fathom. Is it because she's tired and doesn't get enough sleep? She rests in her room a lot—ah, but does she sleep? Could that be it? No, somehow I think it's something else. But just when I'm about to grasp it, my mind slithers onto something, something that has nothing to do with her at all, something frothy and gay as can be, for the days come and go and I smile a lot and tell everyone how happy I am and how wonderful Pat-Pasquale is and how we're going to have six children. How we're going to do this I still haven't figured out, because he's told me he doesn't think he can have children. A horse fell on him when he was playing polo and whatever happened when this horse fell on him makes it impossible now for him to ever have a child—a big plus, he said, when Stella Vara, that actress in those Joe Palooka movies, got pregnant and threatened to sue him saying he was the father, but of course it must have been someone else and not his responsibility. Well, this is another thing it's hard for me to grasp, and I keep forgetting about it along with those other things that slither out of my mind. Yes, they do, isn't that crazy? This forgetting, this pretending none of it's true and that someday, somehow I'll have my six children.

Last night Mummy came to me with something specific on her mind. I was in bed about to turn off the light when she tapped tapped on my door so faintly I thought I was imagining things. But in she tiptoed, hesitant as a wren, to perch on the foot of my bed.

Darling, there are things we should talk about, she said seriously to no one in particular, glancing towards the door as if perhaps Aunt Thelma were expected any minute. But no one was forthcoming and she valiantly scrambled on.

The-the-the wedding, darling? The-the—date—you know what I mean—the exact date in December for the wedding? We have to talk about—that.

Oh sure, I said, any time, any time that's fine with you is fine with me.

Well, no, darling—it can't can't can't—well, it can't be just—any any time—it has to be—well, you must know what I mean—it has to be—be either before or after—after—

Before or after what? I said.

Distraught, she turned away from me, and for a minute I thought she was going to get up and leave, but instead she moved over to the window and stood staring out into the black night. I heard the gentle-soft of her laugh as she turned back to me—

Well, darling, I mean—! Now the words tumbled out, the sound more a smile than a laugh, drawing me close, so close into her beauty that I felt faint.

I mean—I mean—the gentle-soft appeal of it stumbled on—well, I mean—on your wedding night—he'd be saying saying, "But I can't do anything?" And she repeated it over and over again as if I wouldn't know what she was talking about.

Honestly, Mummy! I said. Without hearing me she went right on, and everything—everything—was turned around and I said wildly—

Any time, any time—December December twenty-eighth—

Are you sure, darling, are you sure? she pursued. Maybe we should check a calendar somewhere, and she looked up at the wall over my bed as if perhaps a big calendar might be hanging there.

Yes yes, I'm sure, really sure, as really sure as I'll ever be really sure about anything ever! Rudely I turned over and pretended to fall into a coma.

With all my strength I willed her to leave me be—with all my strength, I willed her to stay, put her arms around me and never go away.

But almost immediately, without hearing the door close, I knew she had gone. And I opened my eyes, and it was true— I was alone.

Masks

We'd been out dancing at Mocambo the night before, ending up as usual at "Uncle" Joe Schenck's for the never-ending game of gin rummy, and now here we all were gathered together again as we usually were on a Sunday. Either it would be around somebody's pool, lolling around doing nothing or floating in the pool doing nothing, or about to play or not play tennis at somebody's court while the usual gang continued on from the eternity of a night's gin game, or it would be for a late Sunday lunch at Romanoff's, which is where I was this particular Sunday, sitting in the usual booth with Pat-Pasquale's usual entourage. These Sundays roll around inevitably as days do, and every Sunday I think perhaps we'll do something different—like take a walk, something like that, but nobody ever walks here. It's all cars cars cars, getting in the car and then driving around and around in the car until the car stops and you get out because you've reached wherever it is you're going to. Only I never do.

What I do have is the feeling of going nowhere at all, and sometimes I get so bored I could scream, although all along I know underneath that what it really is is panic. Panic! knowing I'm getting deeper into something I don't understand. Pat terrifies me with the rages he falls into. Yes, it's like a volcano erupts, only *he's* the volcano and I'm the one that falls in. I try to keep up with him, laugh a lot at the funny things he says—some of them *are* funny, but most of them aren't because they're mean. Still, his being so sure of himself is one of the things—in fact, *the* thing—that attracted me to him. I'm so the opposite, so unsure of myself—more so now than ever. Some days the longing to be back at Wheeler comes over me (I would be there right now) and I think of how it must be with the first snow falling outside the window of the studio, and it's so real to me that Hollywood and Maple Manor and, yes, even Queen Anne and Queen Jonquil are all part of some terrible joke in a nightmare and soon I'll wake up and everything will be all right again.

But then it happened, it happened as we were sitting around that round table in the booth at Romanoff's, laughing away at all the funny-mean things Pat-Pasquale was saying. Something came into the restaurant, a grotesque monster came in the door and spread to the bar, onto a table, and then to another table, quick, so quick, like a fire, but still no one moved, we sat there as it seeped with crackly sounds of flames through dry wood as people stopped talking and then started talking again: people got up and moved back and forth from one table to another, but still no one believed it, trapped as we were by this fire as it spread around and around, for something terrible had happened, and suddenly everyone knew that the Japanese had bombed Pearl Harbor.

Sunday, December 7, 1941—no one will ever forget where they were that day. And the strangers that sat beside me were for an instant without masks: even Pat-Pasquale had looked like someone I might reach out and touch.

The Princess and the Pea

I don't know what I expected when I got back to Maple Manor, but somewhere at the back of my mind was a nameless dread that maybe it had been bombed too and my mother, Queen

Anne of Lace, and my aunt the Queen Jonquil—blown off the face of the earth.

But not at all. There they sat together as usual in the living room, their heads bent close over the task at hand. For these days their knitting and needlepoint had been set aside for more important priorities. The wedding is not to interfere with Christmas, which is just around the corner, and the twins were making "Princess and the Pea prezzies" for their nearest and dearest. Empty cigar boxes were stacked in neat piles around the sofa, waiting to be transformed into tiny beds. Boxes would become four-posters, clothespins glued to each corner supporting tiny canopies, sewn from bits and pieces of fabric, each devotedly ruffled. Mattresses for the Princess's bed were being diligently fashioned from finest silk, filled with Mary Chess tuberose sachet before being placed one on top of the other. The final touch: a single pea placed under the bottom mattress, as the fairy tale tells us. And the princess herself? That was left to the imagination.

Oh, did you hear, darling? my mother said as I rushed in.

Yes yes of course I heard!

My voice came out all funny and they looked up, quite startled.

What's going to happen? I said.

Who knows, darling, we'll just have to wait and see.

Wait and see? But Mummy, Mummy—

Well, it won't stop us from going ahead with plans for the wedding, if that's what you're worried about, Aunt Toto said soothingly as she sewed the rose thread up and down, in and out, up and down, in and out. . . .

Why, the invitations have been sent out. We couldn't change things now, could we? my mother said, looking over at Aunt Toto. It would look too peculiar, wouldn't it?

Much too far along to unravel now, Aunt Toto said matter-of-factly, snipping off the last thread and holding up a tiny canopy bed admiringly. I think this is the prettiest one of all, don't you?

I looked at them both. How contented they were, contented because they were in each other's presence, so pleased with their handiwork, and for a crackbrained instant . . . I thought perhaps none of it had happened, and that everything or anything that did happen or would happen was all just a dream, and suddenly I'd wake up and find myself somewhere real. But where?

Presents keep arriving, and the long mahogany table in the dining room has had to be pushed aside to make room for another long table to hold them all. What will happen when both are filled and there is no more space? Even the Sheraton sideboard has been put to use and cleared of my grandmother's silver tea set and Father's Champion Horse Show trophies, for the doorbell rings on and on, all day long, and Wannsie runs back and forth with a million things to attend to. Mummy stays in her room a lot. To my wedding she's going to wear her wedding dress, the dress she wore when she married my father. It's palest grey with touches of white in honor of my father's Horse Show colors. I look at it hanging in the closet (patiently waiting), and each time I do, a thud comes into my heart, for there is no stopping it now: this wedding. No bolt of lightning from Aunt Gertrude. I guess what I'm doing doesn't matter to her at all at all. I go along through each day telling everybody how much happier I am today than the day before. Why am I driven to prove to everybody, especially to Aunt Gertrude, that the man I am marrying is the most perfect and wonderful man in the world—why? Well, it won't be long now, only a few days until we all drive up to the Santa Barbara Biltmore Hotel, where we will stay the day before the wedding. A retinue of ushers, bridesmaids, Big Elephant, the Little Countess, Queen Anne and Queen Jonquil—not to mention hairdressers and future bride and groom—what a long line of cars it will be, almost like a funeral cortege, only it's a wedding—ha, ha! some joke. There'll be a rehearsal at the Old Mission Church the afternoon before the wedding, and then the next morning the High Mass ceremony, and then, well . . .

maybe something will occur at the last minute. But it would have to be something catastrophic. Yes, really desperate—me running away from the altar down the aisle at the last minute, just as the ceremony is to start. I wonder if I'd have the nerve.

Of course I didn't. Have the nerve. It all happened the way it was planned on December twenty-eighth without a hitch. I walked down the aisle alone as Uncle Harry, who would have been the nearest relative to give me away, kept to his decision and wanted no part of it. Even Virginia didn't come to the wedding, and none of them sent a present or good wishes. But it didn't surprise me. What did, though, was Naney arriving with a complete new set of teeth—one after the other, all in a row, like Chiclets, but she's thrilled with them and flashes smiles around a lot. Especially captivated she is by a picture that appeared in the Los Angeles *Examiner* taken as she descended from the Silver Chief "for Granddaughter's Wedding." Still, up until the last minute I kept thinking I'd have the courage to bolt. All through the ceremony I kept thinking about Howard: the hair on his head, soft and fine to the touch, not like Pat-Pasquale's, which is crinkly like the steely wool on his chest. I had a berserk impulse as Pat-Pasquale and I knelt there side by side—jump up, run to the pew where my mother sat, drag her with me, flying down the aisle out of the church—but then where would we be, and what would we do? It was an irrational impulse, because my mother has been far away in another country for weeks now—even Ketti is out of things, and my mother finds comfort in letting Aunt Toto absorb her. Through it all Aunt Toto's attitude has been Let's get all this over with as fast as we can. Which is just what we did, although the ceremony did go on and on—I thought it would never end.

What was Howard doing that day? I wonder. And Phil Kellogg? Winter Smith drifted back of my mind somewhere and I kept thinking: Was it possible! Only a year ago last December I was at 60 Washington Mews, home from Wheeler for Christmas, and Winter had given me a ring with a stone the color of the sea. I wore it for ages, even to sleep. It was the first thing I looked at every morning when I opened my eyes. That medal of the Infant Jesus of Prague was on my mind too. Winter had it since he was a child and gave it to me that same Christmas (to hold fast for the son we would have someday), small it was and oval. I can still feel the grainy surface on my thumb as I touched it, the molded gold of the tiny Infant. Winter has it now. He asked for it back on that last trip Mummy and I made to New York in November. I left it in an envelope at the desk of the St. Regis Hotel and he picked it up without our seeing each other.

It was the same day I went to see Mummy Anne at the Carlyle—the same day she said I could go and live with her and Cousin Bill so that I didn't have to feel I had to stay with Aunt Gertrude or my mother or get married or be rushed into decisions. But all I could do was shake my head shake my head with no words to say.

And now, I was standing next to this dark stranger who, as the ceremony droned on and on, seemed mad about something. Like I'd done something wrong. But what? He put a gold band on my finger and turned away without kissing me. Together we walked back down the aisle—well, there was no place else to go. For an instant I caught sight of Big Elephant's face . . . weeping. And Naney Morgan (putting a good face on it) still preoccupied with her new teeth. Outside the Mission crowds had gathered. The wind blew my veil around me as Pat-Pasquale reached out to pull it back. If only the wind would catch it like a sail, billow me up, high up in the sky far far away. But it didn't. I kept trying to smile, but my stomach felt empty and my body grounded like lead. Well, no matter what happens, I'll get away from Aunt Gertrude and my mother. I'm free, am I not? But if so, why don't I feel better about things? Just when I think I'm getting out I'm getting deeper in. The bridesmaids (even Carol) all think I'm happy as can be, and it would be like climbing Mount Everest to try to tell them how I really feel. Anyway, it's over, and we're on our Honeymoon, but still I'm thinking, thinking about . . . these things.

And in and out, as I think about these things, other things come to me . . . like the wedding reception at Maple Manor. It was so—well, I can't find a word for it. Like when you're asleep and know you want to wake up from the dream you're having only you can't: that kind of dream. It had to do with seeing the Little Countess and Big Elephant in my mother's house, circulating among the movie-star faces, making everything more unreal than it already was. However, Big Elephant could hardly be said to circulate, settling herself on the sofa as she did to view the passing parade as if she had a choice front row at the theatre. Of course, Queen Jonquil and Queen Anne never sat or stood near either one of them. Not a look or a word between them. To all intents and purposes, as far as they were concerned, the Little Countess and Big Elephant, wherever they moved or sat, occupied a blank space.

Then, of course, there was the question of "Auntie" Palma. I tried to avoid her as much as I could, but it wasn't easy as she kept pursuing me relentlessly, "I'm your Auntie Palma your Auntie Palma your Auntie Palma who wrote your dear mother's book book book." That book which I've never dared read. My mother wrote it about the Trial. I keep mixing it up in my mind with *Pride and Prejudice* in the dippiest way, because of course Jane Austen's a whole other cup of·tea, but my mother's book by this "Auntie" Palma person also has the word "Prejudice" in the title somewhere, hence my torment. "Auntie" Palma is big too, like Big Elephant, but of course not really like Big Elephant at all at all at all (only in a funny way I was drawn to her because she was). Still, I just couldn't shake her, from the moment she saw me it was as if she had something important to tell me and she kept trying to hold me still long enough to hear. But it frightened me, and although I did everything to avoid her she kept after me. Finally I sat down on the sofa beside Big Elephant. "Auntie" Palma didn't want to tangle with that and accepted defeat for the moment by disappearing among the guests.

Rita Hayworth and Betsy Newling are the only ones who look aristocratic, Big Elephant pronounced as she scanned the room. Look at Rita's hands, she went on. They were indeed beautiful, and I looked down at my own short-nailed fingers. Oh well, at least I was thin. But was I thin enough? Pat-Pasquale was of course bouncing around from group to group yakking it up. Mummy, but even more Aunt Toto, was in a state because Lolly Parsons and Dockie Martin hadn't shown up yet and it was getting time to cut the cake. Could something have happened to them on the drive back from Santa Barbara? Time went on

and on and everybody milled around and around until finally
Aunt Toto got really worried and called their house . . . Everything's fine, she said to my mother, returning tight-lipped, so
let's get on with it. Shouldn't we wait? Mummy said, vaguely
looking in the direction of the cake. No-nee, no-nee-no! Aunt
Toto said, as she often did when feeling in a particularly cute
but no-no mood. No-nee-no! she repeated firmly, quite exasperated, at her wit's end you might say as she tried to explain, slowly
and carefully, to my mother that on the way back from the
wedding Lolly had to—had to—go to the powder room. Do
what? my mother said fuzzily. Pee! She *had* to pee! Aunt Toto
said, her voice raised, exasperated. For a moment it grounded
my mother and she kept her eyes on Aunt Toto trying to take
it all in—Dockie stopping the car alongside the ocean highway,
Lolly going down behind a dune to the beach, Dockie waiting
and waiting in the same spot but when she didn't show up he'd
gotten out to search for her along the beach. But she'd disappeared
off the face of the earth and he found himself at the Malibu Police
Station, quite unstrung. Of course, the first thing they wanted
to know was, what was she wearing? And of course he hadn't a
clue so he called home to ask the maid, who said, Oh, but she's
here, do you want me to wake her? Isn't that something? It seems
that after roaming on down the dune she couldn't remember the
spot where Dockie was sitting parked in the car so she'd mean-
dered along the highway towards Santa Barbara until a truck
happened along and she'd hitchhiked back home, gone up to her
room, and fallen asleep. Dockie had been pretty sleepy himself
through it all, and it was all he could do to make it home, much
less go to the reception.

Cousin Tony got really red-faced as he drifted around trying
without success to attach his little self to one group or another.
I tried to think of something to say to him, but he seemed to
have other interests, like peering into glasses left on tables here
and there. Up to his old tricks, no doubt. Oh well, I'd soon be
away from it all. Or that's what I thought then—that is, if you

can call it thinking. (What I think now is a different matter entirely.) Oh! Carol caught the bouquet as I threw it from the staircase on my way up to change into my going-away outfit. I kind of directed it towards her. That means she'll be the next one to get married. I wonder who the lucky man will be?

Who Knows?

"Cousin" Brucie Cabot is lending us his car for the honeymoon. Pat says it looks like Flash Gordon's bedpan, but I try to put that out of my mind. Crowds gather around anywhere it's parked, and however described, it sure is an attention-getter, what with being silver and all, inside and out, hugging the ground with a real speedy look to it. A drive it's to be, this honeymoon, cross-country towards Florida—Palm Beach, to be exact, where we will be the guests of Charley Wrightsman at the Everglades Club for a few weeks before Pat-Pasquale enlists in the cavalry division at Fort Riley near Junction City, Kansas. Yes, that's his plan. He's sure to be drafted sooner or later and he wants to make mighty certain he'll be around horses (he talks about polo a lot) and not just placed anywhere. So by next month I'll be living in Kansas somewhere near the army base, but that seems faraway and unreal to me at this moment as I sit here by Joe Schenck's pool in Palm Springs writing this. And who, I ask myself, am I writing to? A friend, yes! A close close you-and-me friend who knows all about me and understands—yes, everything. I know everything about you, too, and understand. That I don't know your address or your name is of no matter. Even if you only exist in my head I'll keep writing to you anyway. There's always a chance you may turn up someday—who knows? There's a song, isn't there, I remember it from dancing at Miss Bonnie Mae Murray's classes, something about "dreams do so often come true, but outside of you who knows?" Well, *that's* the you-and-me friend I'm writing to.

It's the day after the wedding—think of it. We drove here

last night after the reception, with the top down—windy, very windy—and I sat beside Pat-Pasquale in my Howard Greer going-away suit with the John Frederics hat in my lap thinking about things. Mostly about my feet, which still hurt even though I'd taken my shoes off. There's nothing like having your feet hurt to take your mind off things. It sure took my mind off the too-fast too-fast driving and the wind which got windier against my face like a hot whip the nearer we came to Palm Springs. And now here I sit, Mrs. Pasquale John De Cicco, stretched out on a chaise—you know the kind, puffy to sink into, with a hood over the back—and there's no one here except me. It's hot hot hot, and even though my legs are in the sun and the rest of me is shaded by the hood, I still can't get rid of this pounding in my head. I keep wishing I were asleep. Come to think of it, I'd like to go to sleep for a long long time and maybe never wake up. Of course, I'm not really alone because inside the house behind the glass wall sliding door they're still at it. The whole gang of them.

They were already at it when we arrived here late last night, but "Uncle" Joe, gracious host that he is, took a break to show us to our room. That Gerard man is here too, the one that was married to Betty Boop's voice. Also one of the Marx Brothers, not one of the famous ones, one of the unfamous ones—Zeppo, I think. Come to think of it, maybe it's one of the Ritz Brothers instead. Oh well, anyway, Pat-Pasquale opened the champagne which had been left on the dressing table and we clicked glasses and I kept smiling a lot. Back later, sweetie, he said, you be good now, and out he went into the hall.

I hung up my nightgown on the bathroom door to look at it while I sunk into a bubble bath. It's a real trousseau one with lace and maribou, just a bit, here and there. Boy, was I tired, but I closed my eyes and pretended—oh, something—and soon the bubbles made my skin float away, soft as soft could be, and after a while I got out and after carefully drying myself I put on the nightgown and lay on the bed. Time went by, longer and longer, and I couldn't keep my eyes open—and they never did open until a few hours ago, when I woke up and there was no one there. Not only no one there—the twin bed next to mine was smooth as smooth could be. It was scary, and I ran to the door out into the hall on into the living room, and there they were, Zeppo Ritz and "Uncle" Joe and Eddie Gerard, all still sitting around that table with cards in their hands, and there he was, sitting too—Pat-Pasquale. Money money money was piled up on the table in neat stacks in front of one or the other of them, and big bowls filled with cigarette stubs, and glasses half- or not half-full, for they were still drinking even though the sun had long since risen. They were as glued to the cards in their hands as they were glued to each other and didn't look up or see me standing there, and I ran away, back to the room, threw on a bathing suit, and without even brushing my teeth or combing my hair ran out to the pool and dived in. But it didn't matter— the headache didn't go away and there was nothing to do and no place to go, except swim back and forth back and forth until I could swim no more, and now I'm sitting here in the sun writing to you. If only I could go to sleep and stop thinking about . . . these things.

Nothing seems to please him. We drive and drive over the long flat stretches of land and after a while there's nothing to say. The radio helps, but sometimes, rather often it seems, it blares forth with the same voice singing—

> *From Natchez to Mobile*
> *From Memphis to St. Joe—*
> *There's one thing I know*
> *A woman's a two-face*
> *A worrisome thing*
> *Who'll leave you to sing*
> *The blues in the night . . .*

Yes, it's very popular, that song, and Pat-Pasquale likes it a lot—he turns the volume up louder, gives a cowboy hoot of sorts, and sings along with it, knowingly, as if he's trying to tell me something. I look out the side window as if I don't hear him, because I'm scared of him, of his unhinged temper when he gets black with rage for no reason, like he's going to hit me—but he hasn't. Yet. He smokes those Picayune cigarettes in an endless chain. Light one, Fatsy Roo, he'll say, looking ahead as we speed along the straight endless highways, fast, always too fast. In profile he looks different, but how different is hard to say. Less frightening (maybe) because there's only half of him to see. Twice now it's happened. When I pushed the electric lighter in the dashboard and lighted the Picayune to hand to him—guess what? I gave him the wrong end. I felt terrible (really) because it was of course a mistake on my part. He reached out for the cigarette and popped the lit end right into his mouth. Boy, did he have a fit! He screamed at me, Stupid! *Stupido stupido basta fajol*, or something along those lines, and I cringed down in the seat, praying he wasn't going to hit me. What is it with you! he screamed. What is it with you! And he drove faster and faster on down the long highway as if we were in a race, although there wasn't another car in sight, not another human for that matter, for we were on long endless stretches of desert, driving on and on, as if there was some very important destination to get to—fast, real fast. We eat at diners or coffee shops here and there and when night comes we stop at whatever town we reach around ten or so and check into a hotel, some better than others. We pull up and whoever's loitering around moseys over to stare at the car and ask questions. Then we go into the hotel. I'm all prepared, because he does it every time—still, it makes me twinge as meekly I stand beside him in the lobby while he signs the register with a flourish "Pat De Cicco and wife." That's me, ha, ha!

Once a reporter was in the lobby the next day as we were leaving (we always make our getaway early in the morning, for there's still a long way to go until we reach Florida)—he wanted

to interview us for the local paper. He kept calling Pat-Pasquale "Count De Cicco." It was funny, only it wasn't a bit funny to me. (It's only funny now as I think about it later.) Pat set him straight by saying he wasn't a count, it was his father who had been "the Broccoli King" as he was the first farmer to plant large crops of the vegetable in the U.S.A. But of course it didn't even make a dent, and the reporter kept calling me "Countess Gloria." He must have been kidding, although he seemed rather subdued about it. All newspapers are bunched in my mind with the Trial, and since then I don't read things about myself, but Pat-Pasquale does and is furious at the way he's been treated. Especially *Life* magazine, which had a headline GLORIA MORGAN VANDERBILT MARRIES A MINOR HOLLYWOOD CHARACTER NAMED DI CICCO, and to top it all they spelled his name wrong (he's sure they did it on purpose), which made me feel sorry for him—well, sort of—so I tried to cheer him up by saying they left the Laura out of my name so it's really my mother's name in the headline (how's that for a mistake), but nothing appeases him. Why does it make me more determined than ever to prove to everybody, especially Aunt Gertrude, how happy happy happy I am? But it's a strain, I can tell you. I panicked when a reporter asked me, after Mummy announced our engagement, how my Aunt Gertrude felt about it. Oh, happy happy happy, I lied. Well, at least I got some attention from her, because the very next day a letter from her arrived—

Gloria—

How *could* you have said to the press that I am happy about this terrible thing you are doing?

Aunt Gertrude

That was it—that was her letter—a letter I had no answer to. This may be the last leter I'll ever get from her. But it was my fault—I had lied. If only I could explain to her why. Why I said that or why I wake up every morning to find myself "Pat De

Cicco and wife." But even if I had the chance, even if I saw her
face to face, I still couldn't open my mouth, because if I don't
really know why myself, inside—how will I ever be able to explain
it to her or anyone else?

Honeymoon

Well, we made it to Palm Beach, and here we are at the
Everglades Club, ensconced as it were by "Uncle" Charley
Wrightsman in a big room with a big bed and a window looking
out over a lot of palm trees. It's funny here—Palm Beach, I
mean—sort of like Beverly Hills, flat and flashy, only Old Flashy
instead of New Flashy. All the grown-ups, I mean older people,
all seem same-age-older, as if they all joined the same club at
the same time in the same year. The sameness theme carries
through into the days, for they drift one into the other—like it's
summer all the time, with everyone either at a party or getting
ready to go to a party or having come from a party and talking
about it. There are lunch parties and cocktail parties with hairdressers fitted in somewhere between, along with shopping at
Worth Avenue—there's lots of that. By then it's time to get
ready for a dinner-and-dancing party. Every night there's one
with the same people, the only difference is the costumes they
wear. And the jewels—they change too, because nobody ever
wears the same thing twice. What with all this going on, Pat-
Pasquale's in seventh heaven. Yoo-hoo—yes, there's lots of yoo-
hoos as he jumps around. No one talks about the war at all.

Deenie Hutton's here and she invited me to drop by. She has
a house all her very own to play in called Deen-Wee Cottage.
Some cottage! Her mother built it for her by their big house,
Mar-go-lar, which Deenie lives in when she's not playing. I felt
very funny there and didn't stay long. For one thing, there were
lots of other people around—Deenie's girlfriends from school.
She'd invited the whole sorority and flown them down for the

weekend. There were tons of them. They were all sitting around on the floor playing records on a portable Victrola and munching things from bowls scattered around—Mallomars and popcorn, stuff like that, the bowl of Tootsie Rolls almost empty. Speaking of empty—you can imagine the conversation. Boys boys boys and gossip gossip gossip. They looked at me like I was some freak from Planet Mars. I suppose because I hadn't much to say, plus I'm married, plus to someone who's not the same age as their dippy boyfriends. Anyway, as I said, I couldn't wait to get out of there. But then the minute I left I started thinking about it—the fun they were having—and I feel like I'm missing something. But what? And if I am missing something, why was I so uncomfortable when I was there? They were all so sure of themselves, sure of how they looked, sure of what they wore, sure of what they said, unlike moi who isn't sure of anything at all much less myself. Oh well, at least I'm free. Aren't I? Well, I don't have to go back to school, that's for sure.

One day, sunny as the one before, a yellow envelope arrived—Western Union, unexpected. Even before I opened it I knew it wasn't good news. It was from Mummy Anne and Cousin Bill. It was. The Western Union. Telegram. In answer to the one *I* had sent them.

Only I hadn't. Sent them one—a telegram. Those days, day after day after day, Pat-Pasquale hammer-hammer-hammering on about it. It was awful, but nothing to the awful like it is now. No no no no, I'd said all along and held fast, because I knew it just wasn't right. Cousin Bill has this job in the Government—very important—and Pat-Pasquale thought it might not be a bad idea (was the way he put it) to ask Cousin Bill to recommend him for a commission in the cavalry. That way he'd start out ahead and not have to enlist as a private. It didn't daunt him one smidge that I hadn't heard a word from them, not even Mummy Anne, before or since we got married—but anyway that wasn't the point. The point is it isn't right, and I said I just wouldn't. But *he* did! He sent a telegram without telling me, in *my* name, *without telling me,* and now this telegram has come for me from Cousin Bill in answer, refusing *my* request. I want to scream to Mummy Anne—run to her—tell her what happened. What must she think of me! But every time I pick up the phone to call her, I just can't. I can't. It would all get back to Aunt Gertrude, the whole miserable mess. I'm scared of him. If it's come to this, there's no telling what he'll come up with next.

He says he needs five thousand dollars. Has to have it—fast. But he won't tell me why. Why? Why? I beg him to tell me. But he won't, and there's a feeling in the air like someone is after him. Does he owe money from gambling, maybe? Is that it? Call Howard, he said, five thousand dollars won't mean anything to him. No! No I can't I can't, I tell him. You *must*, he said. Call him call him. I can't I can't, I tell him. You must, he says. It goes on and on like this. Then his mood changes and the way he talks—like he's really scared—makes me feel sorry for him. I've never seen him like this before.

Howard, I say on the phone, I need five thousand dollars. I'll pay it back to you when I'm twenty-one.

A long pause . . . Howard, Howard, I say. . . .

I thought you were calling to say you were coming back to me. . . .

Yes, that's what he said before he hung up.

He keeps after me on and on, it's all he talks about. What about your Grandmother Morgan, hasn't she got some jewelry? It's unthinkable, but then I do. No, she says (thank God). Now he's really desperate and I've asked Dodo for those two diamond rings she always wears. No, she says. Then I find myself wheedling them away from her, hating myself, saying they're so pretty can I just borrow them for a while to wear? I'm too ashamed to tell her what it's really about. Let's go to New York, he says, for a few days, see if we can scrape it together one way or another. I feel crazy.

Pestered till I got the rings. Exhausted. Pat-Pasquale tried to borrow money from one of his rich friends, Dan Topping, but all he got was a suggestion that I go to a pawnshop—there must be family jewelry around somewhere? Pat-Pasquale seems to take to the idea and asked him which one was best. How would *he* know? I wanted to shout, but I kept quiet. The rings aren't very shiny. Dan Topping told Pat-Pasquale it's too bad I'm still a minor, otherwise I could get a loan on my future inheritance. Why can't Pat borrow from Dan if they're such good friends? I tried, Pat-Pasquale says, but no dice.

I went alone. To the pawnshop. Pat-Pasquale said it would have more of an effect. The pawn man gave me a hard time, quite surprised to see me turn up there with such small treasures, but finally he took them. Now all I think of is how I can scrimp and save to get them back for her quickly, quickly as I can. I'd leave, but I don't know where I'd go.

One way or another we scraped the five thousand dollars together. Then he said he has to make a quick trip to Washington. He left in a very good mood and sent me back here to Palm Beach, only now I'm staying at Dolly O'Brien's house and not at the Everglades. It's very castle-y, this house, with a big pool and lots of guests. They're really old, even older than my mother and Aunt Toto, and I've finally given up and said I don't feel well and gone to bed. On it there are flowered sheets, Porthault they're called, and every day the maid changes them, although they are still smooth as could be. While all this is going on I stay out of the way in the bathroom. Food is brought to me on a wicker tray with a set of breakfast-tray china that has flowers on it like the sheets. There's a matching vase on the tray too, holding a flower from Mrs. O'Brien's gardens, a different one every time. It's a strange routine, because I don't feel sick at all, only scared.

Muriel Hemingway came to see me today. It was quite an event. She's married to Marshall, Mrs. O'Brien's son. She's very pretty and seems more like me. What I mean is, she's more like eighteen. How are you feeling? she asked. Better, oh better, thank you. Maybe you should see a doctor? Oh no no, please, really I'll be fine. Then I almost broke down and told her—everything. But I didn't, because after all I only met her two days ago and anyway I wouldn't even know where to begin.

Made myself get up this morning and went down to the pool where all the guests were sitting around. Dorothy and Bill Paley were there and someone else whispered what a bore it was that they have to stick around Dolly's pool every day while the Paleys are here instead of going to the club because Bill's Jewish and Jews aren't allowed there. What does that mean? Kay Chacqueneaux is also one of the guests. Boy, is she catty. About everybody. But then who isn't around here? I sat there for a while and couldn't think of anything at all to say. Miss Pat? Mrs. O'Brien said. Who's Miss Pat? I said. They all thought it was hilarious. Then I got it and said Oh yes, yes a lot a lot, I was just kidding, and I laughed along with them. When what I really wanted to do was drop through the tiles around the pool. Mrs. Chacqueneaux sits under a parasol to protect her white white skin from the sun. She has black black hair and red red lips and sits in the same position for hours like a wax figure. The only thing that moves are her lips as they spout one catty thing after another. You'd think her hands would roast in those white gloves she always wears and that her arms would get tired, not to mention her mouth. They say her husband "fools around" a lot. Maybe that's what spurs her to such heights of cattiness, because in that department she sure takes the cake. Or maybe she's what drives him to fool around. Who knows?—oh well. Now that you're

feeling better, Mrs. O'Brien said sweetly, won't you join us for dinner tonight? Barbara Hutton and Cary Grant are coming. Boy, would I!

Why does just thinking about getting dressed up for dinner make my heart beat fast with hope? Such a dumb thing, but it makes me feel like a girl again. I look at myself in the mirror and don't look too bad even if I do say so myself. All that rest, I guess. Anyway the only thing on my mind now is what in heaven's name am I going to talk to Cary Grant about. Yes— that is the question.

All the pondering was for naught, because I never even got close to them. They arrived late—well after dinner. It was quite an entrance. Even Wolfgang and His Hungarian Musicians in their red coats, who had played lackadaisically throughout the endless meal, shaped up and snapped to. In the arched doorway there they were: Cary Grant and Barbara Hutton, present but not really there, for they were as if set apart on a little stage that moved and turned as they did, and although they had entered the castle, they were only hovering for an instant before turning back and returning to that place where they could be alone once more. Amongst the others, standing around in their Easter egg–colored silks, there was something of the night butterfly about her, for she was in white, diamonds sprinkled at lavish random over gauzy layers of skirt, palest hair fondly pouffed in wings rising from the delicate forehead, so bejeweled that even her face was luminous and appeared to be dusted with flecks of tiny stars. Puppet movements as her hand, with no sign of curiosity, beckoned Wolfgang to approach. Startled, he moved towards the white damask settee where she had alighted, Cary Grant close beside her. The favored Wolfgang smiled and smiled, nodding nodding as he leaned respectfully close to catch her words. Then as suddenly as he had been summoned he was now gently dismissed. With swift compliance he bowed, moving back to where the other musicians waited eagerly. A brief signal and the violins slid into song. Oh, how they played! the music soaring soaring . . . they'll be married soon, everyone says! What was that song? I can't remember it, all I can remember is how they sat there, figures on a Valentine to live happily ever after.

A package arrived for me today. It was small. From Los Angeles. From 7000 Romaine Drive. The medal I gave Howard: Dodo had given it to me to give him for good luck. It's made of silver with figures of Saint Bernadette and Our Lady of Lourdes enameled on one side—and engraved on the other, "G.V. to H.H. August 1941." That's what was in the box when I opened it. Of course, even before, I knew what it was. There was tissue paper around it. Yes, all crinkled up, lots of tissue paper to protect it, you know. Oh yes—I know.

Money's going to be a wee bit of a problem—at least I think it is. I'm not sure just what Pat-Pasquale has, although he sure acts like there's a lot of it flying around—that is, from time to time, on and off as it were, depending on the status of the gin rummy game. But whatever is flying around, when it is flying, flies not really around but away away away. Well, he does like to spend tons and tons of time in Mocambo and Romanoff's. The doormen used to greet us with a "Welcome home"—some home! At least we can count on the seven-hundred-and-fifty-dollar allowance Surrogate Foley gives me from the trust I'll inherit when I'm twenty-one. He was so furious he could do nothing to stop my marrying Pat-Pasquale, I was sure he was going to cut it off. When we went with my mother to his chambers so he could meet Pat, he barked in that fox-terrier way of his, Well, you'll be in the army soon—and then he woff-woffed on, barked out that song—

> *This is the army, Mr. Jones,*
> *No private rooms or telephones*
> *You had your breakfast in bed before*
> *But you won't have it there anymore. . . .*

Pat-Pasquale almost had apoplexy, and he stomped out, leaving Mummy and me to carry on, so to speak. I guess that's why we're on this—well—Honeymoon. Everything is a present in one way or another, this car from "Cousin" Brucie, the two weeks at the Everglades a present from our "Uncle" Charley Wrightsman, "that Sportsman Chuck," as Pat-Pasquale calls him (he likes to have Pat around to make him laugh). Yes, Pat's a laugh a minute to everyone except me. He talks a lot about joining the cavalry division before he gets drafted, then we'll have to really budget ourselves at Fort Riley and may share a house near the army base with Jean and Borden Tennant, which should help towards that. Pat-Pasquale acts like all he has to do is reach up into the sky and money money money will materialize out of thin air, but he doesn't like to talk about it, so we just go on from day to day, driving on and on along these long roads, those endless highways, arriving at day's end to empty rooms. My sketchbook's with me, but I can't seem to fit it into "my busy schedule"—ha, ha. Whenever I sit in the backseat, hoping to get something done, Pat-Pasquale turns the radio up even louder and calls back to me, Let me be the first one to see the masterpiece, Fatsy Roo van Gogh. Well, I'm seventeen and I did something on my own, didn't I? I got married and got away from my mother and Ketti Keven and Aunt Gertrude. And didn't I show Aunt Gertrude she wasn't God Almighty? That's *something*, isn't it? But there's a war and it's terrible and who knows what's going to happen? Not even Aunt Gertrude or Surrogate Foley knows the answer to that. Or maybe they do—maybe they're so powerful they do.

From Washington an hour ago the call came. He was furious. Listen, sweetie, you get pronto on the next train for Kansas City, hear me! What? I said. Fell through, he mumbled, fell through. What? What fell through? Listen, sweetie, mind your business and get your ass moving and on that train Fort Riley enlist have to enlist sooner better hear me! Doberman pinscher just bought a beauty taking him with me. Doberman? I said—what? But with the phone between us I wasn't afraid one bit I kept saying over and over again—*What* fell through? The commission, *stupido!* The commission, he finally shouted—only a thousand dollars more would have done it! What is it with you—told them they could all go to hell—which means you too, Fatsy, unless you get on that train. Stop giving me all this horse shit, hear me—Jesus, what is it with you—what is it with you anyway?

I'm packing. My ear feels as if a trumpet has blown something into the center of my head and it's stuck there so deep it's never going to come out. And that Doberman—it's the one dog that really spooks me. Pat-Pasquale had one when we first met, and he knows we never did take to each other.

.   .   .

I just couldn't. I'm all packed and on my way all right, but not to Kansas City—to Old Westbury Capital to Aunt Gertrude. I called her and she said, Come—I still don't believe it. But in a funny way I do.

That Strange Familiar Place

It's so quiet here. Almost like someone has died. Last night I couldn't sleep, and all through the long night it went on, muffled though it was through doors—the coughing. At first I didn't connect it with Auntie Ger, because at dinner she hadn't coughed at all. I lay there wanting to go in to her with a glass of water to see if she was all right. Twice I got as far as her door, but each time I did, it stopped, the coughing, and with it— relief . . . for the sting of pain within me vanished and I turned away, went back along the hall to my room to lie down, closing my eyes, trying to sleep. But then it would start again. . . . Now that I think of it, she hadn't coughed during the day either, no, not at all.

I get the eeriest feeling that we're here, Auntie Ger and I, waiting. Suspended, you might say. But what it is that we wait for eludes me. She made it clear from the moment I arrived that Pat-Pasquale's name must not be mentioned. Maybe that's my fault. I keep going over in my mind what I'd said to her on the phone when I'd called from Palm Beach. I made the call so fast, so out of the blue, that I can't remember now what I said exactly. One thing I do remember is how casual I tried to sound, about wanting to see her. Like nothing was wrong. But back of it all was *hope*, yes, fervently I hoped that face to face with her everything would be OK, yes OK, and different than it had ever been before, you know—I'd be able to tell her things and she'd understand. Freddy met me at the station, like old times, like I was coming home from school for vacation, only, of course, it wasn't Christmas.

Still, it was going to be all right. But the minute I saw her,
I knew it wasn't. She was stern—more distant than before. Her
manner, everything about her, pulled me back into myself, made
me angry. I want to beat my fists against the marble pillar of
her, force her to open, even a crack, so the light of me can enter
into her, warm her and make her love me and in the loving—
understand. But she has drawn even farther into a distant land,
and that old familiar feeling possesses me once more, makes me
not only draw away but yank away. Hard. I *too* have forces within
me. Her power enrages me, and once more I find myself in that
strange familiar place in battle with someone it is my intent to
love. No—nothing has changed.

This morning Hortense, in her obligatory black dress, brought
breakfast to me on a tray. Such a nice name, Pascal, she said,
pronouncing it the French way. She pulled the curtains apart and
turned to look at me. Pas-cal, she repeated slowly. How exotic
she made it sound . . . Pas-cal. Yes, I said eagerly, isn't it a nice
name? It derives from our French Easter, she added flatly, without
moving. Centuries passed. Has Mrs. Whitney had breakfast yet?
I said. Yes, quite early, and she inquired if *you* were awake yet.
Oh, I said, sitting up straighter, preoccupying myself with the
tray, I'm awake, yes yes I'm awake. She went on standing there,
but this time I held my ground and kept silent. Well . . . she
said, turning to fidget with one of the tassels on a tieback of the
curtain . . . well, I must go to Madame now, I'll tell her you're
awake. Please do, I said. But what difference will it make? Awake
or asleep, there's only one way to get through to Aunt Gertrude—
that is, if I can bring myself to do it.

Well, I brought myself to marry him, didn't I? So if I brought
myself to do that, I can bring myself to pretend how happy I
am. If I can do it to everyone else, I can do it for her, can't I?
I do it—pretend—to everyone else, so what makes it any different

with her? I do goofy things when I'm with her. Like after lunch today as we sat in the living room when she reached for a cigarette I reached for one too. I hate cigarettes, but I used to practice a lot that summer when I first went out to visit Mummy. She and Aunt Toto smoke a lot, and I thought if I could bring it off, it would make me look grown-up and sophisticated. Of course, usually I only give it a whirl at parties, and what with everyone else doing whatever else it is they are doing to impress, no one notices how inept I am, especially when I try to combine it with the long cigarette holder I carry around with me just in case. So far I haven't quite the knack of inhaling, but I can hold the smoke (ugh) in my mouth for a second or two and then blow it through my nose in a quite Lady Moon way. At least I think so—but who knows what impression (if any) it really makes? Anyway, I casually lighted up a Benson and Hedges right along with Aunt Ger just as if it were an everyday occurrence. Some good it did! She didn't bat an eyelash. All for naught it was. Out of desperation, I took a deep breath, made a fool of myself choking, sputtering. But even that wasn't remarked on.

I'm writing this on the train. Soon we'll be arriving in Kansas City. Boy, all those people in Palm Beach who don't know there's a war on should see what the trains are like, the stations jammed with soldiers. As I changed trains in Chicago there was a girl my age sitting on a crowded bench. Her blouse was open and she sat there nursing a baby, but no one gave her a glance. Lost, she looked, no home or place to go. The baby clung to her nipple ferociously, and she sat there without looking down into the fierce tiny face taking great gulps from her breast. Then quite suddenly the baby let go and turned towards me—its eyes squeezed shut, mouth curved down into a huge howl alternating with wrenching sneezes without a moment's pause, fists pummeling the air in rage—a dead ringer it was for the baby in *Alice in Wonderland*. The girl-mother looked straight at me with a sour expression—why, she even held the baby in her lap, loosely, the way the Duchess does in the Tenniel drawing, even her feet in their battered shoes were turned in upon each other in awkward surrender. I almost missed my connection, hovering around in the milling crowds wanting to help her in some way, but I couldn't think in what way, or how to approach her, didn't know what to say to her. So I let myself be carried wherever a wave of the crowd went; then pushing my way back through against the tide I'd return to them, but the howling and sneezing hadn't stopped and now the girl-mother was sneezing too and she looked suddenly old and more like the Duchess than the time before. I wonder what Aunt Gertrude would think. Will I ever see her again—Aunt Gertrude, I mean? She said good-bye to me and I said good-bye to her. But is it really good-bye? Maybe next time we meet it will be hello. Yes, then we could start from the beginning.

It's so overcrowded, this train, fraught with tremors like before an earthquake. Noisy noisy racket without cease, and the wheels of the train keep saying things to me as we speed along, the way they do in some silly movie. I keep thinking about Aunt Gertrude and my mother, and somewhere weaving in and out is that Doberman. God, please make it be not true and just part of Pat-Pasquale's ranting during one of his rages. He does tend to do that—there's always something thrown into his tantrums, unexpected, to give variety, I guess. Are they still sitting there, I wonder, on that bench in the train station? Where will they go, and what is to become of them . . . the baby and the Duchess?

Junction City, Kansas, 1942

It's the coziest house ever! With other two-story houses, low, one beside the other on a tree-lined street, and across the street houses more or less like the house we're in, ditto trees. We have a yellow cat called Gwendolyn, only nothing pleases her and she wanders off a lot. I have a feeling that one day she'll wander off and that will be that. Pat-Pasquale only appears on weekends now and then because he's in officers training camp, and it got so lonely I asked Big Elephant to come visit. So she's here now with Lolly and another very terrible dog, Smokey, a cocker spaniel of sorts, who growls all the livelong day because he hates everyone except Dodo. Oh well—at least he doesn't bite. I get enough of that from Pat-Pasquale. In a way I'd almost rather be alone—or best yet, if only Frances were still here. With her I don't have to pretend—about anything. Or put on an act like I do with Dodo and everyone else about how happy I am being Mrs. De Cicco. Frances, after all, is Pat's niece, and she knows all about everything from the beginning, because his family is used to the temper shooting up like a volcano for no reason at all. They live at St. James on Long Island in a rambling house on a farm. There's Angela (Pat's sister) and Joseph Savino and three daughters, Louise, Loretta, and Frances. Frances came out to California to be a bridesmaid at the wedding, but I didn't meet the rest of the family, except of course Cousin Cubby Broccoli, until after. What a state I was in before I met the others, afraid they wouldn't like me. But it was nothing like the other state I worked myself into anticipating meeting his mother for the first time! What *is* this thing about mothers—anyway, once I was actually there, there were so many of them, what with cousins and all, it went better than I thought. Much better. For one thing, there was so much food to pay attention to, taking everyone's mind off things, and it was so good, everyone talking and friendly and eating eating eating. There was something also about the house painted white with its big porch, as if it had always been there and always would be, set as it is in stretches of farm land, that let me breathe easier. You should see his mother, serene as serene, yes, as serene as serene as it is possible to be serene. Zia, she is called, and she sits quietly—presides, you might say—wherever she may be, her soft hair, grey as a pigeon's breast, piled in a knot on top of her head, and when Pat-Pasquale erupts, all she does is pull herself up straighter, if that's possible, and her neck seems to grow as

though the invisible crown she supports required slight adjust-
ment to hold its balance. So removed from the tirade, it is only
by her hands, which repose as they always do neatly together in
her lap, that you know she is aware of the hubbub—for they give
a little shudder, as though a magnet had pulled together, but
only for an instant. All in the family pay great heed to her,
although she keeps her own counsel and speaks seldom. But when
the one who died young, Pat's brother, Tony, is mentioned—so
full of promise, the light of the family, they say—her face changes
with listening, and though she remains silent it is as if she has
spoken. I try to think of things to say to her but it's not easy.
In the car one day—just the three of us—I said some desperate
making-conversation thing—what, I can't even remember now—
but it set him off—bang bang bang—while Queen Mother paid
no attention, just sat there beside him up front gazing straight
ahead at nothing. If only I could do that! He kept turning around
with that black wall-eyed look I'm getting to know and love (ha
ha) so well, one hand on the wheel, shouting as we careened
along the highway. *Quelle scène* . . . Suddenly he yanked the car
over to the side of the road and all I could do was thank God
his mother was with us, because I don't think he'd dare hit me
in front of her—would he? He slammed the door hard, rocking
us from side to side like we were in a rowboat instead of a car.
It even got Queen Zia's attention and she glanced towards him,
but he started banging at the trunk of a tree and she lost interest,
turned away. For a second I thought she was going to speak but
she only sighed and settled down to watch the cars zip-zapping
past us. I had an insane impulse to jump out, run to him—plead
for forgiveness—but what was he to forgive me for? Then, the
episode in the Muelbach Hotel in Kansas City just before we
moved here. Room service and the eager waiter wheeling the
breakfast table, "Good morning, folks!" hope on his face. Pat-
Pasquale lighting up his first Picayune of the day, ordering the
waiter to pour out the coffee. One sip and that knot of invisible

black rope tightened across his forehead as he swept not just the coffee pot but everything—*everything*—off the table. Mule piss! he shouted. Do you hear me? This is mule piss! It came on so fast, so unexpectedly, so for no reason. Awesome to behold—the waiter, rooted to the spot, was speechless. Well, there is peace and quiet in this house during the week when he's not here. What with one thing and another there's a lot to do—cleaning and laundry, and in the late morning Mrs. Oppy arrives to do the cooking. She's great. Our house came furnished, and I try to fix it up, moving things around, you know, trying different groupings. But the—well, permanence I seek—that's something else, for no matter how you move the furniture around, nothing in this house or on this street or in this town will ever have an air of permanence about it. Right now it's an army town plain and simple, and most of us here, I keep telling myself, are but passing through. But where are we passing through to? Our night tables are orange crates which I painted white, lots and lots of times for a lacquer effect, flowers dotted around here and there with a heart or two for a spot of red, and they're quite OK, what with books and things on. Then the dining room table, two barrels painted green for the base, a plywood tabletop. They look funny with the maple set of chairs but—oh well—I don't think it's fair to copy the chairs Gene Tierney made out of old barrels, painting the kegs white and the iron bands red and covering the seats in red chintz. Why, you'd want them anywhere, no matter where you moved on to. Her house is part of a development, one-story bungalows row on row, all alike, but once you step in the door it's a whole other matter. They come unfurnished, these bungalows (not like ours), and she put hers together from scratch, so it has a certain look to it. She's married to Oleg Cassini who's in OTS with Pat-Pasquale. Every time we've gone there the bed's never been made. Just like they got up from making love to answer the doorbell. She's pregnant and they are crazy about each other and she is very beautiful. I'd really like to be her friend.

But every time I see her I can't think of anything to say, and anyway Pat-Pasquale does all the talking.

When he's not here I'm able to work, but that "Fatsy Roo van Gogh" of his started to get to me so on weekends that all my paints, brushes, everything, are whisked away and he's none the wiser. He always brings home heaps of his friends for dinner whenever they're let out, and Mrs. Oppy cooks up a storm. Dodo putters around in the kitchen with her while Smokey spooks around at her heel growling for scraps. But no scraps for him, only choicest morsels. Mrs. Oppy and Dodo both have the same first name—Emma. Just like in Jane Austen's novel. Or Flaubert's—take your pick. Best not try to unravel that one. When Frances was here we went to the movies once a week on the day the show changed. *China Girl*—so strange, a movie with Gene Tierney and George Montgomery. Sitting there looking up at the big screen, and here she is right now in this town, and George

Montgomery—I wonder where he is? To think I dated him that summer, yes, more than once, that summer so long ago, or so it seems—really, come to think of it, as if it never happened. But it did. I've still got the gardenia corsage he sent me pressed in my copy of Elizabeth Barrett Browning poems. Still it's a fuzzy dream in my head somewhere, one I remember only shreds of, shreds clinging even after Frances and I had our usual soda treat in the drugstore on Main Street after the show. The Big Treat is when Pat-Pasquale and I go to the roadhouse sometimes on a Saturday night, dance to the jukebox. His old favorite "Blues in the Night" usually puts him in a yoo-hoo mood even if it's nothing even remotely like the Saturday nights at Mocambo and Ciro's. Sometimes it lasts, this yoo-hoo mood, other times not, depending on how much he has to drink. Laura and Pete Bostwick have a house just like Gene and Oleg's. Round tables with flowered cloths down to the floor. Pictures in frames and things around to make it like home. You'd never know from the outside what to expect once you set foot through the door, and I keep wondering what the other houses are like inside as they sit row on row on the outside all exactly alike. At parties everyone drinks bourbon and ginger ale in paper cups. It tastes awful. I wonder if Smokey will ever bite Pat-Pasquale? Wouldn't that be something. But it's weird—the war doesn't seem real. No, it doesn't. Come to think of it, what does? Well, the buttermilk. Once in a while I put milk into a mason jar and shake it, shake on and on through the day. I stop, but only when arms get exhausted, to stretch for a minute, then shake again, shake shake, up and down, up and down. It's funny—there's something soothing about this. Just when I think it's a useless activity (not to mention the boringness of it), guess what? A tiny ball forms, a chip of yellow. Encouraged, I shake on, it grows bigger, until it's big as a big snowball, all buttery yellow. The best butter bobbing around in the best buttermilk you ever tasted. Yes—that's real. But why? Now and then when I'm shaking up and down, up and down, my mind wanders somewhere else and Aunt Toto drifts across my thoughts . . . Pearl Harbor and Melba hysterical on the phone saying she'd shoot Melsing in the leg before she'd let her son go to war. Aunt Toto snipping her off—Stop it, Melba—why, if my son were called I'd be thrilled to have Tony fight for his country! Having said this, she was so pleased with herself, pleased as pie—the way an actress would be in a movie repeating a line reading, doing it well. It made me think a lot

. . . but no matter how hard I tried, none of it made sense. Of course, I was only seventeen then. But now I'm eighteen and it still doesn't. Make sense, I mean.

Snapshots

Jean and Borden Tennant had their baby! And guess what? They asked *me* to be godmother. So here I am godmother to Sidney Gale Borden Tennant, Jr. All during the christening I kept imagining how I'd feel if he were my baby, and then after the ceremony lots of snaps were taken outside the church and there I was holding the baby with Pat-Pasquale standing beside me like it was ours. It made me happy to pretend, but it was over in a blink and the baby left my arms, and Pat-Pasquale turned into himself again—a toad, you might say, and me back into a pumpkin—and I knew it was all just silly make-believe on my part.

Why do I keep praying to have a baby when I know Pat-Pasquale can't? I keep forgetting *that*. But why? Does this mean I'm never going to have a baby—*ever*? Why am I surprised every time I get the curse? If only I could talk to Dodo, but all I can bring myself to do is moan about cramps. She says, Lie down, dearie, and waddles up the short steep stairs with a hot-water bottle and then waddles down, and up again with a thimble of anisette liqueur. This will help, she says. But it doesn't.

I had to go to the doctor. I told him I slipped in the shower. And fell on your eye? he said. Well, sort of, I said, and I looked out the window at a pear tree all white in full bloom. What a beautiful tree, I said, what kind is it? You can tell me, he said, and his voice was so gentle I started to cry. One eye was black and blue and I couldn't see out of it, but the other one was all

right. I'd sneaked out of the house without Dodo seeing me, but God—what could I say to her when I got back?

Now that he's a second lieutenant, what's going to happen? Is it to be overseas or another army camp? What is it with you! he keeps saying. I hardly ever hear from my mother. Sometimes when I wake up, the first thing I think about is Maple Manor and Lady Moon—sleeping, no doubt. The shadows of her chamber draw me, and as I enter, a blanket covers me with the dark sweet smell of Brandywine roses I know so well. Why do I long to be there instead of here in this bright little box of a room, my wrists limp with longing—longing for another chance, just one, please, God, to make her love me? Maybe I don't hear from her because she knows Dodo is here. But does she know Dodo is here? I haven't told her. Dodo keeps saying her heart troubles her and she might have a heart attack any day now, but when she says this it's more like me who's going to have the heart attack. Please don't say that, Dodo, please please. Don't worry, I'll be all right, she says and then for no reason at all she'll say I won't have to worry about her future because Aunt Gertrude will always take care of her no matter what. What's all that about? Right now it's all we can do to take care of ourselves and this house and the groceries, so she knows I couldn't give her money now even if I wanted to, which of course I do. The first thing I'm going to do when I'm twenty-one is surprise her with a mink coat. I just wish she'd stop talking about her funeral—making me promise promise promise I'll have Morton Downey sing at it. Sick with worry it makes me every time I hear that record she plays over and over again—the high lilting voice about Irish eyes smiling. But it's the "I'll take you home again, Kathleen" one—that's the one that really puts me on the floor.

Oona's getting married!!! Carol just called to tell me and I'm so excited. She's going to marry Charlie Chaplin. Imagine! How's Bill, I said, what's happening? Carol is more madly in love than ever with William Saroyan, but he wants her to get pregnant before they get married. I don't get that idea at all, but anyway that's the way it is. I always thought Carol would get married before Oona, because she caught the bouquet at my wedding, but now it looks like it will be Oona. She couldn't be one of my bridesmaids because of her problems with her father. He really sounds awful. I can't relate him to the Eugene O'Neill who wrote *Strange Interlude*, the play that obsessed me so at Wheeler. So full of pain—I thought he'd be the most sensitive of men. Instead he pushes Oona away. It's hard to understand, but still, having a father is better than having no father at all, don't you think? Oona and I look alike. We could be sisters. But it's Carol and I who are the sisters, even though we look nothing alike—day and night, you might say. It's funny, though, how connected the three of us are, and all because of Carol. She kind of invents the three of us together, and it works because of this eerie sister look that Oona and I share. But there's nothing invented about Carol and me. From the moment I saw her in the hall that day at Old Westbury Capital I knew we'd be friends for life. If only she could come to Junction City—but of course she can't with this Bill situation. Darling, what's going to happen? I said. I don't know I don't know but I know I'll die if he doesn't marry me, I'll die. Oh, angel darling, I said. He will he will I know he will! And when I hear myself saying it I almost believe it, and so she does too.

Looking for a Happy Land, New York, 1942

It's ruined ruined for me, this dress. I'd saved up to buy it especially to wear in New York on Pat-Pasquale's first leave since he became second lieutenant. A Nettie Rosenstein, black with a plunging neckline, the most sophisticated dress I've ever ever had, and it made me look really old—not eighteen at all—thirty at least! Yes, it did, and now I'll never ever be able to wear it again. Because if I did it would remind me of last night, that horrible night that started out with me feeling great in my new black dress. We met Dan Topping and some girl (his dates all look the same, even though it's a different one each time) at "21" for drinks and then went on to the theatre. We had tickets for *Hellzapoppin'!*, sixth-row center-aisle—the best. It's just the kind of show Pat-Pasquale takes to, and you could hear his laugh zooming out yoo-hooing over every pratfall (you know, gags and then more gags, one on top of the other), lots of clowning around in a circusy kind of way, and there must be something wrong with my sense of humor because it didn't seem really funny to me, but everyone else thought it a scream and there was lots of that—screaming with laughter as they say (ha, ha)—so I tried to keep up with it and not fidget. There was only one intermission, and Pat-Pasquale and Dan Topping hot-footed it out of the theatre with girlfriend and me following behind. They wanted to get to the bar across from the theatre to have a drink before the second act. We sat there at the bar and the first thing Pat-Pasquale said was, Well, Dan, should we give her a hint or—? Dan put his head on one side and looked at me most objectively, giving it thoughtful consideration, but he didn't say anything and after a while shook his head—Noooo, he said, I still think it should be a surprise. A surprise, I said, what? What? What surprise? Pat-Pasquale leaned over to the girlfriend and whispered something to her. She had on a hat with a snood and there was a flower on one side over her ear. Wait, honey, I can't hear, she said to Pat-Pasquale, and he lifted up the flower as if it were a telephone and put his mouth close to her ear. Ooooh! she squealed. What a cute idea! But then another thought came to her—Why don't you think up nice surprises like that for me, Danny Boy? she pouted. What could it be? I thought. What? But no matter how much I tried to wheedle it out of them, no one would tell me. At least tell me when? When will I know? Soon soon soon they chorused and ordered another quick Scotch. Down the hatch, Dan said. We better get back, Pat-Pasquale said, taking the shot in a gulp, Come on, dumplin', get your jelly bottom moving. Of course, I should have known then or suspected, but you know I didn't I didn't I didn't have an inkling. We got back to our seats and it wasn't a long wait because after the curtain came up, the first skit was about newlyweds, lots of cracks the audience thought hilarious, rolling right along with it—and suddenly, suddenly, there I was rolling along with it too, out of my seat, on up the aisle, up some steps and onto the stage, because my name had been called out, not only called out, but now I was part of the things that were happening on the stage, giving an impromptu performance, you might say, and although I was deaf with panic, not hearing what the clowns were saying, through it all I did hear the laughing coming at me as I stood there being handed things, things like rolls of toilet paper that weren't covered, so that when it was over and I was led off the stage and

back to my seat the toilet paper unraveled, leaving a trail behind me. I slumped down in my seat, arms full, wanting to die, but instead I was laughing, trying to go along with it, because maybe that would put an end to it the way it had at Farmington with Bonavishski Buttercup—pretending to be her best friend had shut her up, hadn't it? Hadn't it? Pat-Pasquale put his arm around me and gave me a quick squeeze. How do you like those wedding presents? he hooted. We'll have enough toilet paper to last us a year!

You can see, can't you, why this dress is ruined for me? Why I'll never be able to look at it again, much less wear it? Even if I dyed it another color—anyway, black couldn't be dyed another color, but even if I could, nothing nothing would make any difference.

It keeps going around in my head, some words of Marquand, ". . . looking for a happy land where everything is bright," because every night that's what we're doing, or so it seems, but the search goes according to Pat-Pasquale's taste, not mine. We're at the Hotel Pierre and every day we do more or less the same thing, sleep late, dress up for lunch at "21" again or the Colony, then on to El Morocco to dance the night away. And always with the same people—except last night Orson Welles came into "21" and joined our table. Something happened when our eyes met— and later under the table he kept touching my knee and soon we were holding hands. I didn't feel one bit guilty even though Pat-Pasquale was sitting right there, yoo-hooing away, across the red-and-white checked tablecloth, for I was swept away and wild horses couldn't have stopped it. But today? Where have all the wild horses gone as I sit here fervently hoping the phone will ring, at the same time praying it won't? Won't, because I now know he's in town with his wife, Rita Hayworth, and she's pregnant. She wasn't with him last night because she's on Long Island somewhere at someone's house resting. So I went to B. Altman's this morning and spent my time going back and forth, up and down, on the escalator, over and over again, up and down, to sort my thoughts out. Going up, it would come back to me—how I'd felt in his presence, how it was when we went after dinner to someone's house where a party was going on, the whole group of us migrating, as we always seem to do, in a pack—only this time it was different because *he* was there. I felt alive every single second. . . . Looking for a happy land

where everything is bright—well, look no further, Gloria. *He* is
bright. He made Pat-Pasquale's sallies suddenly cheap instead of
ha, ha. When we found ourselves in a narrow hall on the third
floor of the house facing each other close so close, there was no
place to go except into each other's arms and I melted into them
like cheese under a hot broiler. See—I'm trying to be funny about
it because I'm scared. Afraid he'll call, scared he won't. Those were
the thoughts on the up escalator—on the down escalator it was all
Rita and Pat-Pasquale and the hopelessness of it, all of it. After we
kissed we pulled apart and looked at each other, and in that moment we came right to the center, one to the other, and I knew
that this was not to be. I knew that he knew I'm too serious, and
he knew that I knew he's not serious at all, about me, that is—
well, why should he be, we just met and he's married and his
wife's having a baby and I'm not grown-up enough yet for just one
of those things, and what's more I hope I never am.

Still he possesses me. It's been two days now and he hasn't
called. I think about him all the time. And Rita. *That* helps me
more than anything to forget him. What I *can* forget is Pat-
Pasquale. Wishful thinking, no doubt. He's been in such a good
mood on this trip, but then nightclubs really do bring out the
best in him.

It was terrible, last night. After dinner at Chambord Pat got
the notion to catch the show at the Copacabana. Just as we sat
down a group walked in—people I'd never seen before. One of
them was a man called Harry Cohn, although I didn't know then
that was what set Pat off. Whatever this person means in Pat's
life, it was as if a red flag had been waved in front of a bull. He
jumped up, muttering, I'll kill the son of a bitch I'll kill him,
and he started towards the other table. Just as he did this Cohn
person saw Pat coming towards him and he jumped up, but Pat
was too quick for him and he grabbed him by the throat. From
everywhere people looked and from nowhere two burly men ap-

peared, thugs they were, and tried to pull Pat and the Cohn person apart, but no sooner had they done this than Cohn bounded away, pushing pushing through the crowd, fast, with Pat close behind. There's this columnist, Lee Mortimer, we see around town each night accompanied by a Chinese girl, each night a different one more sultry than the last. He'd been sitting at the table next to us with the evening's companion, but now he was in it too, and I ran to him, pleaded with him not to write in his column about this awful thing that was happening. Even in all the rumpus you couldn't help noticing his companion, who remained sitting at the table, never glancing in our direction, the other way in fact, as if nothing were going on, nothing at all. Mr. Mortimer smirked at me, turned away, but by then nothing mattered because we were all following Pat on up the back stairs in pursuit of this Cohn person, who white faced with fear still nimbly managed to keep a few feet ahead of Pat-Pasquale. But outside on the street Pat caught up with him and a crowd formed—there was noise, flashbulbs going off from cameras suddenly, and a circle formed as it does for fighters in a ring. I ran to Pat, tugged his arm, pulling him towards me—Please please don't, I called out to him, but he didn't hear me and someone separated us. It came to me that my Naney Morgan was only a step away from where I stood on the pavement, yes, for she lived at the Hotel Fourteen, right next door to the Copacabana—for a dizzy moment I started to run to her, but instead found myself running towards Fifth Avenue, running on and on, and it was only when I reached the Hotel Pierre and ran into our room that I knew where I was, knew I was in a room I'll never forget, the room in which when he came back Pat-Pasquale tried to kill me.

What is it with you what is it with you, he shouted as he banged my head back and forth against the wall. It happened before, but this was terrible terrible. That bastard son of a bitch Cohn, Thelma Thelma—he kept it up, over and over again. It didn't occur to me until now that it was Thelma Todd he was talking about and not my Aunt Thelma. Pleading with him only made him angrier, drove him to hit me harder, and I willed myself into a Raggedy Ann doll, hoping to appease his wrath. There might be a chance to work my way to the door, get out, out into the hall, run run, escape anywhere, knock on someone's door, escape escape. Something inside him had snapped, but even out of control he was on to me with the wily animal instincts of the fighter. My head cracked and as I went limp he threw me on the bed. Now listen you, he said—you stay there, hear me, you stay here and don't move off that bed hear me 'cause so help me I'll kill you . . . kill you. I lay there trying not even to breathe, my eyes closed. Then I heard the mattress as he threw himself onto the bed next to mine and the room was quiet, so quiet, dead as if no one was there . . . a long time went by and I slit my eyes open, turned ever so slightly towards him. There he lay in a stupor and more time passed in the quiet of death, but in it hope came to me so that I almost dared lift the phone on the table between our beds—whisper Help! to the operator fast—whisper whisper Help! But no, it was too risky—if he heard me, what then before help arrived? More time went by and still he lay there as though dead. Could it be possible? I lifted myself, concentrating all my being on one thing only—get to the door. I walked a tightrope over the carpet. No you don't—he shot up, gave me two sharp whacks on the head, throwing me back on the bed. I blacked out, and when I came back into the room again it was morning, with the lights still on and the bed next to mine—empty.

I lay there looking up at the ceiling. The windows were closed, and on the bed next to mine where Pat had sprawled the sheets were wrinkled and wild although the covers had not been pulled over him. The dress I had worn the night before clung up around my knees, unfamiliar and strange as I lay there on top of the covers. Through the bathroom door I could see the light still on and makeup strewn about, left here and there, as I'd been late getting dressed the night before. I'd tried to pretend the

Hellzapoppin'! night hadn't happened, and I had—almost—succeeded. I'd felt better about myself since Orson. He did like me . . . didn't he? I'd gone over each detail of our fatal meeting as I'd hurriedly dressed, standing over the basin in a trousseau slip, putting final touches on my makeup. Máybe we'd run into him again—just to see him across the room would be enough. It had hearts, the slip, embroidered around what the salesgirl had called "a sweetheart neckline."

My head throbbed with pain, and I lay there putting off the time when I would have to look at myself in the mirror. Still I felt oddly safe, as if Pat-Pasquale weren't coming back, rescued somehow, as if I'd gotten through a tunnel, through to a place of safety, left him behind in that other place of darkness. Other things kept flying into my aching head: would it be a boy or a girl, Rita's baby? . . . Doctor Davis, I must get to him right away . . . my head. But the door suddenly opened and there he was. . . . What happened, sweetie? he said, looking at me lying there. There was something meek in his manner, hunched over, deflated, truly and deeply exhausted (as well he might be). The phone started ringing ringing but neither of us picked it up. On and on it went until finally he sighed, You take it, sweetie, you take it. There was an edge to it, frightening. Hello, I said. But whoever it was had hung up. You look a mess, he said, did your face get caught in an egg beater? The phone started ringing ringing again. It's Mel Sachs from the *Daily News*, a cheery voice said, calling about the incident last night at the Copa. Oh please, I said, please, it was nothing nothing. OK, he chuckled, can we quote you on that, Mrs. De Cicco? No, wait, wait, I said, there's nothing to say, nothing really, really. Pat-Pasquale took the phone with sudden energy—Listen, you son of a bitch, leave us alone, hear, whoever you are, you just leave us alone! And he slammed down the receiver. Operator, no more calls—Fatso, you tell her, then order breakfast on-the-double, hear—then you better do something about that face, how'd it get that way anyway?

It's the badness coming out in you, hear me . . . exhausted he threw his head back on the pillows.

Nauseated, I got up to open a window. As I did . . . there on the sill I came face to face with a praying mantis . . . it was doing nothing, it was just there. Our room was high up, high up on the sixteenth floor. How had it come to be there—how had *I* come to be there? I walked past Pat-Pasquale sprawled on the bed. He had slumped into a rhythmic snoring that came into the silent room at intervals with so gentle a sound, as if a kettle brewed on the hearth. Now about the praying mantis. You see, they are to me more hated than spiders, feared more than others fear snakes. In my crumpled taffeta black dress I glided away from the praying mantis, past Pat-Pasquale, nothing could have stopped me, out the door I went, down the elevator, into a taxi, for I knew where I was going . . . Mr. Gilchrist. Until I'm twenty-one he is my legal guardian, isn't he? He'd help me, help me out of this place I found myself in, this place, this place of . . .

Those endless halls of Cadwalader, Wickersham & Taft, where Mr. Gilchrist presides . . . how well-remembered the chill, the paneled walls with shelves of books high to the ceiling, a wall of bricks those books in their leather bindings, all the same and yet inside not one alike, for each bears testimony of a different battle! I fear to look at the titles, afraid to find one with my mother's name on it . . . my name. Well, Mr. Gilchrist said as I walked in, what brings you—but his mouth gaped open before finishing the pleasantry. It's true, I must have been a sight. It's Pat, I said, I'm scared, I don't know what to do or where to go. Wait till Mrs. Whitney hears about this, he said, reaching for the phone. No—*you* wait, I said—listen. But he didn't, and soon I heard him going on and on to Auntie Ger until I thought I'd scream. It's not true, I said, grabbing the phone away from him, he doesn't know what he's talking about, listen, Auntie Ger, listen! Gloria, she said, if *you'd* listened to me long ago you wouldn't find yourself in this present predicament. What about your mother? Does *she* know about this? *Does* she? No, I called out, she doesn't, nobody knows, because there's nothing to know—*see*—nothing. I jammed the receiver into Mr. Gilchrist's hand and bolted out the door. I never wanted to see him again, and as for Auntie Ger Auntie Ger Aunt Gertrude . . .

From a booth on the street corner I called Doctor Davis. Come right to the office, he said, I'm here. I started to hail a taxi but instead found myself back in the booth calling the hotel. A strange voice said, I'm sick, sweetie, so help me. Mama's dead, that son of a bitch Cohn, I'll kill him so help me next time I see him—Thelma—where are you, sweetie, Mama's dead, where are you? Your mother's *dead*? I said. It's the badness coming out in you, that's it, that's why you look like you do, come back now, sweetie, get yourself back in shape—Mama Mama's gone—and then through the phone came a sound, the heave of an animal dying, and as it died the animal sobbed, so wounded a sound that it went through my flesh and into my bones and I called out to him—I'm coming I'm coming, don't do anything till I get there—wait wait. . . .

Darling Mummy

Darling Mummy,
      We're back in Junction City after the funeral. The only other funeral I'd ever been to before was Johnny Delahanty's and it was awful. We sat for days in the funeral parlor where Pat's mother was and hundreds and hundreds of friends kept coming in and going out, some weeping, others not. There was a lot of sitting around the coffin on ballroom chairs and lots of going to one house or another and eating eating and drinking drinking and then back to the funeral parlor again.

Pat took his mother's wedding ring off and has it on his left hand. It's gold, kind of like mine, only thicker. Mummy, there are so many things I'd like to tell you about, but I don't know where or how to begin. I thought it would be easier in a letter, but now that I'm writing—everything's flown out of my head. Oh, I did see Mr. Gilchrist in New York, actually the day Pat's mother died. Did he say anything about it? I know he wouldn't have directly to you but maybe through Mr. Crocker? If he did please write me about it. What he said I mean. Mummy, is there any chance you could visit us in Junction City? It's nothing fancy, but it's cozy and I've tried to make it look like a real home even though it's not of course. How is Aunt Toto? Is she still seeing a lot of Edmund? Maybe she could come with you? That is if she'd like to. What do you think, Mummy? It would really be great to see you.

Lovingly,

Gloria

P.S. If Mr. Crocker hasn't said anything to you, maybe you could call and ask him to call Mr. Gilchrist, just to see if he had anything to say about the time I saw him in New York. It was at Cadwalader.

Hugs and kisses, Mummy

Gloria

Gloria Darling

Gloria Darling,

Please tell Pat how deeply I sympathize with his great loss. I'll be writing a letter of sympathy to him but please tell him, darling, in case he doesn't receive it by the time you get this.

Things are more or less quiet these days what with the war on and all. We went to Cobina's Saturday night for dinner and

I must say it was a lovely party. The next night a quieter dinner at Veneta's, but Pepe d'Albro was there and you know how amusing Pepe can be especially when he's feeling no pain after a few glasses of champagne. He did his woof woof imitations and it really is something you have to see to believe, especially the Pekingese one. Wish you and Pat could have been there, darling. Tomorrow we're going to Tamara's cocktail party. Remember you went to her studio once. She always asks about you and of course I tell her how happy you and Pat are even though you're in Kansas and there's this awful war on. Speaking of that, darling, it's really hard for me to get away right now. For one thing Thelma has terrible sniffles. In fact I don't even think she'll be well enough to go to Tamara's but, darling, as soon as she feels better, who knows we might just pop up one day on your doorstep. Until then, darling, I am always your loving

Mummy

J'Attendrai

He's going to be sent overseas. Suddenly he becomes someone else—an actor in a movie. Maybe he'll be killed and I'll never see him again, and it makes me panic. Dodo's back in Freeport at the Schillers', and Mrs. Oppy is helping me get our things together. That song of Jean Sablon's, "J'attendrai"—in my head I keep hearing it, on the record I used to have—

> J'attendrai
> le jour et la nuit
> J'attendrai toujours, ton retour
> J'attendrai, comme l'oiseau qui
> S'enfuit vient chercher l'oubli
> Dans son nid. . . .

I hadn't thought of it until now, not since Johnny Delahanty died. I played that record over and over when I was allowed a few days off from Wheeler to go back to Old Westbury Capital for the funeral . . . over and over until Winter Smith was at his wit's end. But still I played it for the comfort—as if Johnny really would come back to me. But then it all scrambles up, and in my center a terrible sense of loss; but around this, over and around, are layers of—yes, *relief*. It's a strange feeling leaving this town—Junction City—this place I have in some ways come to call home, because I never really feel at home anywhere. Not since the Caravan with Big Elephant and the Little Countess . . . You and I together, Love—Never mind the weather, Love . . . together in the Caravan no matter where we roamed. . . . And working in the studio at Wheeler—*that* was home. It's funny to think maybe I'll never see Mrs. Oppy again. She gave me her recipe for Angel Pie, something to remember me by, she said, American Gothic—the woman in Grant Wood's painting is so like her, in the eeriest way. And the main street of this town with its straight lonely flatness—a painting by Hopper—especially late, very late at night. (I didn't know that then, but I do now.) I wish this war were over. Maybe I'll come back. It won't be an army town then, it will be a home town, a place where people live instead of just pass through. Gene and Oleg are leaving too. They're having an auction to sell everything in their house. I'd give anything to get those red-and-white barrel chairs, but we don't have the money, and besides where would I put them? Right now I don't even know where I'll be living in New York when Pat-Pasquale goes overseas. What I want more than anything is a home. A real home and lots of children. Everything's packed and the furniture's moved back in place the way it was the day we moved in. Will this house be here thirty years from now? I know I won't, because I can't imagine living after I'm thirty. But most people do. Grown-ups live on forever. There's this full-length mirror on the back of our closet door, and Pat-

Pasquale spends a lot of time in front of it in his second lieutenant's uniform, most solemnly looking at himself. Once I came
up and stood beside him. There we were, two cutouts staring
straight ahead, afraid to catch each other's eye. We're going to
New York for a week's leave before he goes to Georgia, from
there—destination unknown.

A Message

I went to the post office to mail a letter, a letter to Auntie
Ger, and when I got back Mrs. Oppy said there had been a phone
call long distance for me and to call back soon as soon as possible.
I got him right away, Mr. Gilchrist, and he said
    I have sad news—
    What? What? I said
    There was a buzzing in my brain, my heart throbbed so fast,
his voice coming through water—drowning I called out for help—
    What? What?
    I kept calling but no sound came and he didn't hear me
    Is it Dodo Dodo Dodo?
    But ocean pounded through me and I struggled great gulps
of air
    As far as I know, he said, the nurse is in Freeport. . . . Nooo
nooo, he said through a hundred years, it's not the nurse . . .
it's Mrs. Whitney
    Dodo—Auntie Ger? Auntie Ger? I said
    She's dead
    Dead? I said, she can't be dead dead I just mailed a letter a
letter to her Auntie Ger Auntie Ger
    Well, I'm sorry to say, she is
    I don't believe it, I said, someone like Auntie Ger doesn't
die
    Well, she *does*—
    and she is—Dead. He was quite put out with me

This dead is said to have taken place in Doctors Hospital
That's what he said
Then he went on to say that the viewing would be at 60
Washington Mews and the family, my Aunt Gladys, Cousin
Flora, and all of them said to give me the message
The door would not be closed to me if I cared to go
That was the message: all of it
I keep hearing her coughing, the sound of it through the
doors
maybe if I'd brought her a glass of water
at Old Westbury   coughing
but only at night
during the day she didn't cough at all at all
The thin tall coldness of her—her face; the tiny crossways on
the upper lip, the rust-color lipstick blurring, russet hair, but
most of all—
her Aunt Gertrude hat
and a voice comes to me . . .
warm and loving, but it is not hers and there are no words
to the sound. . . .

I went into the kitchen, where Mrs. Oppy sat at the table
by the window. She was staring out at the rain, having a cup of
tea and resting her feet. My bunions always act up in this weather,
she said. That call was about my aunt I said, my Aunt Gertrude.
Is she the one lives in Newport? Mrs. Oppy said, settling back
in the chair, tucking a strand of hair back into the bun on her
head. No, I said, it's the one who lives at Old Westbury. Oh,
that one, Mrs. Oppy said, impressed. Dodo talked to Mrs. Oppy
a lot about Aunt Gertrude. That's too bad, she said, what did
she die of? She used to cough at night, I said, and I put my
hands over my face. It's good to cry, dear, she said, it'll help.
But as soon as she said this my heart hardened and my mind slid
to other things—what to do with the orange crates I'd painted,
things like that. Mrs. Oppy, would you have any use for those

night tables—you know, the ones I made from the orange crates? Why, yes I would, she said, my daughter could use them in the baby's room, that'll be real nice. . . . We sat there not saying anything for a long time. . . . Where's the funeral? she said. In New York soon. Oh, she said and gave a deep sigh. Then more time went by and the phone started ringing. It was Naney Morgan. When are you arriving, Little One? she said, all energies directed towards the crisis, giving orders in her most Naney-Napoleon way. Wait, Little One, wait, she finally said. Dodo's here, and I'll put her on now. Big Elephant came on the line but sounded not like herself, and her voice kept fading away. We're leaving tonight, Dodo, I said. Will you meet me at the Park Lane Hotel tomorrow? Please, I said. Yes, lovey, I'll be there, and then she hung up. Of course, my mother hasn't called, but that's OK because I don't expect her to. No other word since the one message from any of the others: Auntie Ger's children—Flora, Barbara, Sonny—Auntie Gladys, my father's sister . . . from Gerta—cousin, unquestioned friend—not a word.

I wanted to go straight to 60 Washington Mews from the station, but then I knew Big Elephant would be at the hotel waiting for me. And she was. But she's in a terrible state. She sits staring ahead, struck dumb as it were, because Auntie Ger didn't leave her any money in her will. No matter how hard I try, I can't get through to her to tell her—it doesn't matter because I'll always take care of her. But she doesn't hear me, just sits there in the same chair in the Park Lane Hotel, won't even eat when I call down for room service. Not even profiteroles, which Big Elephant is most partial to, tempt her. Money turns people into strangers. No surprises, though, from Pat-Pasquale, who sulks around, quite put out that the only thing Auntie Ger left me in her will is "my pearl and diamond bracelet which I almost always wear." But why *should* Auntie Ger leave me any-thing? I certainly didn't expect her to. The Cartier bracelets—

yes, I can't remember a time when she didn't wear them, pearly twinkly cuffs, one on each wrist. That's proof she loved me. Isn't it? This bracelet is one of a pair, and the other is to be for Cathleen. It makes me feel close to Cathleen again, knowing she'll be wearing one while I'm wearing the other. Connecting us like she really is my sister after all. I wonder if she'll go to the funeral. After she married Ramón she never leaves Cuba, and since she broke her promise to me telling Aunt Gertrude about Van Heflin—well, I'd kept putting off getting in touch with her. But now if I see her it will all be different. Pat-Pasquale's main concern as evening rolls around is finding nightclubs that are out of the usual rounds, places we can slip in and out of without being noticed. What he means is that he doesn't think it's smart for us to be yoo-hooing the nights away while in the same city Auntie Ger lies dead. Last night he insisted I go with him to some hole in the wall, but tonight he's gone out without me—I have a pain in my sawdust, I told him. What does *that* mean? he said. It's what my Raggedy Ann doll used to say to me. Well, Fatsy Roo, you never were very smart, were you? You be good now, he said waving toodle-ooo and yoo-hooing on out the door.

The funeral is at Saint Bartholomew's—tomorrow. Pat-Pasquale fumes around over pros and cons of whether he'll go or not. I keep quiet, wanting him to be by my side, but praying to God he won't. It's late now, but Dodo under a spell just sits here in the same chair she's sat in every day without moving. If I don't get to 60 Washington Mews now—right away—it will be too late and I'll never see Auntie Ger again. That letter I wrote her—will anybody read it, or will it just be torn up and thrown in a wastebasket somewhere?

Auntie Ger lay in her bed at 60 Washington Mews. She lay there like she was asleep. Only she wasn't. She was dead. Everyone was there. Except Gerta. Why wasn't she there? They were cold to me, but they didn't shut the door in my face. Black figures milled around and around those rooms I know so well. I feel dead-sick and want to cry but can't.

On our way to the funeral, in the hotel elevator, Pat-Pasquale just-like-that said he was going to "21" instead. So I went on to Saint Bartholomew's alone. The usher sat me in a pew next to Mummy Anne and Cousin Bill. It was a tight squeeze. The church was crowded. I could see Auntie Gladys and the others, the backs of them, all in a row, one black dress after another, hats with veils. The men cousins all in black too. I tried to make out which black back was Gerta but gave up. Someone was chewing gum—Cousin Liana? Is that possible? . . . I kept re-membering how I used to call her Cousin Leelee until that day at Old Westbury Capital—she was having tea with Aunt Ger-trude, in the living room. I started running the tub to take a bath. And I went to do homework, forgot I'd turned the water on. Suddenly a wild thing—Cousin Leelee—came into my room. You stupid girl! What have you done! I ran past her, down the stairs, through the open door of the living room I caught a flash of the water seeping down through the ceiling, maids with pails, mops, Aunt Gertrude standing in the door gazing up at the drops as they drip-dropped down like rain—on and on I ran down the hall to the cottage, up the stairs to the topmost room, the room in which later Winter and I loved each other. But Cousin Leelee ran after me, found me sprawled on the bed, pillow over my head. What made you do it do it? She was trying to pull the pillow away from me, angry angry. You stupid girl girl girl! Didn't mean to, didn't mean to, didn't didn't, I kept saying, but she kept shaking me. How they must hate me . . . not surprised at all when I went against Aunt Gertrude and married Pat-Pasquale. Even though I couldn't see his face, I knew the tallest back in a black coat was Cousin Gerta's father—the un-pleasant Bozo Bean. How especially pleased *he* must have been, proving all along how right he was in not permitting Gerta to associate with me because, as he said—I might turn out like my mother.

Come with us, we'll drop you off, Mummy Anne said when the funeral was over. I sat between her and Cousin Bill in the limousine. He stared out the window and nobody said anything. Mummy Anne took my hand. My eyes closed and we shot forward; on a roller coaster roller coaster and I wanted more than anything to get off, but I couldn't couldn't and then it was too late too late for me to stop crying. The roller coaster fast fast fast—the traffic slow slow. When we got to the hotel it was still going— the roller coaster—on and on it sped, couldn't get off, out of the car, up the elevator, along the halls to our room faster faster. . . .

And there he was—Pat-Pasquale getting ready to leave for overseas. Don't worry, sweetie, he said, I'll be back. He thought it was for him, this endless ride. But it's not—or is it? this bottomless pain for something I've lost. Only I can't remember what it is. Maybe I could if I could only stop crying.

Roses

This hospital isn't really a hospital, more like a . . . place, an outdoor stage set in which four walls have been put up and a ceiling plopped on haphazardly at the last minute so that all at once there exists an enormous room with beds placed row on row, each in its own time, if necessary, transformed by curtains into a roofless tent granting privacy to the dying soldier. It is within one of these tents within this enormous place that I sit, imagining that it is Cathleen who lies in the bed I hold vigil by. But of course it is not my sister and we are not in Havana. We are in an army hospital at Mitchell Field. Hours before he was to go overseas Pat-Pasquale collapsed and was sent here with an illness from which the doctors say there is little chance of recovery . . . septicemia. Long and narrow he stretches out, the sheets around him smooth as a shroud, so still, so quiet, I find that I am no longer afraid of him. Sometimes his eyes open and float aimlessly around our little world like two jellyfish in a bowl of still water, drifting by me as if I did not exist. In illness he has become docile, and I believe—yes! I do—that if I can bring him back to life . . . things will be different, transformed into something real and lovely and not the nightmare it has become. The dark anger will be shed and in its place a prince will be revealed, someone who is loving and kind, someone to talk with about most secret things, a man who will never strike me again.

I sit beside the bed holding on to his foot, anchoring him to life, fervently praying to God and Saint Theresa that he will not die. Frances has come to hold vigil with me, and we go to Saint Bridget's Church, strangers, knock-knock-knocking on the door, searching for a miracle. And although I know Father Feeley is no longer pastor there, still it is eerie to see another standing in his place. Yes, Father Feeley too has been lost, he too has died, and the new pastor receives us, averting his eyes from our grief, embarrassed, wishing for the dark anonymity of the confessional . . . keep praying keep praying, he says over and over, until soon there is nothing more to say and he heaves himself out of the chair muttering, Other matters other matters to attend to attend to attend to. . . . No matter no matter about those other matters, for as he heaves himself out of the chair . . . roses, yes! roses, roses like the roses on the statue of Saint Theresa's marble likeness which presides over her shrine at Saint Patrick's Cathedral where I go to light candles, roses like the roses she holds in the painted cover on my prayer book. They are strewn about, stenciled there on the fabric covering the chair, and I kneel down to touch the pillow, for surely the dim flowers are the sign we had prayed for . . . the message from Saint Theresa.

When we return to the bedside the doctors are there, their voices come to me muffled by the roses I saw on a pillow, as they talk about a drug . . . a new drug, a drug they are saying may be the breakthrough they've been looking for—it's made from molds and might work, it's hard to get, but we have—enough to treat him. . . . What is it, doctor? I call out—what is it? It's called penicillin, he said. Yes, penicillin—and he took the syringe and gave Pat-Pasquale the first injection.

My half-sister Cathleen's son, Harry Cushing, and I were born in the same year, and it is strange to know my nephew is the same age as myself, strange to think of him now in Havana by his mother's bedside. I too would be by her side were it not for Pat-Pasquale. Does Harry sit as I do by Pat-Pasquale's bed, lightly oh so lightly holding Cathleen's toe? Does she speak, or does she too lie silent, lids closed, lost to us? Pat-Pasquale's fever has abated somewhat, but his face has not changed, and his breath—ah, yes. His breath, one nurse whispers to another, smells It smells of—Death. But I make myself into a sieve, and the blackening shadow passes through my body, for if I hold on to his foot this cannot be, I root him to life, my breathing timed to his, his breath taking strength from mine. As the moments go by, tendrils take root in my energy, we become one person, and I am possessed by—hope: hope that he will not abandon me as my father did, for this time I am no longer in a crib at Sandy Point Farm helpless as my father lies in the next room dying . . . this time it will be different.

A silent messenger beckons me follow. Past rows of beds on and on down long corridors until we come to a door, enter a room small with telephone . . . from far far away a voice comes to me . . . Harry telling me Cathleen is dead, funeral tomorrow, burial tomorrow in the communal grave of Ramón's family, will call me when he returns, Good-bye, he says, good-bye good-bye, and we are cut off cut off cut off. I click the receiver back and forth, but the buzz of dial tone leaps into my head, splinters into zigzags of color, comes at me from edges of my eyes. Forms assemble, but as they are about to be identified, apart they zing, pushed by pain aside, other shapes more dazzling—hurt—zigzagging dazzling than ones before. From feet, needles go into streams of blood, quicksilver on up through body, lodge into head, faster, around around . . . run run escape, forget Cathleen forget Pat-Pasquale everything gone—nothing anywhere   pain

Pat-Pasquale sits up in bed yoo-hooing at the nurses, yoo-hooing at Fatsy Roo (for that is once again my place in life), yoo-hooing at the doctors and being impossible in general to the stream of people who stop by his bed on and off through the day. He is a big Star and his recovery will be a landmark case in the annals of medicine, one of penicillin's first triumphs. He is to be discharged tomorrow, not only from hospital at Mitchell Field but honorably from the U.S. Army. From here we will go, accompanied by a trained nurse, directly to an apartment on the East River where my cousin Sonny Whitney, Aunt Gertrude's son, and his bride, Eleanor, have given us their apartment to rent. I say "given" because the rent they have asked is so low it is really a present. I always felt that Sonny liked me a lot and now I know it. I can't grasp that this is our last day here. Frances and me. It seems as if we have again been in this limbo forever and that we'll never be young again.

A *Place by the River*

A place by the river most beautiful: duplex with stairs winding to a hall where all is spacious, quiet, doors leading into other rooms of ordered beauty. The bedroom, a corner room papered in silvery Chinese tea paper, windows facing the river—boats glide by bearing mysterious cargoes, at night the wail of steamers.

A silvered screen hides bed from view as you enter, on it etched flamingoes, pink, their long legs poised in pools of aqua where water lilies drift. The bed is also silvered: magnolias—painted petals of white—open, nestled in vines twining around the headboard; sheets of white linen, lace bordered, each monogrammed in spidery arabesque—gWv. These initials of Aunt Gertrude's embellish vermeil spoons and forks, china, even a beaded needlepoint pillow, and every place the eye rests brings to mind how it used to be long ago at Old Westbury Capital, and it is as if I had stepped back into that Kingdom . . . belonged there at last.

We have a butler called Orlando and a maid called Katie. He is sweet and she is sour. But he recommended her for the job and they get along fine by communicating with as few words as possible. Katie is German, short straw hair frames her face in rigid waves, a face that has one expression only. How angular she is, moving quickly, in her every gesture the anger of women in a Munch painting. Orlando speaks gently, his voice warm with sunlight. He has a daughter my age, but his wife is never mentioned. So the days have started fitting into place, one after the other, and there are times when I believe, even with the terrible war going on across the sea, that it does belong to me, this life of—beauty . . . order. Almost.

Almost, because as the days pass and Pat-Pasquale gets better, all is as it was before the illness. It's walking on eggs most of the time with Pat-Pasquale, and just when I think things are OK (calm, you know), the tiniest thing can set him off—What is it with you! he'll shout, because I put on the white sweater I thought he liked instead of the brown one. What is it with you? No, nothing has changed as eggshells start breaking all over the place, cracking in the old familiar way. But I have my little ways of tempering this. I keep everything around me neat as neat can be, in its place. Just so. In less than a second when I come into a room I can tell if anything has been moved, yes, even a fraction of an inch. My dressing table no one touches but me. Every day it gives me great satisfaction to take off all the jars, perfume bottles, enameled pink brushes, mirror—everything, dust carefully, oh! so carefully, and then—everything back in place just the way I want it. It's such a small thing, but it makes me feel each time (please don't laugh) that I've come to a decision.

Summertime, Quogue, Long Island, 1944

Summertime and the living is easy—or so it says in the song. The wooden house we've rented on the beach nestles flimsily in the dunes and appears from the outside to be small, which is misleading, for there are many rooms, too many rooms from my point of view, rooms which are never empty. But not because a family lives here, for this is not a house which is a home, it is a house that is a hotel with guests coming or going not just on weekends but during the week as well, staying either for a few days or longer—it matters not. It matters not to me. No, no! it doesn't. Not anymore. I don't care I don't care. So if I don't care, why do I feel angry about it?—because I do. Angry at Pat-Pasquale that he has turned this house into a hotel where his friends can bring their girlfriends, a different one each time. Girls with not much to say for themselves, who only smile in that knowing way. Girls who usually appear at mealtimes because they spend all the hours of the day in rooms with Lex Thompson or Billy Sussman or True Zuckerman. While in the living room Pat-Pasquale gambles all day long with Halibut Steak (for some reason that's what I call Hal Sims), Lee Mavis, and whoever else happens along. Days of sun go by, one after the other, but they rarely go out these guests, not even for a quick swim, so absorbed are they in their various recreations. The girl Lex Thompson brought here last week, blond this time, didn't even bother to greet me when they arrived. Come on, Lex honey, she said, peeling off her dress as we stood in the living room, come o-on. She swirled around in a polka-dot two-piece bathing suit, itching

to go for a swim. Around her body was a golden chain, delicately circling her sun-tanned waist, neatly clasped together by a golden heart. It hung loosely below her navel, and dangling below this heart swinging to and fro as she wiggled around there was a little golden key to open the padlock. No, Wanda, come here! Lex said, impatiently running his hand around the golden chain, Let's unpack first, and he took his finger and poked it through one of her Shirley Temple ringlets. Oooooh—all right, she pouted, flouncing away and glancing around the living room as if this might be the guest room. Where'll I put my stuff? No, it's this way, I said, leading them up the narrow stairs. Well, that was the last we saw of them until dinner time. Pat-Pasquale and his gang settled into their game of cards, and as I went out to the beach I heard him call out, Hey, Lex boy, quiet up there, you two, hear! We have to concentrate! Yoo-hoo! Gin! he yelped, slapping down a card. Upstairs it was suddenly quiet. I walked out of the house on along the wooden ramps to the beach and sat down on the sand. Already it was hot and the day had hardly begun. I stretched out and looked up into the sun, testing how long I could stare into it without turning away, thinking about what we could have for lunch along with the egg salad sandwiches, but tears came and the soles of my feet still smarted from the hot sand so I jumped up and ran into the sea.

There's a lull in this week's activities—quickly I suggest we invite some other friends for a change. Pat-Pasquale says OK, Fatsy, but remember Hal Sims is staying on so don't give his room to anyone else, hear me. Oh no, I said, of course not, and I quickly get on the phone to arrange things before Pat-Pasquale changes his mind. Now it's all set and I'm making lots of plans for picnics, outings to choose lobsters from the fishermen's wharf, things like that, maybe even a movie Sunday night.

Everybody's here: Carol and her sister Elinor (a mirror image of Carol is what I expect every time I meet her, but it's always a surprise the second I see her—why, they're not even related!), Maggi McNellis and her adoring beau, Clyde Newhouse. He's crazy to marry her but she's not sure. Ham Nelson's name pops into the conversation rather often, because, Maggi confides, "he wants to marry me too—you know he was married to Bette Davis before he fell so madly in love with me—the Ham is short for Hamilton, yes, Hamilton Nelson, that's his name," she says, matter-of-factly examining her perfect manicure. Anyway, they're all here, and so is Frances. Now Pat-Pasquale has Halibut Steak all to himself, and he's on a roll which puts him in the best possible mood. If only the rest of the gang were here to see him as he yoo-hoos one gin game after another, which isn't easy, because Halibut is some sort of wizard at bridge and anything pertaining to games of chance, making competition fierce when he's around. This incessant game occupies all their time with pause for only a few hours' haphazard sleep. Then up and to it again as they face each other in fevered concentration, hardly taking time out to eat, absentmindedly reaching for the snacks I leave at their elbows. What a relief to be reasonably safe, knowing Pat-Pasquale's focused on the gin game with little that anybody could do to provoke his wrath—why, I could leap over the moon and he wouldn't notice, much less pick out weekend guests, as long as we stay out on the beach and don't distract him.

Tonight I've planned a bonfire picnic. Clyde's digging a pit for it now in the sand. Seaweed has been spread out to dry in the sun and should be ready at dusk to steam the lobsters and fresh ears of corn. It's really hot here without a single cloud in the sky; not a breeze even, so hot, people lie face down on the sand without moving, there's just the sun and yellow beach and blue of the sea and the only thing that's moving besides Clyde, as he shovels the sand like a gravedigger, are the waves breaking, now and then, in a slow, hot way, rhythmically, far down at the rim of the sea. It makes me want to move down and lie at the edge of the water, let the waves lap over me, nudging my body out each time the tide recedes, yes, each time a little more, inching me out, pulling me into the ocean, and in the doing draw out this feeling I harbor within me so that I will be free, free from this feeling that something is . . . *missing*, something I have no name for, something that has nothing to do with now or this time and this place, no, it's something much deeper than that, something from long ago, much deeper and more impor-tant—oh, yes! much much more important—but . . . what? It's hot, too hot to move, and instead I look up, circling the bowl of blue sky, and wonder if that's where heaven is, and if my father's there. And I go over and over again the conversation I had with my mother last night when she called from California. She's coming to live in New York, or so she said. Maurice Chalom is finding an apartment for her. Oh Mummy, I said, how won-derful! When? Soon, Pooks, soon, her voice trailed off vaguely.

Will you be here before summer's over, in time to visit us here in Quogue? Of course, darling, she said, and I look up where heaven might be and my heart leaps with hope.

It shook me up so that finding it seemed the most important thing in the world, like my life depended on it. There we were, late at night on the beach, sitting around the bonfire, the heat of day turned chill, so chill we had put sweaters on over our bathing suits. We had a big slippery beach ball and Clyde got up and started throwing it up in the air and I jumped up and then the others did too and there we were all throwing it back and forth to each other. Pat-Pasquale was still hooked into the game with Halibut Steak and hadn't set foot out of the house all day long. We were laughing and horsing around, but after a while I said, Come on, let's go in for a swim. The waves were phosphorescent in the moonlight and at every stroke hands skimmed the water, making sparkles like the sparkles that flare from wands on July Fourth nights. There we were, in the beauty of midsummer, and in joy I held my hands high, high up above me, jumping up to touch the moon, so close it seemed, a perfect globe of milky white in the black sky. I looked up at my hands and in the moonlight, clear as if by day, I saw each finger, saw that the plain gold band I always wore was—gone. I ran my hand up and down the ringless finger, but there was no mistaking it. Gone. I called out, a cry of despair. Suddenly we were back around the bonfire, searching in the sand, searching for my wedding ring. It was all haywire, because maybe it had slipped off in the waves, but maybe not—Help! Help! I called out, and to comfort me Clyde said, We'll narrow the area down to where we've been, put posts at four corners, strings between—keep looking. Suddenly from far away along the beach a light bobbed up and down, up and down as closer and closer it came. What you folks up to? a voice called out, and the light was suddenly flashed in our faces. Help us help us, I reached up to the tall man, he was in uniform and because of this, wildly, I hoped that it gave him power—

my wedding ring ring, gone, lost somewhere around here, and
I pulled him along the sand. Let me get some of my buddies to
search around with me, he said, and they waited there, Frances,
Maggi and Clyde, Carol and Elinor, while I ran back to the house
to tell Pat-Pasquale. *Stupido!* he shouted at me—Can't you see
I'm in the middle of a game?! Leave us alone, if you're dumb
enough to wear a ring on the beach, what the hell do you expect!
Halibut Steak paused for a moment and looked at Pat-Pasquale—
Listen, the kid's upset, why don't we take a break and go to the
beach? Nothing doing, Pat-Pasquale said, raising his eyebrows
as he shifted into a philosophical mood—Let Her Reap What
She Has Sown. He raised his eyebrows and nodded his head
pontifically in my direction and turned back to his cards. Halibut
Steak started to say something, but I ran away, away from them,
out of the house, back to the others. The beach was now flooded
with lights and men from the Coast Guard were raking the sand,
but it was hopeless hopeless hopeless—and through my head
trudged the Walrus and the Carpenter walking close at hand,
weeping like anything to see such quantities of sand, if seven
maids with seven mops swept it for half a year, do you suppose,
the Walrus said, that they could get it clear? I doubt it, said the
Carpenter and shed a bitter tear. Thank you thank you, I said,
running back and forth from one to the other. How astounding
that these unknown Coast Guard men would do this for me,
search with hope through the hopeless sand, I'll never forget
it, no, not if I live a million years. Frances and Carol and I
made sandwiches and coffee to bring to them, as on and on we
worked, sifting through the sand, and it was only when the
moon fell out of sight and the sun came up over the rim of the
sea, orange and hot, that we gave up and said farewell to each
other.

Pat-Pasquale and Halibut Steak were still at it when we
struggled into the house. Did you find it, sweetie? Pat-Pasquale
said without looking up. I walked past them and went up to our

room. From the window I could see over the dunes to the sand where we had searched so urgently. Somehow it still seemed important to me—the ring. It meant something to me that had nothing to do with Pat-Pasquale. It had to do with something else, with the something that was . . . missing, the something I had no name for. I went back out onto the beach and sat there looking out at the ocean. I sifted my hand around into the sand and all at once, just like Little Jack Horner who sat in a corner eating humble pie, stuck in his thumb and pulled out a plum and said what a good boy am I—there it was, a gold ring—just like the wedding ring my mother wore, but this one was mine, shiny and damp with sand.

Summer's End

Good-bye, House—good-bye, Beach—good-bye, good-bye— I'm glad the summer's over. Rented houses aren't really homes, no matter how one moves the furniture around or adds a touch or two of oneself here and there. In a moment all is back as it was before we moved in, and the house will be abandoned without a trace of our having been there. I look around the nameless room. Mummy was in this room, she sat in that very chair, the one I noticed had the cigarette burns the first day we got here. I sit in it one last time for old times' sake. She was here only for a few days with Maurice Chalom who's moved from Paris to New York for the duration. He's even more attentive than when he sent Mummy those bouquets of red roses in cellophane at each stop the Super Chief made when Tootsie Eleanor and I were with Mummy on the "California Here We Come" trip, but whether she's in love with him or not is one of the mysteries. He's a whiz at decorating and buys houses here and there, fixes them up and then sells them for a fortune. He's going to help Mummy fix up the apartment she's taken on Seventy-third Street. Queen Jonquil's staying on at Maple Manor to be near Edmund, and as far as I can tell Ketti Keven is out of the picture. Boy, am I glad. When Mummy and Maurice were out here we went to the Montauk Inn for dinner, a big long table because we had the usual full house. Pat-Pasquale and Mummy still get along great. Of course, she knows nothing about—well, you know—and every time I hope to be able to talk to her about things she looks vague and starts talking about the weather, and it gets too complicated to even try to bring the conversation around to Pat-Pasquale and the dark of things. My fear sometimes gets so that I want to run and hide somewhere where he'll never find me.

Mummy and Maurice weren't so hot for the beach during their visit. For one thing Mummy still likes to sleep late—well, she always did, so I shouldn't have expected it to be different now. She did set foot on it once, late in the afternoon. Maurice brought a huge tin of Beluga caviar and we made a celebration of it, taking a bottle of champagne out on the dunes as the sun set. That was the same evening we went on to the Montauk Inn. The Lady Moon got quite dreamy-eyed at dinner, sitting directly across the table from me between Halibut Steak and Pat-Pasquale. She started talking to Halibut about me, and by leaning forward ever so slightly I could hear every word. My daughter, my little daughter Gloria, she sighed, fluttering her eyelids, she's everything I could want, isn't she lovely, she's she a pooks—not only that, she's—she's—I strained forward—she's—sentimental—yes, sentimental, Mr. Sims—isn't that divine? I drew back and looked at her across the ketchup bottle. She caught my eye and her mouth slipped into that half-crooked smile of old, the one I knew and loved so well. Ah, yes! so well. I love you, Pooks, she called to me across the table as she lifted her hand and wiggled the long mahogany-lacquered nails in a salute of sorts.

But I do believe they had a good time, Mummy and Maurice, at least I hope they did. Pat-Pasquale kept himself in a good mood while they were here—well, the walls were just boards nailed together, and you could hear what was going on in the other rooms if voices were raised. I guess most beach houses are that way. Not like New York. Nobody there hears what goes on behind the closed doors.

Bonwit's on a Rainy Afternoon

It was pouring rain and we were on our way to meet Pigeon and Ted Gossett at Grand Central Station. Pat-Pasquale was looking forward to the football game we would see in New Haven, not to mention the other games he and Ted would occupy themselves with on the train. I'd brought along *The Fountainhead* by Ayn Rand. I'm really involved in that book, reading it slowly, loath to come to the end. But when we got to the station and I saw the two Gossetts standing there ahead of us in the distance, waiting—it wasn't only two Gossetts I saw ahead. It was the day ahead: Ted and Pat-Pasquale, Scotch-and-sodas close at hand, playing gin; Pigeon, her manner to me grown-up to child, me straining to be polite. Then: sitting sitting at the stadium (dare I sneak *The Fountainhead* out of my bag to read instead of watching the game?), the dinner after, more yoo-hoos over Scotch-and-sodas before the late train ride back with cigarette smoke, gin games, and more yoo-hoos. (Well, you get the picture.) There they stood, Pigeon in her tweedy suit, smart and hatted as could be, alligator bag glistening with gold hardware, and Ted, spotting us, waving in that flabby way of his, calling out, Hey, fella, hurry up, we're gonna miss that train! No, I couldn't couldn't, and they stood there gaping as I spun around and ran ran away, fast up the steps, fast fast through the station and into a taxi. I looked back, but there were only strangers hurrying in and out— not a shadow of Pat-Pasquale.

The taxi left me at Fifty-seventh and Fifth and I went into Bonwit Teller and called Frances from a phone booth. I'm at Bonwit's in a phone booth, meet me please soon as you can,

hurry! Are you all right? she said. Yes, I said, but hurry. Surely
Pat-Pasquale would have supernatural powers to track me down,
and although people were waiting outside the booth to get at
the phone I sat there talking away as if there were still someone
on the line. Suddenly a face pressed against the glass door, tap-
tapping on the pane. I jumped up! The face loomed through the
cloudy glass so close it appeared to be that of a stranger. But no,
it was Frances, and together we hurried to the elevator, up to
the fifth-floor lingerie department—Bras, 34B or any size, I told
the salesgirl, any color, it doesn't matter—and I grabbed them
from her and Frances and I went into a fitting room where I told
her what had happened and why we came to be huddled in this
closet of a room with handfuls of bras we had no use for. But
eventually, of course, we had to move on, and we did—but it
was a big store, and we stayed there until it closed at six, going
from one floor to another, pretending we were shoppers with lots
to spend and not a care in the world. Then it was closing time
and there was nothing left to do but go back. I kept saying to
Frances, maybe he had gone on the train, the prospect of a game
with Ted Gossett too good to pass up maybe maybe maybe?
Maybe, but maybe not. Frances didn't answer, and we took each
other's hand and in no time at all there we were, right back
where we started from. Although I had my key I rang the bell.
Surely in front of Orlando . . . but as the door opened there he
was—Pat-Pasquale, as if he'd tried to get there before him. He
looked at me and he looked at Frances standing by my side and
without a word walked past us out into the hall. With his back
to us he pressed the button for the elevator in and out, in and
out, hard. As the door opened he turned and nodded at me—
You, he said, I'll get to you later—and then he was gone.

Frances was going to stay overnight with me. Everyone but
Orlando was off and he fixed us dinner. We sat in the dining
room eating pasta Romano and looking out over the river at the
jewels of light from the bridge and the boats passing, and didn't

talk much. All at once there was a racket, a noisy noisy racket, voices, and cutting through it—a laugh. He was back. We could hear them setting up for a card game in the library. Thank God, I said to Frances, it'll be all right. And in one way it was, but in another way it wasn't all right, and it never would be.

Autumn in New York

Another weekend at Lorelle and Bill Hearst's in Manhasset. So many weekends there, always the same people, the men always playing gin or backgammon while the women tell catty stories about their friends. Janet Stewart is always there, with her Botticelli grace and every strand of her pale lemon-yellow hair devotedly gathered at the nape of her neck in a loose chignon, cool madonna that she is—especially to me (is it because her husband, Will, was once in love with my mother?). Morton Downey's nice. I like him. The last time we were there, snow was on the ground and Pat-Pasquale regaled everybody during dinner with a tale of how on the drive up he'd had to get out of the car to pee and how in a snowdrift he'd peed a circle the way children draw a face, put two slits for eyes, a portrait, he said, yes a portrait of Fatsy Roo called "Wee-Wee Holes in Snow"—they all got it right away because of my Javanese Vanderbilt eyes and thought it hilarious. All except Morton. He didn't laugh. Anyway, on those weekends I do get a lot of reading done and stay in my room as much as possible. Other times, when I'm not reading, Dominique Francon is on my mind even though I finished *The Fountainhead* weeks ago. I'm going to try and be as much like her as I can—that is, the way she was before she became Mrs. Howard Roark. She didn't want to feel things or get attached to anything or anybody because then she'd be free and couldn't be hurt. Yes, that's how I'm going to be, like Dominique Francon.

. . .

During the week we hardly ever stay home. It's either "21" or the Colony for dinner, sometimes Chambord, but whatever restaurant, we're always, like it says in the song, "off on the road to Morocco"—Elmer's, that is, ha, ha! The "we" I refer to of course means not only the De Ciccos but also the six or eight or nine others who migrate with us en masse from one restaurant to another, usually winding up at our place for a game that goes on and on through dawn. Couldn't we stay home one night? I asked Pat-Pasquale. Sure, dumpling, next week. But next week never comes.

Without telling Pat-Pasquale I found a place to work, a place of my own—to paint, to be myself. I can't believe my good luck. Until now it was Bernard Lamotte's studio, perfect light from a skylight on the top of a six-story house on East Fifty-third Street across from Rockefeller Center. One room with fireplace, closet kitchen and bathroom. There's a roof terraced with a lattice arbor where vines grow and a tree has been planted, a chinaberry perhaps? Perhaps not. I'll have to wait till spring to find out. Beneath it, a well has been sunk for wines to cool on ice. I've read of gatherings at Lamotte's and picture myself among the guests, as we sit around an unpainted table. Curious coins have been set into this table, which is carved with the names of Lamotte's many friends, and we are gathered around it over cocktails, in the sweet dusk, talking. Dinner begins with bowls of the hors d'oeuvres made from the herbs he grows in pots. Soon Lamotte will grill slabs of thick steak on his primitive charcoal grill to carve on the French diagonal for dinner, served on a plank. There will be a salad, cheese with crusty bread, and later inky-black coffee in tin cups. And then in the spring night Sablon sings or Claude Alphand plays her guitar, or Sieyès talks of the Free French, or Antoine de Saint-Exupéry does his inventive card tricks (no gin rummy for that one). Oh yes! Yes! This is how an evening should be after a day of work. At last I'll be able to work after the fruitless summer, after Pat-Pasquale making fun of me every time

I'd start to take my paints out onto the dunes. Soon it will be my twenty-first birthday, and I'm full of hope—yes, hope.

Snow

Snow sifts silently on the skylight as I work. Every day I come here in the afternoons after Life class at the Art Students League. Our teacher is Robert Beverly Hale, and once we enter the studio all else is shut out, for it is a place of most singular intent. Will these days be remembered by me when I am old— the snow as it fell over the grey-white city, will I remember? Will I remember how it felt as I walked home through the dusk on the brink of my life with heart full of longing, thirsting for tomorrow, bursting with love and aching to find a place to put it? I will remember, won't I?

Carol is wounded like an animal dying. Bill is going to be shipped overseas, and her grief is terrible to behold. Oh, how she loves him. It's as if her body were being ripped open and her insides falling out, strewn on the floor. It's as if once he goes— she'll be nobody. All of her self exists in him. Their son, Aram, is two years old and she tries to hold herself together for his sake, but her eyes are red with weeping and her face mutilated with pain. It is as if a knife were stuck in her heart and she bleeds and bleeds but there's no stopping it. Let's go to a movie, I said, and we went to see *The Hunchback of Notre Dame*. Charles Laughton plays Quasimodo, and the moment he appeared we both got the giggles—he looked exactly like Bill Saroyan and Pat De Cicco cloned together in grotesque caricature. No kidding. Well, it sure took our mind off things. After the movie we walked along Madison Avenue and stopped at a place to buy Apples-on-a-Stick. We ate them moving on through the snow, still talking about Quasimodo . . . the snowflakes as they stuck to the lacquered sugar frosting the lips with cold sweet surprise. Will I remember?

. . .

Every day snow keeps falling falling on the city. Carol and I look out the window at the river as it swirls down through the grey sky, over the grey water, over blocks of ice cracking apart as boats pulse their way slowly out of sight. We sit cross-legged on the floor, having tea and talking. Talking about Pat-Pasquale and Bill and listening to a record of the *Warsaw Concerto*. Other times it's the train music we play, the Rachmaninoff, over and over again. Carol calls it that because it sounds the way you feel on a train as the wheels turn along the track in and out, through tunnels, over bridges, on through the night when all else is quiet. Carol doesn't know who her father is. She thinks about that a lot. That's why we feel so close to each other. She tried to find out from her mother just before she gave birth to Aram. Who is my father? she said to her mother. But Mrs. Marcus wouldn't tell her. There's nothing I couldn't tell Carol, for she is my sister, myself. Will I remember when snow kept falling falling through the days . . . will I remember how it felt before we met—the White Knight and I—before we came face to face, before I knew that my life had begun?

December 1944

Carol and I spend all the time we can together. It's like before the war, before we married—fun that flashed by in a minute and was gone. Why, in a week we wore out a pair of silver Delman sandals, dancing. But that was a hundred years ago—Winter Smith and Carol's beau, Kingdon Gould, the holiday dances, the weekend at Choate, tea dancing at the Plaza—the only thing that's the same is Chanel No. 5. Then there are mornings, coming out of the sea of night I wake trying to remember what I dreamed about. But it eludes me and all that remains is the waiting, suspended, waiting for *it* to happen, waiting for someone wonderful, someone extraordinary to discover me. Yes, that's what

I longed for, someone like no one else in the world who would discover me and believe in me and love me. And when that happened I'd never have that gone-away feeling again, because he'd always be there. No, he wouldn't—ever—go away, would he? And on those mornings I'd think, *Today* might be the day, the day it might happen. Dodo says I have my whole life ahead of me, but I don't know what she's talking about. Oh, I understand the words all right, but they mean nothing to me. What about *now*? I ask her.

But it's come back to me, the feeling, every morning now as I wake, that it's about to happen—maybe this very day—and hope washes over me as it did long ago. And it's all because Pat-Pasquale is in California that I wake no longer afraid. It's like being on vacation from school, that second when you first wake up and think you're still there—then realizing you're not, knowing you're home and can do anything you want the whole livelong day.

To have gotten married at seventeen . . . it's different for Carol because she's now and forever in love with Bill. What with him and Pat-Pasquale away, we have days and days together, and in the evening there are dinners and seeing people and important decisions of what-shall-I-wear? and sitting on the floor at parties in front of one fireplace or another, being mysterious, and saying to some man we've just met "I live instinctively" and things like that. I don an over-the-shoulder bag and it has an air about it (why I don't know) that makes me feel most Dominique Franconish, so much so that even I get carried away and forget it's only make-believe.

Last week for a lark Carol called up a man we don't know. We picked his name at random out of the Manhattan directory. At first he was annoyed but then he got quite caught up in the whole thing and now we have an ongoing conversation with him several days a week, usually late at night, sometimes for hours. Carol usually talks to him first and then she'll hand the phone

to me and I'll take over. He calls Carol "Fluffy" and me "the Philosopher." That's because I'm always talking about weighty things. Carol keeps it on the light side. He's a photographer named Plucer and we now know quite a lot about him—mainly that "Plucer is painting again." He often talks about that, always referring to himself in the third person. Of course he doesn't know our names, and we have no intention of telling him because it would change everything. It's fun just the way it is, and by now he really wants to meet us. He lives near Carol on Sutton Place, and one night when we were calling him from her place we told him we'd meet him between Fifty-sixth and Fifty-seventh. He really took to that idea, and sure enough ten minutes later we went out on Carol's balcony and looked over the railing. There he was, walking his Afghan just as he said he'd be. We got fits of giggles and ran back into the living room, although we were so high up he never could have heard us. It was mean, I guess, to get him out on false pretenses, but it probably was time to take the dog out anyway. Well, after that it got boring because, well—where was it going to lead? Nowhere, and besides we were tired of hearing "Plucer is painting again." So we started calling Reba Feezel. Rather Carol did. We also picked her name out of the phone book by closing our eyes, opening it, and putting a finger on a page. I never got a chance to talk to her because she wasn't just annoyed she was plain furious, especially after the tenth call, and said she'd report us to the police (well, who needs that?), so we gave up. Anyway, Pat-Pasquale has gone to visit "Uncle" Joe Schenck in Beverly Hills. Gone gone gone, and now that he has, I'm not scared. Well, maybe a little. But that's just because I know he'll be back. Maybe a miracle will happen.

The Messenger of Light

We went to a party. Carol and I. It was at someone's house, someone we didn't know, but Paz Davila, a friend of Carol's, invited us. There was a man standing in the hall as we arrived and he started talking to me. As he did, another man went up to Carol and said his name was Ted Van Arsdale. And I'm Scott Rutherford, the other man said. He was wildly attractive, and Dominique Francon really got to work (luckily I was wearing the over-the-shoulder bag). We found out later they were in medical school at St. Luke's. But by then it didn't matter. It didn't matter because we moved on through an alcove into a large living room and there at the far corner I saw someone, someone like no one else in the world, someone who inhabited my imagination like a tree, tall so tall, a tree rooted in beauty, stretching up into the sky far above me with white clouds in a halo around his head (yes, that's how he was in my brain before we met). He turned towards me as if I'd signaled to him and I was flooded in the radiance of his light. But I turned away, trembling that he would not come to me. A woman's voice was saying, Gloria, this is Leopold Stokowski, and I turned and met his gaze unafraid and he did not turn away, and that evening he stayed by my side although all words were blown from my mind and I could think of nothing to say. And I still can't and I count each hour since last night because it's now five o'clock and he hasn't called. Maybe it's all just in my head the way the tree is, maybe he really didn't like me at all.

A call came but it wasn't him. It was Scott Rutherford asking me out to dinner. Ted Van Arsdale's hoping Carol can go too. Yes, I said quickly—anything to get away from this silent phone. At the Biltmore under the clock at seven, OK? he said. OK, I said, and once Carol and I were on our way there in the taxi, it was OK. I guess because I could talk to Carol about Leopold Stokowski, because that's all I think about. Do you think he likes me? I asked her for the thousandth time. Darling, he's in love with you, she said for the thousand-and-first time. But I still can't believe it and I know I'll never ever see him again ever and my life is over over just as it started. Then, there was Scott Rutherford standing under the clock, making me forget for a moment, because—well, he was so good-looking. In the tidal wave I'd forgotten that, but now it all came back to me. What also came back to me was Pat-Pasquale, because he'll be back the day after tomorrow and a week from now it's Christmas.

My Name Is Called

Why did he keep saying I had no sense? Carol and I were sitting in her living room talking about guess who and going over each moment of that momentous evening two nights ago. He didn't say that! I said. Yes, he did, Carol said, when the three of us were sitting on the sofa, I was looking at my face in my compact and he said I was like a Marie Laurencin painting—that was just before he said "She has no sense," and he didn't just say it once, he said it twice, remember? Oh, sweetheart, I said, he wasn't saying *that*, he was saying *"Quelle innocence, quelle innocence"*—you know, French for What innocence, what innocence. Oh! she said, are you sure? and taking the same compact out of her bag she searched her face. Yes, I said, positively absolutely sure. Do you love me, darling? she said. Do you think I'm beautiful? Oh, angel, you know I love you and you know you're beautiful. No, I don't I don't, she said and started to cry. The phone rang and she dabbed the peachy puff over her white nose, quickly around her eyes as the floury powder sifted over her black sweater where it settled in a grey mist. Darling, shall I answer it? I said. No, it might be Bill, and she jumped up off the floor and ran over to the desk. Hello, she said, in a fuzzy voice, hello. Then her eyes got enormous and she looked over at me—and I knew it was *him*.

I thought I'd fainted but instead I was by her side holding my breath. Not only was it Leopold Stokowski, but there was no mistaking he had called Carol for only one reason—to talk about me—because I heard Carol's voice saying amazing things like Oh, I know she'd love to see you, and then, years later, You can ask her now because she's right here, and she handed me the phone and I heard a voice saying Gloria and another voice (could it be mine?) saying Yes Yes . . . And now it's almost here, that moment of peril when we will stand alone and face to face.

Prayer

"My mother says you ought to wear something like Garbo did when she was with Leopold in Ravenna—you know, when the photographers were chasing them all over Europe." Carol's with me as I'm frantically trying to decide what to wear. Something about "dirndls," her mother said. Dirndls? Mrs. Marcus said dirndls? But they're for summer, I said, aren't they? And besides I don't have any (just as well, because how could I ever compete with Garbo?).

Wait till *my* mother hears about this. This will really impress her. Garbo's her ideal, and if Leopold Stokowski likes me and he was in love with Garbo—well, that ought to mean something. A Big Something.

"You better hurry, darling, and decide, it's almost time to leave." Hurry, yes, but I'm fainting and my knees are water. It's lucky I'm going to be seeing him first from a distance. It'll give me time to collect myself. I haven't let the ticket out of my hand since it arrived. One ticket for Leopold Stokowski's concert at City Center. Yes! and after that I am to have supper with him at his house. Just me (I pray).

Oh what splendor there is in the world! I sat there listening, and my eyes never left him. Surely he is not mortal and has been sent as a gift to walk amongst us, a messenger to transmit through the beauty of his music the answer to all things.

There was no one else there. The supper was already prepared and the table set. Soup was warmed in the kitchen and put in bowls of pottery. Before that, little squares of pumpernickel with something tasty spread on the top and slivers of carrot, pepper,

and radish dotted around. These are called kanapki, he said. My!
I said, really? There was a wine I'd never heard of, Château
d'Yquem, a cold ambrosia, the color of topaz. We sat on a sofa
and there was no time or place and I listened to him talking
about countries he'd traveled to, weak with longing.

He touches my face, my eyes, and I am no longer blind, my
flesh is clay, his hands on my breasts and my nipples rise to meet
his lips as he calls my name. I put my hand back against the
wall, pushing against it hard so that he can come deeper into
me, yes, deeper, only him will it be, only him will I know,
deeper each wave brings him closer into me. He pulls back and
looks into my eyes . . . oh God, beyond boundaries, none! as a
wave covers me I cry out, for in the letting go I die, still another
carries me high over mountain, higher it lifts me, on and on,
swift, until all mind is lost, disassembled, fragmented into atoms,
my eyes dissolve, he comes to me and I am finally broken and
as I break, without armor, without skin, I am born whole, and
forever this shall be, forever I will be him, always and always,
for without him I will not exist.

To be loved by this man, to be with this man for all the days
of my life, this is all I'll ever ask for, dear God, please. Please,
I humbly beseech Thee, make me worthy, and if you deem that
this is so and grant my prayer I'll give up desserts, not just for
Lent but to the end of time, and I'll be good for the rest of my
life.

A Merry Little Christmas

He wasn't aware that I saw him from the taxi, but even from
the back, walking along our street, I could tell he was telling
Halibut Steak one of his yoo-hoo stories. The two of them were
moseying their way towards our apartment on the river, and from

the look of things he was in a good mood, no doubt in anticipation of a gin game. He was back from the visit with his "Uncle" Joe—since this morning, to be exact, although I'd not been home for the arrival. Not because I was frightened—quite the contrary, for the mantle of love I wear strips him of weapons, protects me . . . no harm can befall me. No, I was not there because I had an appointment—a most important appointment with Mr. Gilchrist at Cadwalader, Wickersham & Taft. Well, he said smugly after I'd told him, I'm surprised it lasted as long as it did—three years, isn't it? Yes, I said—three years. Three thousand years or three seconds, what does time have to do with it? Plenty to do with it, he said—Reno. And that takes six weeks, it's required procedure, residency in Nevada for six full weeks before divorce is granted. What about an annulment? Dodo says I might be able to get one because because—there are reasons—Pat can't have children. An annulment takes longer, much longer than six weeks, he stated. *How* much longer? That's impossible to predict. The Church moves slowly, and the Vatican has a great deal to contend with. It could take years. Years? I said. Perhaps not, but who knows? (If I can't wait a minute, how can I wait years?) Reno is most advisable and airtight. Mexico is not even to be considered. No one can query a Nevada divorce. (Six weeks! six million years parted . . .) And what does De Cicco have to say about all this? He doesn't know yet. I seeee, said Mr. Gilchrist, spreading it out towards the silence that followed. How do you think he'll take to the idea? It doesn't matter to me one way or the other how he takes to the idea, because this is something that *has* to be, it's as simple as breathing (you understand now why I'm not scared, don't you?), breathing, in and out, as natural and inevitable as that. Will you tell him now or wait until after Christmas? Now, I said, as soon as he gets back—today.

Where were you, Fatsy Roo? he said chattily, glancing up from the fan of cards in his hand. Halibut Steak, sitting across the table from him, held the usual cigarette while the other hand, preoccupied with cards, waved in my direction. I stood in the doorway looking at the two of them and thought, Who are these people? And why are they here? Hey, what about the tree, Fatsy? What *about* the tree, I said. Why isn't it up, *stupido?* he said, starting to get dark all over. I turned and walked up the stairs to our room. He had unpacked his suitcases and thrown them into the hall for Orlando to take down to the storage room. No. It wouldn't do. It wouldn't do at all—I couldn't stand it another minute, and I went back down the stairs into the library. Pat, I said, I've got to talk to you about something. Look, sweetie, put your glasses on, can't you see Hal and I are in the middle of a game? And anyway, Fatsy Roo, I've got something to say to you too, and if I can wait till later, so can you, OK? No, it's not OK, I said. Now listen here, you, just a minute! and he put the cards down. Where the hell were you anyway when I got back this morning? Halibut Steak got up, mumbling about being back in a minute. No, sit down, sit down, Hal, Pat-Pasquale said smoothly before shouting at me—Jesus, what is it with you, now you look here, smarty, let me tell you something. Uncle Joe made me go for a checkup while I was out there, see, about headaches I've been having, and I may have to have an operation, something since the septicemia, some complication. No big deal, and I'm only telling you now so you'll leave us alone so we can finish our game. Right? he said to Hal, who had sat back in hunched dedication over his hand. Huh? Halibut Steak grunted absentmindedly, peering into his cards without looking up. Pat-Pasquale settled down across the table from him and picked up his deal—No rush about anything, he said, after Christmas is time enough. I'm going back out there the next day, have it done at Cedars of Lebanon. Uncle Joe's doctor's the best. Listen, do me a favor, will you, tell Orlando two Scotches and some of that smoked turkey from "21," OK, and on the double. And get the tree up, Fatso, hear me, deck the halls, Christmas is almost here—bah, humbug and yoo-hoo!

· · ·

Every time I start to say "divorce," something stops me. What if he really is sick? What's to become of him? I'll be twenty-one soon and I'd be able to give him money. I'd want to do that. At least then if he is sick he'll have something to fall back on. I'll be able to give Dodo and Naney money too, and fur coats. Both mink. They're already ordered with the understanding I'll pay for them on my birthday. And Mummy. Of course, I'll be taking care of her too, and I'd like to give her a really nice present. A bracelet, maybe, of diamonds, Yes, diamonds with emeralds. Mummy's most partial to emeralds. And Carol—I'm having a pin made of diamonds clustered in a design resembling a bunch of grapes with matching earrings (she likes grapes because Bill does, and he likes them because they remind him of a vineyard in Fresno owned by some Armenian cousin). Frances too must have a present. Oh, what fun it's going to be!

"Have yourself a merry little Christmas, make the Yuletide gay, next year all your troubles will be miles away"—that's the song Judy Garland sings in *Meet Me in St. Louis*, and it floats in the air over the holidays, heard in snatches at unexpected moments, from a taxi radio perhaps, even Christmas shopping at Lord and Taylor in the Fantasia department it comes tinkling forth from a music box. Round and round it goes in our heads, Carol's and mine, and we'll never hear that song again without remembering Christmas of 1944.

Signs and Portents

Leopold and I meet at Carol's. It's safer until things are put in place. It's the most amazing feeling to wake up every day of my life and go through the day not feeling frightened one single moment. Every time Pat-Pasquale's about to slide into a tantrum, something gives him pause. Something in my bearing, in my

manner, is an incantation—I *know* it's there, elusive though it may be to define. Although of course it's not really, for surely I must appear to others as crystal—a crystal vessel with love shining through me, and there are no dark or secret places left within me, for I have given them all to Leopold.

He tells me he is Polish and that his mother, Maria, came from Lublin and his father from the nearby city of Cracow. His mother died when he was an infant and soon after he was taken to live in England among strangers. There he was cared for by a nurse who gave him love. . . . I keep waiting and waiting but so far he hasn't elaborated upon this other than to imply the Hapsburgs are in it somewhere (noble birth, maybe?). I'm dying to know more, where they lived and so forth, but he never talks about his father either, other than to say his name was Antoni Boleslavowich Stokowski. It's all most mysterious but I don't question because his silence must mean that it's too painful to talk about. That will come later, I'm sure—when he knows how much I love him. He believes in a Divine Mother whom he prays to. I'm going to pray to her too (as well as to God and Saint Theresa) and ask her to make him love me forever and ever. I haven't met his children yet, or any of his friends for that matter. Soon as Pat-Pasquale leaves I'm going to have him meet Dodo—that'll be after Christmas. And—my mother! I can't wait for that! She doesn't even know yet that I've met him.

He has three daughters—Sonia, older than I am, and then Luba and Sadja, the youngest. Luba was at Wheeler, but only for one term. I remember her because everyone knew she was Leopold Stokowski's daughter and must be interesting, but then she left before I got to know her. Just think of that! I see them in my mind's eye each one more beautiful than the one before, each a Princess in a fairy tale as depicted in dazzling colors on a Palekh box of black lacquer from the Ivanovo region of Russia. I do hope they're going to like me. He doesn't seem all that friendly with their mothers. Especially Sonia's mother, Olga

Samaroff (he really can't stand her), although he doesn't go into the ins and outs of it. Sadja and Luba's mother is called Evangeline (must read that Longfellow poem again), and she's presently married to a Georgian Prince of sorts (according to Leopold). He seems to tolerate her more or less (with a strong accent on the less). Of course I want to know everything, everything about him—the smallest thing that touches his life is of utmost significance to me, and I squirrel away each detail as it's revealed to me so that I may ponder over it at leisure, seeking signs and portents. Yesterday Garbo came up! Not by name, but I knew right away who it was when he referred to "a beautiful person" he had been in love with. But it came to an end because she was "too melancholy." Well, he won't get any of that from me, you can be sure—although had he intimated he liked even a sprinkling of melancholy, here and there, now and then, just for a change, you can be sure I'd be capable as Garbo of adding it to my repertoire, for I want only to please him and make him happy. He's very suspicious of women, and the more beautiful they are, the more men have to be on their guard. That's what he says, and I worry about it because he thinks I'm beautiful! He said he'll never marry again and right after that he said, Who needs a little piece of paper to prove you love someone? So although I'd die to marry him, if we don't ever get married it matters not to me as long as he loves me and we can just be together. I think he's been hurt by a woman, terribly—perhaps more than once. But soon all that will be changed, because—I'm different—yes I am, and soon he'll know it too, oh yes, he will he will, and he'll never ever be afraid of being hurt again. I swear it.

Excerpts from a Diary

December 26   What a sham—but it's over. Christmas. It's over and I told P. wanted a divorce. He refuses to believe it and says to wait until after he's had the operation and we'll talk about it then. Feel trapped, in prison. Went to see Naney at Hotel Fourteen. She took out the ermine cape from the trunk under her bed and said if I was going to a party New Year's Eve I could wear it. They still don't speak to her—Mummy, Aunt Thelma, Uncle Harry, or Consuelo-Tamar—not a one since the Custody Trial. I don't risk talking to her about things that matter to me, although I'd like to. She's so worldly she just wouldn't understand, and it makes me shrivel up inside. She wants to give me a big party on my twenty-first birthday as a present and invite lots of European royalty. Please don't, Naney, I said, let's have petits fours and tea at the Plaza that day, just you and me. That's what I'd really like.

December 27   L. says there shall be no compromise between us in our love. It will be All and Everything. He pronounces compromise "com-pro-meese" in the French way and it thrills me. Told Mummy about asking P. for divorce. She was more than surprised. Why, Pooks, she said, I had no idea, he's such a handsome man—what happened? Oh, well—you know, Mummy, it's complicated. You know, darling, she said—men aren't really meant to be monogamous, they stray now and then—it means nothing—a night out on the town with the boys and who knows what bit of fluff comes along, and if that happens best look the other way, it's soon forgotten. Oh, it's not *that*, I said (although I think Pat-Pasquale did fool around with Bridget Prichit). But I know she thinks I'm just trying to cover up out of pride. Was going to tell her about L. but didn't.

December 28   L.'s love surrounds me. His strength becomes mine. Yes, surely goodness and mercy shall follow me all the days of my life. . . .

December 29   P. has gone. Yesterday he left—so subdued. Felt suddenly sorry for him. Maybe he really is sick? Told Frances about L. how much I love him, how I must be with him till death do us part. She understands, more than anyone she knows what it's been like with P. Maybe those rages he has come from some imbalance in his brain? Maybe he can't help himself, maybe when he gets all dark like that something happens in his head and he's possessed by something he can't control? I've never dared talk to anyone about Thelma Todd—but she's been at the back of my mind somewhere ever since that time at the Hotel Pierre with the praying mantis. Remember? That's why I'm scared.

December 30   Letter from P. today written on the plane. Says he loves me, and no matter what happens hopes that God will always be my "running mate." Folded up the card table, took it out of the library, and Orlando's put it away. What a relief—one less reminder that since I've known P. it's been one long continuous Gin Rummy Game.

December 31   Joe Schenck calls says that P. has to have operation. Is it serious? I say. Can I help, does he need money? No, the doctor says it's not serious, but yes, Joe says, he does need money. How much? Two hundred thousand, Joe says. What about the divorce? Yes, Joe said, yes he'll give you a divorce. Although I wanted to help him, this does seem a lot of money, doesn't it? And now it's as if the divorce depends on it.

Later: L. says he'll give P. the two hundred thousand dollars. That he would want to do that for me makes me die of joy. Of course I refused. In two months now I'll be twenty-one and I can take care of it myself with my own money. But that L. offered to do this makes me the happiest girl in the world! Tonight it's New Year's Eve. L. has a concert and after we'll have supper together. Thank you, God and Divine Mother and Saint Theresa, for making me worthy.

Surprises

Mummy, I have a surprise for you, I said. Oh! she said, I
love surprises. Well, come to a party Mrs. Marcus is having for
Carol—tomorrow night. I can't tomorrow night, darling, Maurice and I are dining at the Colony and then we're going to see
that new Bette Davis movie *Mr. Skeffington*, and besides Mrs.
Marcus is someone I hardly know, hardly an acquaintance even.
But Mummy, I said, she's *Carol's* mother. I don't see what that
has to do with it. But Mummy, I said, this is important, really
important, the most important thing that's ever happened to me.
Surely it can wait till another night? Maurice and I have been
going out so much lately we wanted a quiet evening. Mummy,
please, I said. Oh, all right, darling, I'll try to rearrange things
and we'll come by for a minute after dinner. I'm beside myself
anticipating this fateful meeting between my mother and Leopold. She'll be bowled over when she knows that he is in love
with me. Nothing in the world could impress her more than
this. Oh, hurry hurry, time, only a few hours and I will be
saying—Mummy, I'd like you to meet Leopold Stokowski.

It was a surprise all right, but not the kind of surprise I
expected it to be. I'm shattered and confused, because Mummy
clearly wasn't thrilled and impressed the way I thought she'd be.
I never ever expected her to feel this way, and I don't understand
any of it. Anyway, it doesn't matter, it makes no difference at
all at all, no it doesn't it doesn't. But still it makes me so angry
the things she said later. That he's old enough to be her father—
meaning *her* father, not mine—that his name is really Stokes and
that nobody knows what his "origins" really are. She didn't say
any of these things directly to me, but it all got back to me
because those were the things she was saying to her friends. I
don't know or care how old Leopold is or what his name really

is or where he comes from. What I do know is that his genius is admired and respected all over the world. Ah yes! but it is *me* he loves and I love him and and—Mummy Mummy please! But she was hardly even polite to him when they met. It was awful awful and I was so excited because I thought she'd be so happy for me—but she wasn't. She isn't, she isn't, and she never will be.

I tried to talk to L. about my mother, about what happened in the Custody Trial, but the more I try to explain it the more he leans toward Aunt Gertrude (maybe I don't explain it right), on her side, so to speak, against my mother. So I try to explain it again, over, from the beginning, but it comes out more mixed up than ever. Well, it was pretty mixed up, still it's my fault for not being able to explain it right. But how can I when I don't know myself really where to begin, what's right or not right?

Sometimes it sounds as if I'm against my mother when the opposite is true. L. was very put off by her when they met. And why not—her manner cold, disapproving. He's suspicious of her, I can tell. It's all topsy-turvy and not at all the way I'd thought it would be. Why would she approve of Pat-Pasquale and disapprove of Leopold? Half of me wants to believe she's the best mother in the world, and the other half—well, it wasn't even a question of *hoping* she'd be thrilled and impressed that Leopold is in love with me—I'd have staked my life on it. Yes, I would have. And what was meant to be the ultimate surprise for her instead turns out to be the ultimate surprise for *me*. Mummy, talk to me, talk to me please as if I'm real . . . your daughter. I am, aren't I?

Today, Yesterday, and Tomorrow

Mr. Stokowski says he's going to marry you (Mummy keeps referring to him in that formal way) as soon as you divorce Pat?

Mummy Mummy, I said, I'll marry him, live with him, anything he wants as long as we can be together. Well, that's what Mr. Stokowski informed me of at Mrs. Marcus's party. Then she said huffily—Don't you think it inappropriate that Pat's niece, Frances, was sitting right there on the sofa during the party when you were making goo-goo eyes at him—how do you think she feels? Mummy, I said, I wasn't making goo-goo eyes at him, and Frances already knows all about it, and she may be Pat's niece but she's also my friend. Mummy looked up senselessly at the ceiling without comment and lit another cigarette. We were sitting in my studio, where she'd come to "talk things over." Is it true that you're going to Reno? No, yes yes, I said, maybe I don't know, yes! my heart was pounding and I could hardly breathe, for all I could think of was—*he* told my mother he was going to marry me marry me marry me. . . . Mummy Mummy—I love him, don't you understand, please, Mummy, please. Then to my amazement she said, Would you like me to go to Reno with you? Thank you, Mummy, I said, but it's best not. I was dying inside with the wanting of her to come with me—part of me, that is, but the other part knew it would never work—how could I be alone with her in a hotel in Reno, Nevada, or anywhere else for that matter, and not be able to talk of my love for Leopold? I would fair burst with torment.

I'm not going to tell Naney about L. My mother's reaction throws me for a loop, and I even don't dare risk his meeting Dodo. But still I'm going to chance it. Tomorrow afternoon at four he's coming to the apartment. It will happen then.

She stood by the bay window in the sitting room next to the bedroom. Her back was towards us, for she was looking out, at the river. Leopold and I walked towards her and as we did . . . she turned and waited there by the window without moving. Dodo, this is Leopold, I said, and as I did, her eyes filled with tears. Why is she sad? I thought. Why? The three of us stood there, not long, a few minutes, or was it longer, much longer? I was silent while Leopold talked about unimportant things, making conversation, putting Dodo at her ease. Then he said— I love Gloria and I'm going to make her happy. Take her on picnics, Dodo said, smiling suddenly, she likes surprises. Later she said to me, He'll cherish you, won't he? Yes he will he will and I'll love him all the days of my life. But why did her eyes tear?

Carol's having a birthday party for me. So is Maggi McNellis, so are my mother and Maurice. Flurries of parties and I'm full of plans, only they go off in different directions and how will I ever be able to pursue each one? Part of me sometimes has a fantasy of a house on Sutton Place, living in New York, giving myself time lots of time to get a bit older. The war will soon be over, I'd make a life of my own, days at the League and in the evenings friends to see and things to do. But—Leopold, how does that plan fit in with Leopold? It doesn't fit in at all at all, and I know then that I only muse on the other plan because I'm so afraid maybe L. isn't really serious about me. He hasn't said anything definite about the future—*really*. No he hasn't. Then I think about Scott Rutherford, how attractive he is (and I know he's attracted to me—you can always tell), and somewhere there are other persons in the world, people I haven't met yet and maybe I'll be missing something. But those thoughts are just more protection in case L. stops loving me (they are—aren't they?), and I only have those ideas when I'm away from him, because the moment we're together there is no doubt in any part of me that his love for me is as great as mine is for him.

There's a shiver in the air these days of spring coming, although the nights are chill as if snow is about to fall, but in the morning one wakes to feel shoots of green are about to burst on the trees in Central Park. Mostly we meet at his house. He wears Japanese kimonos of silk and I too have been given one to wear.

There are hours together when we enter each into the other and there is no one in the universe but we two, rather it is—one— for I have merged into him and no longer exist. I didn't know anyone like this walked on the face of the earth. He is godlike to me. A giant. He's not coming to Carol's party. It's best we are not seen together until I am free.

The party started at ten o'clock. Carol had yellow roses in bowls all over her living room. Walking into a garden, it was like that. The cake was white and fashioned to resemble a book, on it an inscription of yellow icing—"I could write a book"— from the song

> *If they asked me*
> *I could write a book*
> *About the way you talk and whisper and look. . . .*

It was so gay, and again I felt on the brink of my life and maybe I should wait, not make decisions until I had recovered from the years with Pat-Pasquale. It had all happened so quickly. Don't be so impulsive, Gloria, Dodo's always saying to me. All during the party at Carol's I kept thinking about the past months when we had been girls again. They were here at the party, the friends we had been having fun with—Penelope Sack and Robin Maugham, Ted Van Arsdale, Paz Davila and Hurd Hatfield, oh so many, and Artie Shaw whom we call Dark Blue because of the way he looks in a navy turtleneck sweater, John Gunther—oh, and Scott Rutherford, yes, he too was there. But then Leopold came to me—where was he right that second, and did he miss me?—and at the thought of him, all else was diminished into something small and unimportant, until it disappeared and there was no one else in the world but him.

Soon I'll be twenty-one, and when that day comes I'll be really and finally grown-up, so everyone says, but it's so strange, because, somewhere inside, I'm still a child—back there where

I was long ago, only the long ago isn't long ago at all it's right now, not only today, but . . . yesterday and tomorrow. Maybe when I open my eyes on the morning of my twenty-first birthday—it will be different, like when overnight I've lost weight. You know that feeling? Yes, I'll wake up and tons and tons will have sloughed off mysteriously, just like that, and I'll be free and a hell of a lot thinner.

The Ring

Talking about signs and portents, he asked for my ring size—left hand, third finger—and we all know what that means! Not a word about a date or anything definite—yet—but time will tell. That is, if I don't die of suspense. Maybe the ring doesn't necessarily mean we'll get married, maybe it's a love ring, just to wear. Leopold has brought up more than once (as if he doesn't think I heard him the first time, ha, ha) how unhappy he was married to Olga Samaroff, later to Evangeline Johnson, ending the subject by saying he'd vowed never ever to marry again no matter how much he fell in love. Still, I'm bursting with hope and take this event to be of great significance. It is also of great significance that after a concert he asks me to have supper with him at his house although each time it is decided at the last minute. I have seen how he is after the music, as though his very skin peeled off and he must be alone until it returns to his body. But since we met, after a concert—each time—the call has come, and I take it as the most incredible gift that of all the people in the universe he could be with—he chooses me.

Pat-Pasquale called in a rage yesterday saying he was coming to New York to see me. Please—don't—there's nothing more to say. But then I got frightened and talked to the elevator men in the building that if he showed up here not to let him up. Later, Joe Schenck called and said it would be best for all concerned if a separation agreement was signed. Yes yes, I said, sooner the better, but what about the operation? Oh, the operation, they—the doctors, that is—haven't decided yet when it's to be. Please, Joe, tell him there's no reason for us to see each other. Sure you won't change your mind, Gloria? Are you absolutely sure, because I think Pat wants a reconciliation. No! Joe, I said, never. Well, all right, I'll tell that to Pat—and this time I knew that he knew it was really over.

The ring is on my finger—twenty-four-carat beaten gold, a solid nugget shaped like a dome, big and primitively molded. This is a most serious ring, yes, a ring of most fateful intent. As the years pass, time and wear will put their mark on the gold, blurring it to a soft patina. I look at it in wonder. No matter what happens—we are married. This is a ring to last forever.

Bill Saroyan is back. Carol is ecstatic. He's out of the army and they're going to leave for San Francisco. I, too, shall soon be leaving. It's a funny feeling. In many ways I'm going to miss these past two months, and Carol will too, for we came to know what it could be like without Pat and Bill, and in these months there were glimmers of the way it was before the war, when we were sixteen and lovely things happened every day. But it lasted only a minute, we got married and the war came and it was—over. But now the war is ending and these past few months are ending, because Bill's back, and Leopold—we have a plan. I'm to meet him in Los Angeles this summer where he's to be conductor of the Hollywood Bowl Symphony Orchestra. No mention yet if I will stay in his house high on the mountain of Beverly Crest or rent a house of my own, but I will be free and we will be living together. Sometimes I throb with such impatience for that life to start now—right away—I think I'm going to die. There's no sense of time anymore about anything, and the feeling is that if we don't have it soon—we never will.

.   .   .

Leopold did come to the party Mummy and Maurice gave for me—unexpectedly. The room was crowded and I was at the far end at the piano. Someone was playing and a group of Mummy and Maurice's French friends had gathered round as is their wont, singing one song or another—

Longtemps longtemps longtemps
Après que les poètes ont disparu—
Leur chanson court encore dans les rues. . . .

He had come from his concert and there was that about him stripped and bereft as he stood there so suddenly in the doorway, tall so tall, his eyes going straight into mine. I ran to him and without a word he took my hand, pulled me out onto the street, into a car that waited for us. I didn't think until later how upset Mummy would be and how rude it was of me to leave like that in the middle of a party she was giving for me. But there was no choice, and I would do it again in full knowledge of my action. In the car driving to his house and later as we lay together in the secret dark, still we did not speak, for there was naught to say. And after, in the kitchen, as we prepared the supper—a change had come to him, for he had returned once more to the world of people, with the skin settled back upon him, resting in grace. But to me nothing had changed, and it was as it had been before, because he had revealed himself to me naked and full plain: I knew that he had trust in me and that I had trust in him, and that this trust would belong each to the other, as long as we both shall live.

A Hotel by the River

Dodo's with me and we're on a train going to Reno, and although it's only been two hours, eight minutes, and two seconds since Leopold and I said good-bye, already I've become a girl who doesn't exist. How can I get through a day, much less six weeks, without him? Everything ended and cut off suddenly, and although I want to be free of Pat-Pasquale more than anything, there is this desperate feeling that I'm trapped on this train, trapped at the Riverside Hotel where we'll be in Nevada, Dodo and I, and it won't be six weeks, it will drag on and on

into eternity. I'm twenty-one, but it didn't happen, that overnight grown-up feeling that was supposed to happen—maybe
tomorrow? L. teases me and says that now I'm a grown-up lady
I should wear my hair in a formal manner, swept up, not waving
around my face as it usually does. He wants me to grow it long,
as long as can be, and of course the minute he said that I decided
never to cut my hair again. A diet is also in the offing—just to
lose a few pounds. But will I ever be thin enough? I want to be
perfect for him. Yes, perfect as perfect can be.

We were met at the station by the lawyer, Mr. Summerfield,
who settled us in at the Riverside Hotel. It's even worse than I
expected. Flat—flat as a plate that has no rim around it—instead,
faraway mountains in a miniature circle all around the horizon,
a barrier far as the eye can see. We have two corner bedrooms,
Dodo and I, with a living room between. She makes bowls of
junket, oh so creamy, in a kitchen fitted behind a closet door.
We have this at night before going to sleep with cinnamon
sprinkled on the top, nutmeg sometimes for a change. Her birthday is May twenty-seventh—I'll be sixty, Gloria, she said. That's
not so old, I say in a joking way to make her feel better, while
inside I'm screaming, Don't have a heart attack, don't don't die
and leave me. On the train she wore the mink coat I gave her,
but since we got here she hasn't worn it much. The Colorado
River flows right by the hotel, grey and cold, but so far we
haven't seen any wives throwing wedding rings into the water
as is the custom on divorce day, or so I've heard. My wedding
ring's gone back to Pat-Pasquale along with the peridot engagement ring. Somehow this confirms that I never was married to
him, no not at all.

There's space in the bedroom, not much, but enough to set
up a folding easel. L. believes I have a gift, one that I must
nurture and develop, and oh! how I will with him by my side.
Dodo and I take walks and go to church, and then there are the
driving lessons I've been taking every day, soon I'll have my

license. What freedom, to drive oneself! Independent, knowing in the car only you are responsible, knowing no one in the whole world can reach you or find you. I'll be driving L. this summer to rehearsals at the Bowl and so forth. Of course, he drives, but it will make me happy to know that when he's working, I'll be able to take this off his mind because all he'll be thinking about is his music (and *me*, of course!). But the high point of the day comes with the post, for there is a letter every day—sometimes two! The thrill when I see that dearest writing with "Madame De Cicco" penned on the envelope. Letters in which I am called Divine Beloved, letters which make me die with longing and the missing of him, each word engraved on my heart and soul as with poems and messages of great import. I talk to Dodo about him all the time, but of course she never knows what's inside the letters, for they are just for me. Then there are the phone calls from Mr. Leonard Stanley, one of the names L. uses to be incognito. Culture, Dodo says, he certainly has culture. Oh my, yes, I agree, culture and everything.

Whistle Stop

Carol and I sat on a bench in the railroad station at Reno, where her train was making a stop on its way to San Francisco. Bill's already there and she's going out to meet him. I've missed her so, but at least we have twenty minutes before her train takes off again. She saw Leopold the morning she left and all he did was talk about me. Did he say anything about getting married? I said. No, darling, he didn't but— But what? What? I said. Darling, he's madly in love with you, of course he'll want to marry you. How's Bill? I said. Bill's fine, only he—he rages around a lot and calls us the Gold Dust Twins. You mean you and me? I said, laughing. Darling, it's very difficult sometimes with him, and I never do the right thing at the wrong time—I mean *right* time, and well, it's just hard to please him no matter what I do, and darling, you have to understand—he—he made me promise I'd give these to you. She delved into a huge bag and fished out a box which she put in my hand. I know this box well, for it is the one made for the diamond grape earrings and pin I had given her. Oh! please, Carol, they were made only for you. Sweetheart, I can't, he won't let me. And I know there is nothing more to say or do and that it would only make it more difficult for her if I tried. Why doesn't he like me? I said. He thinks we tell each other things, Carol said—talk about things that I don't talk to him about, and although it's true, in another way it's not, because after all he's a man and—with him I have to make-believe all the time, pretend, so he'll love me—whereas with you I never have to pretend or make-believe about anything. With Bill it's like I'm playing a game all the time and it saps me, drains my energy, but I have to keep on with it, even when I'm asleep, otherwise he'll leave. . . . I know he will, oh, darling, do you feel that way with Leopold? No—I don't, because I don't know who I am except through him, because—I've become *him*. That he loves me is a miracle, sometimes I don't think it's really happened.

Carol sits for a long time, silent. . . . I feel that way too, like I'm no one, that I won't exist if Bill stops loving me, that's why I have to pretend to be what it is *he* wants and that has nothing at all to do with the way I really am, it's why I'm afraid every second and have to pretend, otherwise I lose him and then I'd be nothing, nothing—it's—it's like living off of someone else's smile. You're afraid of him, I said. She didn't answer, and I opened the box and we sat there looking at the grapes as they lay on the velvet. Would you like coffee, darling? I said, and I poured from the thermos I'd brought with me to the station. I'm afraid of Pat, I said, but not of Leopold—with Leopold it's as if I'm absorbed, absorbed by—by some *great* thing . . . and since this has happened, I'm protected for as long as he loves me—I am safe. And you don't have to pretend, ever? No. I'm drawn into his strength, and because he loves me I feel clear, clear as crystal is clear to receive the love he pours into me, and soon, very soon now, everything that happened long ago—all the ugliness—will be erased because he loves me.

All aboard! All aboard! rang out, and we looked at each other and I held her in my arms. She ran from me up into the train. Through the window her face pressed like a white moth, wraithlike, against the glass. There was no need to say good-bye.

Plans

The plan is set. Immediately after the divorce I'll go directly to California, where rooms at the Beverly Hills Hotel are reserved. Leopold will be ensconced in his house on Beverly Crest Drive—expecting me. Carol's sister, Elinor, is on her way to Reno, and she'll be with me for the summer. We don't know each other very well, but being with her will be like being, in a way, with Carol—almost. At least that's how I imagine it will be. Maybe we'll rent a house in Beverly Hills—it all depends on what happens with Leopold. If it's terrible, at least I'll be near Carol in San Francisco and Elinor will be there and we can make a life, see friends, and—what I really mean is, I'm scared he's going to stop loving me and these other plans are only protection in case this happens. Dodo's packing to leave the day after Elinor arrives. She's going back to the Schillers in Freeport, but may come out later in the summer to California, or I may go back to New York, depending on what happens.

A phone call and all is changed! Leopold is coming *here*—to Reno the week before the divorce. Does this mean we are to be married? I don't know I don't know I don't know, but there are log cabins at Zephyr Cove on Lake Tahoe in the Sierra Nevada mountains, and one, with four rooms, waits for us. We'll be together, without a soul knowing, until the divorce. Of course now that Elinor's here she's not like Carol at all, the exact opposite, and now that L. is coming I wish she weren't here, no matter who was here I'd want her not to be, because the only person in the whole world I want to be with is Leopold. I keep hoping she'll suggest leaving, but she hasn't. Anyway, nothing matters at all at all—soon we'll be together.

Everything is arranged. I'm keeping our rooms at the Riverside Hotel even though we'll be at Zephyr Cove. The rented car I've been using will be kept, although I bought a secondhand Cadillac sedan which I'll only start driving when I pick L. up at the station on Thursday. Yes, Thursday, April twelfth at 3:30 a.m., the Overland Limited—that is to be the day my life begins.

Joe Schenck called from California. He says Pat-Pasquale's lawyer, Jerry Geisler, is all riled up, and ditto for Pat-Pasquale— and have I been talking to the press? No, I said, they've been calling but I don't take the calls. Well, Mr. Geisler thinks you have, about the financial settlement. That's not true, Joe. Well, I don't think Pat will believe that. Joe, I don't care what he believes, why are you calling me like this? Well, Pat's denied it of course, but I just didn't want you to be upset by things he said when the reporter questioned him about you and Stokowski, about your being "impressionable and not really very smart," he also told them he has to undergo a brain operation sometime next fall . . . maybe sooner. Look, Joe, please—I don't know about this because I don't read anything about myself in the newspapers . . . after what happened . . . it was the only way I could hold— hold onto myself. Gloria, what d'you mean, has something happened we don't know about? Joe, I'm talking about long ago— the Custody Trial. Oh, that, Joe said—well, best keep your pretty mouth shut far as the press goes. . . .

I don't know what to do. Everything set, thought out to the last detail, and now it's all crazy. This man has arrived at the hotel, suddenly—Hello, Gloria—as I stepped off the elevator into the lobby—I'm Bill Berry from the New York *Daily News*. It really throws a monkey wrench into things. L. hates personal publicity and has stressed to me that if ever questioned by reporters I'm to keep repeating, no matter what, "I never answer personal questions I never answer personal questions I never answer personal questions." Bill Berry is a constant companion, following me everywhere, friendly as pie, questioning me as if he knows nothing about anything so I'll be drawn into explaining things to him and talk a lot. L. is already on the train, and I'm desperate as there's no way to warn him. Snow keeps falling falling, stops for a while, but then falls again, on and on, through the hours, endlessly. Snow I love, so beautiful, but each flake as it falls piles on window ledge, on streets, higher and higher. Luckily I did a test run of the fifty-five-mile drive from the log cabin along Lake Rim Road to Truckee station, and although there was no snow that day I know the turns of the road and what to expect. Make it stop, dear God, please, the snows melt, the roads made passable, the train arrive . . . blood drives me, governs me, moves me forward as I walk the knife edge. . . .

The rented car I've used these past weeks is left parked on the street outside the Riverside Hotel—fat chance it'll fool Bill Berry (still it's worth a try). Maybe he'll be asleep when Elinor and I start out in the Cadillac for Truckee at eleven. That's giving us five hours to make the thirty-five-mile drive in the snow from Reno to the station—with luck we'll be safe in the log cabin by dawn.

All went as planned and no sign of Bill Berry anywhere. On and on the snow fell as we got to the highway, and although there had been few hours of sleep, necessities had been reversed and the hours awake were what my body craved. To be conscious is food, for the waking air gives me thought of him. In sleep I am deprived of his light, since try as I will, I am unable to bring him into my dreams. Instead, it is Pat-Pasquale who sometimes seizes my spirit. So real these dreams that when I wake it is as if sleep were the real life, and the time awake the dream. But more often at night it is my mother who inhabits my dreams, and each time I wake sobbing, unable to stop until I reach for the photograph of Leopold beside my bed, hold it close. He knows of these episodes, for I tell him everything. They're just scrambled eggs, he says, pray to Divine Mother, she is a mother who will never fail you. I think about that a lot. So the hours awake bring energy to me and I am not tired, but Elinor is, and her head falls back beside me on the seat, where she sleeps limp as a rag doll, the little feet placed side by side, as though she had taken off her shoes and put them neatly on the floor before retiring for bed. They are white, these shoes, open sandals, with black socks peeking through, and in the darkness they appear separated from her body. The clothes she'd brought to Reno were California clothes, the slacks she wore, summery pongee. There was something surreal about us, inching through the snow in the car, the windshield wiper tick-tock-ticking, back and forth, against the flakes as they smashed against us through the glass. I kept thinking of Mrs. Mosier, the music teacher at Green Vale School, who came once a week to give me piano and singing lessons at Old Westbury Capital. Her metronome rested each time in the same spot on top of the piano, tick-tocking, back and forth, just as the windshield wiper did now against the snow. It was something to hook onto, tick-tock, tick-tock, something to ground the wildness within me, so I drove slowly along the slithering road instead of pressing on the gas pedal as I longed to do—hard, oh so hard, speeding us ahead.

How quiet and still it was as we drove along the main street of Truckee! No one in sight as we parked beside the filling station shuttered for the night. It was next to the railroad, and I turned off the lights and we sat there in the dark . . . waiting. Elinor?

I whispered. But she didn't hear me, and I wanted to shout Wake up, wake up, I wanted to jump out into the snow, take great armfuls, rub snow on my face, over my body, to cool the fevered joy. Instead I took deep breaths and prayed to Divine Mother, God and Saint Theresa. And immediately almost upon us—the whistle of a train—It's here, Elinor, wake up, wake up! She blinked quite dazed but got out of the car according to plan, her little feet sinking into the snow, and she stood there looking down into the drift to find them. Hurry, I called out, hurry, hurry! She lifted one leg up slowly, one after the other, maddeningly, making her way forward. Someone was beside her suddenly, not Leopold but—guess who? An eternity—and there he appeared, wearing a hat, the hat he wears for disguise as it covers the white crown of his hair. He thought Bill Berry was a railroad employee as he grabbed L.'s hand—Leopold, welcome to Truckee, the back door to Nevada. I represent the New York *Daily News*. L. choked while Bill Berry went on—Are you going to marry Mrs. De Cicco? Leopold stood there and said, What is there to say? Here I am. Where is Gloria? he said to Elinor. There she is, Bill Berry said, pointing to the car. Come and get him, Gloria! he yelled. I eased the car over to where they stood and put the clutch on as Leopold crossed in front carrying two suitcases—but my foot came off the brake and the car lurched forward. Release your gears! Bill Berry shouted as Leopold leaped out of the way. But it mattered not, nothing did—snow, earthquakes, Bill Berry— nothing could part us now, and the blood raging through me became a stream with trees on either side, coursing along valleys through the filtered sunlight to the sea. He was in the car by my side, and as we glided away I heard Bill Berry call out, I wish you all the happiness in the world. Oh, thank you thank you, I called back through the snow. I felt such love, for Bill Berry too, yes I did, for the love I feel for Leopold embraces all the world. It does it does and it always will.

A Death in the Family

Schéhérazade, Leopold called out to me, don't forget to put bran on the list. I was on my way out the door to get groceries at the supply store down the road. I ran back to where he stretched out on the sofa in front of the fire and knelt beside him. We looked at each other and he put his arms around me—Lublu, he said—and my cup runneth over. No matter how much I have of him, I'll never be satiated, for as my thirst is quenched, it needs replenishing. Each time I am filled, floating with love, but if he touches me his desire reawakens mine as the fire now flames before us and the logs split in heat. We are close, so close, yes, surely goodness and mercy shall follow me all the days of my life. . . .

It is still and cold, cold as on the feast of Stephen when the snow lay round about deep and crisp and even. The sun ricochets from whiteness, blinding me as I walk to the car. The other log cabins seen through the trees are empty and deserted, and there is only one chimney with smoke drifting up into the silent air. Again I try to guess which one Garbo and Gaylord Hauser lived in one summer three years ago, or so the agent said when Dodo rented our cabin. How different this place must be in summer. Perhaps Leopold and I will return, years from now, to this same cabin, have picnics with our children under the trees, sitting at one of the redwood tables now laden with snow. Yes, our children—for we are to be married. And fair bursting, I got into the car and started along the road. Sure enough, behind me another car and the smiling face of Bill Berry as he waves good morning. As time passes I've come to feel differently about him, connected in some way, friendly almost, you might say—puzzling indeed when his pestering is abhorrent to me and I wish him out of sight. He glued himself to my presence as I wheeled a cart by the racks of groceries. Anyone seeing us might have thought we were a team doing some sort of survey, for as I picked each item from the shelf Bill Berry would jot it down carefully in his notebook. Well, at least yesterday I'd shaken him long enough to send telegrams to Dodo and Carol telling them in ecstatic code that a wedding was to be! But by now I'd come to know Bill Berry's little ways, and this morning I could tell that he was deflated about something, yes—definitely a wee bit depressed. Well, he sighed, as I finished shopping, this really knocks my story off the front page of the *Daily News*. I was going to let it pass, but curiosity got me and I said, What? *What* puts your story off the front page? Didn't you hear? he said, Roosevelt died. The President? Yes, four thirty-five p.m. yesterday—just as my story was ready to roll—now it's on page four, he said morosely. Yeah, it happened suddenly in Warm Springs, Georgia, everything fine, sitting there having his portrait painted when he said "Have a terrific headache," keeled over unconscious, and two hours, twenty minutes later—dead. Just like that (he snapped his fingers), knocked me right off the front page—well, you can't win 'em all, can you? What's going to happen now? I said. Oh, I'm still on the story, he said, although it's cooled down a bit. No, I meant to our country? Oh, a new President is what it means, yeah, a new President—Harry S. Truman. I couldn't believe this. Why, Franklin Delano Roosevelt had been our President forever and ever—ever since I could remember. He had always been there. But now he wasn't . . . gone. For a minute I forgot Leopold. Snow had started to fall again, steadily it fell, sure and steady, it would never stop. But it would. It too will disappear, and there will be nothing left of it save in memory. Was Leopold really somewhere in a log cabin waiting for me by the fire, or would he too be gone?

To Carol—Airmail Special Delivery

Darling Angel,

I'm sitting in the patio while L. is working in the house
on his scores and there's so much to tell you I don't know
where to begin. First, I hope Elinor is OK? and that her
summer is OK? I think she was bored being with us and why
wouldn't she be when all L. and I wanted was to be alone
with each other. I haven't seen a soul since we got married,
except Aunt Thelma, who I had lunch with two days ago at
Romanoff's. My mother's still in New York with Maurice
(I guess) and isn't coming out here until later, but seeing Aunt
Thelma is a lot the same as being with Mummy and I was
dying to shout my happiness from the rooftops. You'll never
guess what she said just as we were finishing lunch, she
winked and said—Your Mummy hears Garbo's in a snit
because *she* had wanted to marry Stokowski, only he told her
he'd never get married again. I couldn't believe my ears and
said—What? just so she'd repeat it over again and she did!!!

Now, darling, as for me, you're getting a letter from the
happiest girl in the world. But I'll start from the beginning,
from the day I got the divorce. There was this reporter Bill
Berry from the *Daily News* following us every moment, it was
impossible to shake him and it threw off all our plans which
were to drive to Calexico on the Mexican border and be
married by a Judge—they were top secret these plans and the
last thing in the world we wanted were reporters following
us. Phil Kahgan, L.'s business manager, had worked all the
details out and would be meeting us in Calexico. Right after
we would drive to L.'s house at 9330 Beverly Crest Drive.
Darling, this house is the most fantastic place. It is private as
private can be and from the road you'd think it was just an
adobe wall, shaded by eucalyptus trees, for there are no

windows looking out onto the street. L. designed the house and built it on land high on the mountain and when you go inside it's like entering a secret garden. The rooms are built around a flagstone patio with tall glass doors opening out onto a garden. There's a high gate at one end of the patio which can be opened out to a balcony with view of trees and flowers and the city far beyond, or kept closed to wall in the secret garden. It's a dream, but then everything about my life seems like a dream and I still can't really believe I'm Mrs. Leopold Stokowski. Oh, darling, to think he's the most wonderful man in the world and he loves *me*. Together, he says, we are going to find the Ideal.

The other house he built in Santa Barbara is called The Monastery, haven't seen this yet but we're going there before rehearsals start. He also has orange groves in Redlands and beach land at Santa Monica—darling, I don't spend a cent of my own money (except for clothes) and I feel so protected and cherished. But—where was I? Oh, yes—Bill Berry—he was something! And it was because of him L. changed the plan at the last minute and chartered a plane to take us to Calexico. While I was at the courthouse with the lawyer, Mr. Summerfield, Bill Berry of course spooked around in constant attendance, not knowing that L. and Elinor were already at the airport in a plane waiting for me! Right after I got the divorce Mr. Summerfield and I went to a restaurant and after we sat down I went into the ladies' room—then through a back door, through the kitchen out onto the street right into a car L. had waiting for me with a driver whisking me straight to the plane. I was fainting up until the last minute that something would happen, but it didn't and soon there we were flying up into the sky waving good-bye to Bill Berry who drove up just as we were taking off. It was a rattly plane and sputtered a lot. Especially as we flew over the Sierra Nevada mountains. It kept getting worse and worse and Elinor got jumpy. L. was calm as could be so of course I was too. Just as we got over

the mountains the plane started going down down down and
we all knew we were going to crash. But it didn't bother me
one bit because L. was in the plane and that meant nothing
bad could happen. Still it was some crash. Elinor got
hysterical and the pilot wasn't in such good shape either but
it was mainly nerves and no one was hurt. L. was above all of
it and as we got ourselves out of the plane he looked around
at what he calls "the beautiful nature" as if we had landed
smooth as cream. Oooh! he said, leaning down to examine a
cluster of wildflowers almost hidden by the grass. "Tell me,"
he said to the pilot, pointing, "can you tell me the name of
these flowers?" Of course, the pilot didn't know them from
fruitcake, but it did take his mind off things for a minute. By
then Elinor had calmed down too and we made our way across
the field to the highway. L. had his hat firmly down over his
head so no one could recognize him and after about fifteen

minutes a car drove by, saw that we were hitchhikers and stopped. "Where you heading?" the man driving the car said and when L. said Calexico he said, "jump in 'cause that's just where we're going." The pilot wanted to be let off at the nearest phone and after that, there we were, L. and Elinor and me sitting cozily in the backseat merrily rolling along, with the two brothers sitting up front. "Where you folks from?" the one who was driving said. "We're farmers from Connecticut," L. said, "tobacco, we grow tobacco." No one said anything for a while and then the other brother said, "Don't know much about growing tobacco." We waited for L. to speak up but he remained inscrutably silent staring out at the blackness whizzing past us. I thought we'd never get there but finally we did around ten o'clock at night and after that all is fused in my mind as one big burst of joy that at last had come to be. I was being swept along into the hallways of a great house to a room full of people with the Judge standing behind a desk, carved and ornate. There were papers to sign as the witnesses stood by with quiet dignity. Then I took the ring off my hand and gave it to L. who put it back on my finger. It was a moment most solemn, and I floated with him back along the great halls into the backseat of the car with Phil Kahgan at the wheel. L. put his arms around me and the kiss we gave each to the other was most fervent and I stayed in the circle of his arms, our hands entwined, as we sped away. It was the most perfect moment of my life. It all went like a dream and there was not a reporter in sight, nor was there any, after driving all night, when we arrived the next day at four in the afternoon at Beverly Crest—Home!

Oh, darling, he's so wonderful, I'll never ever as long as I live find words to tell you because they just don't exist. All that exists is my love for him and the feelings that possess me. He just came out now to the patio asking when lunch would be ready. So I've got to stop, angel, and fix the salad. I've become quite a cook, mostly casseroles with a little bit of this

and a little bit of that, different each time. We have a fig
tree, imagine! They're for dessert with sour cream and brown
sugar. I love you, sweetheart, write soon please. I miss you—

Gloria

Family Matters

The days settle one into the other in perfect bliss with not a
moment apart, for I go with him to rehearsals at the Hollywood
Bowl and listen through the hours as the music takes form and
soars into being. Our lunch is a picnic hamper and we feast in
his dressing room or sometimes under a tree on the mountain
high above looking down on the rainbow arc of the stage far in
the valley below. We see very few people and go out seldom and
there are moments when I miss the fun Carol and I used to have,
but they pass fleetingly, in and out of my happiness, as memories
from long ago. I think it's wonderful, he said, that you would
just leave everything behind and come away with me. What an
amazing thought, for to follow him, to be with him, to become
him, is all I longed for since first we met. I had a letter the day
after we were married from his daughter Sadja, wishing us happiness, it was lovely, and quite a bit later one from Luba. Sonia
is another matter. She's to be wed soon and wrote to L. saying
she was determined not to make the same mistakes in her marriage
that her parents have. That didn't make me feel so hot. Then
she went on to say she'd like an automobile, preferably a Lincoln
Continental, as a wedding present. L. had an absolute fit and
instead I went out and bought some really beautiful silver and
wrapped it all up in white paper, kind of patent-shiny looking,
really pretty, with silver ribbon and orange blossoms festooning
the bows, and sent them to her with a card I drew—you know,
silver bells and so forth. He was so furious at first, calling her a
"busybody like her mother," that he wasn't going to send any
present at all. Well, maybe taking the matter into my own hands

was a mistake, maybe he was right, because the presents, all of them, came back, unopened—every single package. What a slap—but I was a bride too, and I opened the packages and Mr. and Mrs. Leopold Stokowski now own a pair of tulip-shaped goblets chased with seashells by Gorham and Company, Providence, Rhode Island, circa 1858, an extremely rare Strawberry and Pudding dish by Thomas Hammersley, New York, circa 1760, and, last but not least, a tapered cylindrical beaker by Paul Revere II. L.'s also enraged by a letter he got before he came to Nevada from his former wife the Princess Evangeline, informing him that our marriage must not take place. A bit much, don't you think? It really isn't any of her business. But once the sting tapers off, none of it matters, because I'm his wife and that's what's important and real. As for my mother, she's finally arrived in Beverly Hills and we're going there for dinner tomorrow night. I know L. doesn't want to go and is doing it just for me. Maybe that's a mistake too. I don't want anything to shake my happiness.

After agonizing over what to wear, I decided on the Hattie Carnegie—it's white and quite formal, more like for a restaurant in New York, but Mummy likes white, at least I think she does, because she once said I looked pretty in that silk blouse I wore with the Howard Greer suit, and that was white—the blouse, I mean. Anyway, I took hours getting myself together and even went to Arden's to have my hair done plus a manicure. The hair came out curly and awful, but I wetted it down and that helped a little, but not much. Oh dear oh dear oh dear, what can the matter be, but anyway L. looked splendid in one of his electric royal-blue shirts and a burgundy tie and I was finally ready (on time) and off we went. L. was driving and I said, I wonder if anyone else will be there or will it be just the four of us? I was also agonizing about what we'd talk about, not that I ever have much to say, except when Leopold and I are alone together, with other people present I'm mostly silent, listening to him.

Sometimes I feel threatened by things, like last week when

we went to Boski and George Antheil's for dinner. He's a com-
poser so controversial that L. had to fight to perform his Fourth
Symphony on NBC a year ago. I knew L. respected him and I
wanted to be the best I could be. And I did feel that way, even
though Hedy Lamarr was there with John Loder, looking like
she did in *Algiers*, remember? The conversation got on to Europe
and how now that the war was over it would come alive again
artistically even more powerfully than in 1919 when it had its
great artistic renaissance, Paris would be the artistic center of the
universe, young French composers would break away from their
present imitations of Stravinsky's *Symphony of Psalms*, which had
been very much à la mode during the war as a model. The way
L. talked made me suddenly fearful, uncertain. He said perhaps
we would leave America, go and live in Europe, Paris maybe, or
elsewhere. I panicked as I listened to him saying the press hounded
us and that the antagonistic and totally incorrect publicity about
cancelled Mexican concerts, growing difficulties with the new
orchestra in New York, the cancellation of his NBC contract the
year previous, made him think we should leave the United States.
Antheil kept going on and on about what a great man he is,
never satisfied with one accomplishment, always creating something else once a goal has been accomplished—the Philadelphia
Orchestra and then the All-American Youth Orchestra, two of
the finest in the world, the countless composers he'd discovered,
and even now he was forming a new orchestra which will be even
greater than his previous creations—that is, if he doesn't leave
the country before then. All through this I kept nodding in
agreement. . . .

There was silence around the dining table after this. It was
a hot, hot night, and Hedy lifted her arms to sweep the dark
mass of her hair high up in a pile on top of her head as she leaned
back and closed her eyes. There were dewdrops of perspiration
like a necklace garlanding her throat, and she looked so incredibly
beautiful that we all turned to gaze at her—It's so hot, she
murmured, stretching her arms up as her hair rippled back across

her shoulders. The spell was broken, everyone started talking at once—that is, everyone except John Loder and me. He had spoken as little as I had throughout the evening, and I wondered what he was thinking, or if indeed he had a thought in his head, for he appeared bored and oblivious even to Hedy.

As for me, I was stunned. The Paris I knew as a child dwelt within me still and I feared the cobbled streets, the patterns of light reflecting from the passing cars on walls of a room at night as Big Elephant and the Little Countess hissed and whispered behind the door. No, I couldn't go back, I couldn't, no matter how much I loved Leopold. I wanted my own home, my own children, my own family in one place, here in America, I didn't want to be a wanderer again, ever, for here in America I'm home, at home as much as I ever will be. Europe, no! I felt threatened, alone suddenly . . . but then I looked at Leopold and his eyes bathed me with such tenderness and love that . . . maybe this time it would be different, this time I'd find the words to tell him so that he'd understand all, all that had happened. But I didn't, not later that night as we drove home, nor later still as we lay touching in the secret dark. And now here we were, almost there, almost at Mummy and Aunt Thelma's, and he still didn't know how daunted I felt, how alarmed, chill.

It was a mistake, going here, and although L. doesn't actually say anything against my mother I know he's more suspicious of her than ever. It's odd, but there's something hovering around that reminds me of Naney Morgan. I wouldn't dare say this aloud—but there *is* something of the Naney Napoleon in Leopold, except L. of course doesn't overdo it the way she does, for Naney Napoleon always ends up going too far. You know—deep sighs, silences pregnant with meaning (to coin a phrase, ha, ha). Only it's not ha, ha at all at all. No, there are no ham-actory performances from L. like the ones Naney sometimes indulges in. But still . . . the way Naney holds things in, like she knows things, things about my mother, things so terrible they can't be spoken, and they hang over us in a delicate balance and must not be put into words, for if they were our little world would shatter and we'd be blown to smithereens, exploding into the sky in one great firework.

As usual, L. says—Pray to Divine Mother, she'll help you. And I do pray to her, but I can't quite get the knack of it yet, and I do much better with God or Saint Theresa. She's best really, I can really get to her.

There was no one else at the dinner, and it proceeded as follows: Leopold, Imperial; Mummy, Opaque; Aunt Thelma, Hoity-Toity; Me, Apprehensive, yes, most apprehensive indeed. And so it loitered along with L. sitting with the cloud of his hair held high in the air as Mummy and Aunt Thelma chitchatted around us. I sat sinking, as the minutes passed, down, down, slowly, into the depths of a bottomless well, and like Alice I had plenty of time as I sank to look about me and to wonder what was going to happen next. And in this wondering it came to me that Mummy hadn't called me "Pooks" in ages (come to think of it, not since I met Leopold). Well, so what! It wouldn't be hard to resign myself to continue on Pooks-less for the rest of my life—it was a silly name anyway, and not all that special— she scattered it around a lot. I have rehearsals early tomorrow, L. said, standing up unexpectedly, we have to go. Good night, Mummy, thank you for a lovely time, and Aunt Toto, thank you too. So that's what happened next, we left abruptly, just like that. Wannsie hadn't even brought coffee in yet. Out on the street on our way to the car L. stopped and put his arms around me and we kissed right there on Linden Drive, a long kiss, before making our way, without saying anything, to the car, and without saying anything we drove home . . . and now it's next day and the moment's passed and it's too late to say anything at all.

Days in July

Leopold sent twenty-five of my poems to Blanche Knopf and a letter came from her today rejecting them. I'm not too disappointed, because I didn't really expect her to publish them. For one thing, they're too influenced by H.D. and Ezra Pound, and I must keep working to find my own voice. L. believes we should develop the talents we are born with and he encourages me in everything I strive for. It took ages before I could bring myself to tell him about wanting to be an actress, but when I did he not only listened seriously, he talked with Gabriel Pascal and another producer, Boris Morros, about a screen test. It's only talk, but now I'm going twice a week and working on scenes with the dialogue coach at Paramount Studios. Of course L. thinks acting can't be compared to painting and writing because it's an interpretive craft, but I'm drawn to it because I have an instinct that in each part I played I'd discover parts of myself so that one day, presto! it would all fit together like pieces in a puzzle and I'd know who I really am. Not to mention all that love, waves of it as they say, that actors get, and you can never have enough of that, can you? ha, ha.

I never got to first base talking to Aunt Gertrude about any of this, and now that Leopold loves me everything's changed and none of it seems so important anymore because, well—I've merged into him, haven't I? . . . Except, except sometimes—sometimes silly things threaten me. Like yesterday when I was in the bathroom taking a long soak in the tub, happy as a lark. L. knocked and I chirped, Come in, darling. He closed the door and said, Garbo's here. What? I said. Yes, she just stopped by unexpectedly, to ask if she could rent The Monastery in Santa Barbara—come out, sweetheart, and meet her. I put the washcloth over my face and said, I can't I can't I can't. Of course, I was dying to, so why did I say that? Shaken suddenly, as if she were the one L. loved and not me. She wants to meet you, he said, please do come out, just for a moment? No, no, I can't and I froze inside, chill spreading along my limbs pulling me down to the bottom of the sea. He went out of the bathroom and I lay there as the water got icy, unable to move. How would I know when she had gone? But, more to the point—would she go? Perhaps

not, perhaps I was the one that was to go. Just when I thought
I'd die there was a knock on the door. He came in and said she'd
left. Are you going to rent The Monastery to her? I said. No,
because Beryl Markham's rented it for a year, and we're going
there next weekend, Beryl's expecting us, I want you so much
to see it. He leaned over and took my face in his hands. I love
you, Divine Beloved, he said, and all at once I wasn't afraid.

That night we went to a dinner party at Mrs. Franz Werfel's
house. It was quite an event because we go out so seldom. Thomas
Mann was there, and when Faye Emerson was introduced to him
she bobbed up and down in a curtsy. Paulette Goddard didn't,
but she and Burgess Meredith held hands a lot and I was quite
giddy with it all—you know, the novelty of being at a party-
party—and what with one thing and another Garbo was quite
forgotten. And the minute we got home, everything fell back in
place again and we were happy, so happy, Leopold and I, just
the two of us, alone together.

Wednesday, July eleventh: Last night was Leopold's first concert at the Hollywood Bowl. The Love Music from Acts II and
III of Wagner's *Tristan und Isolde*—his transcription—was for me
alone. As it ended I slipped away quickly to get back to his
dressing room before the curtain calls, no one else is privileged
to enter and a guard is stationed outside the door. I wait there
after every performance with towels and water, for he arrives from
the stage after the concert dripping wet. Even after he has changed
he prefers not to see visitors, and we leave through the stage door
immediately to avoid the people that flock back hoping to talk
to him. It seems rude, but if only they could see how raw and
unprotected he is after the music, they'd understand. Last night
he made an exception for Frank Sinatra, who came backstage after
the concert. L. received him in the dressing room for a minute,
where Sinatra kept glancing at me as they talked as if I was about
to say something. But I have nothing to say when I'm with
Leopold, to be by his side speaks for itself. Soon I drove him

home and in no time there we were in the starry patio partaking of the supper I'd prepared before we left. L. keeps teasing me that I cook enough to invite the entire orchestra to dinner, and I'm doing my best to make the casserole portions smaller, but I get carried away by all the fresh vegetables and things at the Farmer's Market. It's the improvising and not following recipes that leads me astray and why we get stuck with a lot of leftover lunches and dinners.

Wish Mummy had been at the concert, but she and Aunt Thelma have gone to New York on their way to London. Also had hoped to show her the trailer L. and I are crossing the country in when the season at the Bowl is over. We call it our Gypsy Caravan and it's just like a little house on wheels with every modern convenience. L.'s crazy about travel and talks all the time about the places he's going to take me to—so many dozens and dozens with names I've never heard of that sometimes it's hard to keep track of them all. What about home? Where will that be? I ask. He doesn't know yet, but one thing he's certain of: if we do settle in one spot, it will be someplace in "the beautiful nature," no city for us, not even New York. So right now, who knows when I'll get to see Mummy again? But I did get to talk to her on the phone before she left. The rental on their Beverly Hills house is up and she doesn't think she and Aunt Thelma will be coming back again. They're probably going to live in Europe, but who knows? As we were saying good-bye, she mumbled something about setting up a trust fund for her instead of sending her the money I do every month. Sounds like a good idea and I'm going to talk to L. about it. Oh well, even though she'd have been impressed last night at L.'s concert, she's really not that wild about classical music, so maybe it's just as well after all that she wasn't there.

Had lunch with Oona today. She's pregnant—soon, soon—wishing wishing—praying, soon it will be me. L. hopes for a girl exactly like me and she will be called Maria (his mother's name), but that will only be one of the names, for she will have many many names, including Linda Bonita, so when she grows up she'll have numerous choices to select from in the event Maria doesn't please her. After lunch Oona and I went to see a movie with Rita Hayworth. She seemed so remote up there on the screen, as if I'd never known her, and it brought back the time with Pat-Pasquale and that also seemed so long ago and only comes to me sometimes in dreams. I push out of my mind last week what happened on my way back from the market—there he was, bang! right beside me in an open car, waiting for the red light to change. Gloria, I want to talk to you, he shouted, jabbing his finger, pointing to a parking lot across the highway, pull over pull over, he kept shouting, his face all dark and my heart filling with dread pounded as the light changed and I shot ahead. He pursued close beside me, shouting, but I pressed on and made a quick turn and he gave up, didn't follow, and soon I was home. Leopold took me in his arms and said it was so strange, how he had felt while I'd been away . . . the room became you, everything I looked at—you! This room became the world and it was you encircling me. As he spoke he started drawing and what he drew were initials—an L inside of a G, like this

So long ago and far away, but I have it still.

Every day for half an hour L. does yoga exercises he learned from a guru in the Himalayas. Someday I'll take you there, he says. He studied Sanskrit and he tells me about the Shakti (which means Energy) cult, based on the female principle of the universe. Among Hindus the worship of a deity is placed above that of his wife, but in Shakti worship this is reversed. Siva's wife, Parvati, is the central object of Shakti worship (*love* that idea!), and she has many manifestations—Devi, Kali, Bhagavati, Durga, and other personifications of the "great goddess." L. says it's impossible to define Hinduism or to detach it from the caste system. It's hard to understand what it must be like to be born into a system where your position in life can never, ever be changed, but L. says it's all intimately connected with belief that the deeds a person does in a previous life determine his position in the present life (karma). These deeds include sin (papa), merit (punya), salvation (moksha), and morality (dharma). Finally the soul goes on until it attains moksha, or salvation. This moksha is differently conceived by each sect, but all believe that the perfected soul is freed from the need to die and be reborn again and that it lives forever intimately with God, absorbed in him. I told L. the one thing I do understand is the ancient rite of the funeral pyre and that if he should die I would want to die too because I couldn't live without him.

Doves dwell in our patio. Their fantails open in the moonlight, white and lacy as a bride's veil, leaning against each other, coo-cooo-cooo, in the jasmine-scented night . . . the moon shifts suddenly and they are in darkness, as close so close we are bathed in light, turning towards each other. His eyes gleam with love, but a cloud passes over the moon, leaving us to touch in darkness, and all at once the doves are still . . . will I remember?

The Caravan

Leopold's music scores are all packed, the paintings I've done this summer strapped up onto the ceiling of the trailer—everything is set for our departure. Soon we'll be on the road. And I start to dream things like . . .

Leopold in the car driving along the highway—me in the Caravan wearing a Broomstick skirt and long golden earrings, preparing the dinner of trout from a mountain stream caught at sunrise, table with yellow-and-white check cloth, candlelight glowing on the blue jug of wildflowers gathered in a meadow at a stop along the way.

. . . I tap on the window to Leopold in the car ahead—he

smiles and waves before maneuvering the Caravan into a forest primeval where we will bide the hours of darkness.

. . . Come, Gypsy—he takes my hand at dusk, leading me through the still pines—far ahead a deer pauses an instant and leaps for shelter . . . later, something close by, flashing white in the darkness. I look at Leopold and dare not speak—a Unicorn. . . .

All through the night delighting in each other, frost at dawn, my feet cuddle against his, toasty warm as in a cup of hot chocolate. Pancakes for breakfast, with honey, before we pack up and move on—My turn to drive, darling, I call out.

. . . In the Caravan Leopold does his yoga exercises while I am at the wheel speeding us on towards another paradise. . . .

I'm writing this in a trailer camp where we're parked for the night. In New Mexico, somewhere near Albuquerque, I think. Our dog, the wee Buffalito, barks constantly at every little thing, and it's a pain in the you-know-what, especially at night when we're trying to sleep. Our neighbors aren't so keen on it either— Keep that dog *quiet*! they shout at us. None of it's turning out as we thought. For one thing, no one can be inside the trailer when it's moving, because everything jiggles and jangles, vibrating, up and down, so you'd end up jelly. Things have to be removed from tables, kitchen pots and pans—everything put away and battened down before taking off. Then comes the driving—most iffy, the driving, because the car we have is too light to pull the weight of the trailer. More iffy when going up hill and down dale—down dale's scariest, the Caravan speeds ahead alarmingly, bumping against the back of the car. Then up hill we're being pulled back by the weight of the trailer, so there's no control either way. By the time we got to Flagstaff, Arizona, L. decided to sell the Caravan on the spot and continue on with just the car, but this got so complicated what with his boxes of scores and my canvases that we decided to take our chances and keep going. Then there's the food problem: while driving there's no electricity, so things in the icebox spoil. As for finding spots of "beautiful nature" to park overnight—we're lucky if we find a trailer camp. There's also the hat situation with Leopold—he has to keep one on so people won't recognize him, ever since that first night when we pulled into a trailer camp in Salome, California, and a woman in curlers hot-footed it out of the trailer next to us, all excited, calling "Hey, aren't you Mr. Tchaikovsky?" He didn't answer, but she was relentless in pursuit, and finally he said most courteously, You are mistaken, my name is Leonard Stanley. The woman didn't believe any of it for one minute and ran all around the trailer court like a chicken with its head cut off spreading the news that Mr. Tchaikovsky was here—"You know—the one that wrote 'Full Moon and Empty Arms.' " That song's been on the radio a lot this summer, a big hit, stolen from a theme of Rachmaninoff with dippy lyrics tacked onto it, lyrics that stick in your mind the more you try to forget them. I really wanted to put a muzzle on her along with one on little Buffalito. We'd like to go to a movie tonight but Buffalito would go ape. Maybe tomorrow we'll check into a hotel just to get a night's sleep.

Leopoldo and Lorenzo

Leopoldo! Leopoldo! a woman called out, waving frantically, as she ran across the plaza towards our Caravan. It's Brett, Leopold said, slowing up and looking around for a place to stop. We had reached Taos after another night at a trailer camp and I felt apprehensive (perhaps because of little sleep), threatened even, by this Brett person flapping around the window of our car as Leopold maneuvered over to the side of the road. She was of indeterminate shape, quite interestingly pulled together, with high boots of tooled leather over men's corduroy trousers, a vest of Indian woven design, man's shirt and cardigan, and to top it

all a wide-brimmed sombrero on a grey, rather pinlike head. I
didn't know it then, but later heard it said that in her trousers
she carried a long stiletto, the better to ward off fantasies of
assault. There was in her manner towards L. the gushing of the
fan combined with the intimacy of—yes, secret implications, as
if they had a past together—one that excluded me. The Brett
cast a long shadow, and it got even longer in the days that
followed after I met Mabel Dodge Luhan and Frieda Lawrence,
for although Lorenzo, as they referred to D. H. Lawrence, had
been dead for fifteen years, these three still fought in death, as
they had in life, to possess his soul. Down, Reggie, down! Brett
kept calling out to the dog who bounced beside her alongside
the car. He was big, this Reggie dog, and most friendly, competing with Brett for attention, as he put out his tongue in an
attempt to lick L.'s face in slobbery greeting through the open
window. It's a different Reggie this time, L. said amusedly, as
he asked me to roll up the window—Brett always has one dog
or another, but *plus ça change, plus c'est la même chose*, they're always
named Reginald, after her father, the second Viscount Esher.
Oh? I said. It was quite a thought.

I tried to imagine having a dog and naming it Reginald—
for that too was the name of my father. Maybe it made Brett feel
close to him because she missed him so much—then again maybe
not, because there was no getting around it, Reggie was getting
more and more irascible minute by minute, for attention must
be paid, and right now it was clearly Brett who was center stage
with a little crowd gathering around to witness our arrival. Reggie
was most displeased, and the welcoming tongue now alternated
between barks, hostile barks you might say, yes, definitely verg-
ing on the hostile side. And yet at first there had been a certain
appeal about Reggie, an endearing mixture of this and that,
bulldog, Afghan, peppered here and there with a smidgen of the
Buffalito. As I leaned over to roll up the glass Reggie didn't take
to it at all and the barks slid alarmingly, there was no mistaking
it now, into definite snarls. Buffalito was going batty in the

backseat, hurling himself at the window, trying to get at Reggie. I tried to picture Buffalito as a Reginald—no, it wasn't a good idea at all, a sort of desperate tribute that would never work. As a matter of fact, there was something creepy about the whole enchilada.

Boy, has the Brett got a crush on L. It's infuriating. She hardly acknowledges I exist, much less am his wife. If only I were older I'd be able to put all this in its place, but I can't, and it's as if I'm in silent battle to hold on to Leopold, body and soul, for they all clearly worship and adore him and why not, what's not to adore, but it shakes me up when they call him Leopoldo, simpering and leaping around him as if he's Lorenzo in Taos, arrived as the new messiah in New Mexico to start the utopian community D. H. Lawrence dreamed of long ago—the Rananim, the title chosen from a line of a Hebrew dirge—which was to be in Florida, with disciples John Middleton Murry, Katherine Mansfield, S. S. Koteliansky, Mark Gertler, and, of course, Brett, as charter members. And although it never came to be, Brett still dreams about it, holds on to it as if Rananim were still ahead of her and not behind her. Only now it's to be the Leopoldo as the Lorenzo replacement and I am to be the Impostor.

Brett has done dozens of paintings of L. conducting and otherwise, and years ago followed him to Philadelphia where she was permitted to sit backstage during concerts and attend rehearsals, and I listen to these reminiscences, my skin turning prickly green with jealousy and fear—yes, fear that he doesn't belong to me, and if that happens it will be the end of me, for I will no longer exist. But it's only in my head, of course, because later at the Don Fernando Inn where we're staying, he jokes about them, Brett, Mabel, and Frieda, mildly teasing the three of them—nothing more. He's especially taken by Brett's endless preoccupation over his nose, the beauty of which she finds impossible to capture on canvas due to its composition, or as she puts it, that most difficult of combinations—very big, but very delicate too. Yes, there are endless ponderings over the renderings of the nose, for there are to be many paintings, ah yes, many, not just one, and the collection is to be called—the Stokowski Symphony. Between—for nose relief, no doubt—she makes tracings of his hands by putting them flat on paper and drawing round them. Her eyes never leave L.'s face, and the ear trumpet of brass she carries to hear through (for she is partially deaf) is held in trembling anticipation like an elephant's trunk towards the sun and moon of his face. Quite frequently, the name of Evangeline, the second Mrs. Stokowska, pops into the conversation as Brett enthuses over the fur coat, which she still has, and the pair of lovely pajamas E. gave her. Can you beat that! Well, she'll get no fur coat and lovely pajamas from *this* Mrs. Stokowska. But still, isn't it funny, there is something familiar about her—it might be that she reminds me of someone?—and secretly I keep wanting her to like me, as I long not only to be part of Rananim but a most important part. After all, I'm Leopold's wife and I'm entitled to this privilege, aren't I?

It's much easier to be around Frieda Lawrence because she has her own fish to fry. There is something about being with Brett that constantly, though silently, calls out "feed me feed me." Frieda, blowsy in a somewhat Tyrolean outfit, higgledy-piggledy hair piled on top of her head with strands waving about like tentacles, is far less needy—in fact, not needy at all except for the cigarettes. I've never seen anyone smoke so much, one cigarette right after another, forgetting one unpuffed in an ashtray while absentmindedly lighting another. Brett drove us to lunch along with Reggie and Buffalito who have made peace with each other. Mrs. Luhan was also supposed to accompany us, but at the last minute declined, due to a sudden tiff with Mrs. Lawrence, or rather Mrs. Ravagli, for Frieda is now married to Angelo Ravagli—a quiet one, stays as I do, silent and listening. He's on the outside of things, sort of just there, because when all's said and done Frieda's really still married to D. H. Lawrence.

These are all Lorenzo's paintings, Frieda said, waving a trail
of smoke from her cigarette at the walls without looking around.
There they hung, all around us, huge and oddly Thurber-like
although they're oils and not small line-drawn cartoons. Satyrs,
who look like Lawrence, pursue zaftig naked women, who look
like Frieda, through coves and glens in fruitless chase. Another
cigarette is lit as the talk shifts and Frieda ambles up to heave a
trunk from under her bed. Ach! she says, opening it to letters
and copy books thrown in at random. His manuscripts, see!—
she opens a book as the ashes from a cigarette sift over—Ah!
Lady Chatterley, this one, and I gaze mesmerized at the writing,
so precise, on and on as it neatly fills the pages. He would sit,
she bellowed, with us, like we are now in a room, everybody
talking away, and still write as if no one was there—ach! he was
something! Suppose there were a fire, shouldn't the trunks be in
a museum? But I didn't speak up and only did later, when I
tried, without success, to bring the conversation around to Katherine Mansfield. Ah, yes—Katherine, Frieda said, and it dropped,
as they say, like a stone into a well, with no one to fish it out
as the conversation bounced back to Lorenzo. But I liked Frieda
because she acknowledged my existence and didn't make dippy
cow-eyes at L. Well, maybe—but only a little. You can't be
blustery like Frieda and pull off cow-eyes with even a small
success. As we were leaving she gave me her book *Not I but the
Wind* and signed it "Frieda Lawrence for Gloria Stokowska—
September 45" in a big scrawl in pencil. I have it still.

The last of the trio I met last night—Mabel Dodge Luhan.
Tony Luhan was not present, nor was Frieda, the spat with Mabel
still hanging in the balance. But Brett was there. Clearly Mrs.
Luhan also still has Rananim on her mind, no doubt activated
by L.'s arrival in Taos. I felt like a child permitted as a special
treat to sit at the grown-ups' table, a table onto which Mabel
put her cards pronto. You should stay longer, Prince, she said

to L. (me too?). Why not linger longer on this trip, move to my house, later perhaps more permanent ties? That's kind of you, L. said smoothly, but we're gypsies, we must move on—tomorrow we're leaving at sunup, aren't we, Schéhérazade? He smiled at me with such love that I came back to myself again. Yes, I said, oh yes—tomorrow tomorrow. . . .

A big fat orange of sun was ahead of us as we drove along the great mesa, past the deep mountains. Above us the sky, oh! as it got light, so much sky, I've never seen so much. On and on we drove until we came to the Rancho de Taos, a mission church of adobe, built by the Conquistadores. It's like sculpture, perhaps Brancusi, and in the fresh dawn we stopped and entered into the cool of its quiet. At the altar L. took a taper and I put my hand on top of his and together we lit a candle . . . that old familiar heady mix of wax and smoke as I closed my eyes and made a wish, the same wish I always make when I make a wish . . . the wish that we'll have a baby. As we left there was no one else on the face of the earth, only we two—but suddenly from nowhere a figure appeared, of indeterminate shape, scurrying straight towards us, very fast, a black shawl over its body. For a crazy instant I thought it was Brett following us in the dawn, pursuing L., donning a shawl of black at the last minute in hasty disguise. But suddenly I stopped dumb—for it was Dodo, of course! No wonder I had been drawn to Brett, for she was another version of Dodo . . . even the ear trumpet Big Elephant could have managed with aplomb. And the dog Reggie was . . . the crabby Smokey. But of course the bundled figure sliding past, unaware of us, wasn't Brett, wasn't Dodo . . . and it disappeared into the black hole of the church without a trace. I wanted to turn back, back to Taos, find Brett, find her and tell her I loved her, but instead I called out to L.—Hurry, let's hurry, and I got behind the wheel and drove fast fast on down the highway without looking back.

dear Duncan

Pittsburgh Detroit New Orleans Urbana San Francisco Houston Mexico City Seattle, etc., etc., etc. It seems like years, as indeed it is, that we've been traveling. Why, I could fill pages and pages with the et ceteras as we have gone and continue to go to and fro, back and forth, either to a city where Leopold is guest conductor or to and fro back and forth across country just for the heck of it. The Caravan has long since gone, much too cumbersome for our purposes, and we are free as birds migrating here and there, taking our nest with us, only instead of a nest or a house it's a car. Yes, a Chevrolet has become home, or so it seems to me right now as I sit writing this in the Drake Hotel in Chicago. I don't mean to sound cranky, and if I do it's because I'm tired waiting in this hotel room for L. to get back from rehearsal, plus I just got my period so I'm not pregnant. I want more than anything to have a baby and have a home with L. in one place instead of this endless to-and-froing on these endless highways. It's like we're always going somewhere but never getting there. I know that he must go where the orchestras are, but let's face it—he really loves this travel, even when it's not to an orchestra, and he's champing at the bit, itching to cover Europe as soon as it's on its feet again after the war. Even talking about this scares me, because it looms over my dreams of HOME. That's not to say that our Chevrolet isn't homey, for it is, homey as can be—we even carry our very own portable library consisting of two well-read books. By now I hardly need refer to either one, for I know by heart all the restaurants suggested by Duncan Hines in *Adventures in Good Eating* and by heart I know the hotels he recommends in *Lodging for a Night*. Ah, yes—dear Duncan! But it's not lodging for a night that I want to know about, it's lodging forever and ever and ever—that's what interests me.

. . .

Later: Forget what I wrote in my cranky mood. It came on me as it usually does just before I get my period. I had a good cry and feel OK again. Yes, because I know L. loves me, adores me, and all we both want is to be together, we two alone, and we have that, so I'm really mad at myself for beefing about anything. And who knows—maybe next month I'll get pregnant.

An Empty Room

All through the toing and froing—or, as Lady Moon and Queen Jonquil would put it, hither-and-yonning—I've kept my studio on Fifty-third Street, where we've stayed whenever we've touched base in New York. But now we are to leave, for Leopold is to be the regular conductor of the New York Philharmonic and we are to be in one place and have at last the home I've been longing for. In many ways I hate to leave my studio, but we need more space not only for ourselves but for L.'s scores, which are now stored in a back room on the floor below us. Yes, in a few weeks we will be moving from this place. So much has happened here—I will never forget this skylight room with the chair of strawberry chintz placed by the fire, never forget last night. . . .

We had been quiet for a long time, loath to move from each other, loath to pile another log on the coals, loath to do anything at all but be as we were. I sat on the floor beside him, leaning against him, his arms around me. . . . There's something I'm going to tell you, he said without moving, speaking slowly . . . something that no one knows—no one in the world. It's about myself. He was looking past me at the glowing coals, that naked look he has after the music, when he steps down from the podium, stripped to the center—the center that is mine. Close so close we were, and I looked at him, opening to him in that trust I had given since our eyes first met at the party across the room, even before we had spoken. And now I trembled, for I knew he was to give his trust to me, and that the core of him would in full measure belong to me. He was looking into the fire as if mesmerized and for a time said nothing. Then he whispered— I've never trusted anyone until I knew you and what I am to tell you must never be repeated to anyone, ever. I promise, I promise! I said. So close we were at that moment I thought I would die of it. But as I spoke—he pulled away, stood up, and in an instant all was changed. Yes, he said, putting a log on the fire, later— someday—this isn't the moment. But it is, it is! I wanted to scream, but no sound came into the room. It was as if it were empty, inhabited only by a bed, the empty strawberry chair by the fire. Nothing moved except the log as it suddenly caught flame. He has all of me . . . everything, everything, and I'll never rest until I have all of him. I believed he had trusted me with all of himself, but now I know I've been mistaken, know it's because he's been hurt in the past—he's suspicious, afraid to be once more betrayed. But with me it's different. He'll know this in time. The force of my love will reach through to him, and when it does he'll understand that I am not a betrayer, he'll trust the truth of me, and when he does I will possess the soul of him as he now possesses the soul of me.

Where Are You, Lady Moon?

The best way is to send her a cable in London, Leopold said, you can always follow it up with a letter—remember, Thelma has money—and anyway, let her work to earn her living like most people in the world do. But—but—but, I kept saying. It was weird what was happening, because in all the buts—the biggest but of all was that my mother was getting further away from me than ever and I feared her once again as I had when I was a child. It was as if I had been pulled back in time by L.'s suspicion of her, yanked back to that place I knew so well, the land of foreboding, innuendo, and dread, where all things were

possible and nothing safe. There was only one difference—now
at least there was one thing I had control over: money, for indeed,
now it was mine. Leopold spoke of my mother, when we did
speak of her, which wasn't often, much in the same way that
Naney Morgan did, only his interpretation of her was simpler
and more clearly defined. Naney was Proustian, Leopold—Western Union. She never gave you love, he would say, Dodo gave
you love. And of course it was true. In some ways . . . in other
ways not. The ways not, I came to understand only later—much,
much later, when I came to understand her, understand that she
was incapable of giving me the love I yearned for and endlessly
sought from her . . . the love that (as I write this day) I still
seek from her, although she has been dead these many years. If
I had understood that then, it would have been different and I
wouldn't have sent the cable. (Or would I?)

LOOKING THROUGH MY BOOKS AND ACCOUNTS, OWING
TO HEAVY EXPENSES, I CAN NO LONGER CONTINUE YOUR
MONTHLY ALLOWANCE.   GLORIA

Two days passed before her answer came.

DEAR GLORIA WHAT YOU TERM "MONTHLY ALLOWANCE"
IS MY SOLE MEANS OF LIVELIHOOD. PLEASE RECONSIDER.
LOVE, MUMMY

Now's the time to follow it up with a letter, Leopold said,
and he dictated it on the spot to the secretary he works with
every day during the morning hours.

Dear Mummy,
There's really nothing more to say than I've already said
in my cable. Surely Aunt Thelma, who you live with, has
more than enough for two, so certainly money will never be
a problem with you.
Gloria

She typed it up with great dispatch, and as I signed it there came to me again that feeling . . . but what? It's only now I know—Melton Mowbray, the "rare bease" letter, a letter also dictated to me, but by Big Elephant . . . but most of all—it's Naney Morgan I can't forget.

Mummy's flown from London and she's in New York and it's terrible what's happening. She's said to the newspapers that I've cut her off without a cent and told her I don't care if she starves to death and I keep saying to Leopold that maybe Thelma, the Queen Jonquil, doesn't have as much money as he thinks she does and maybe what we're doing is the wrong thing. But he says he doesn't believe in trust funds, which is what she wants, and it's all gone so crazy with reporters trying to get pictures of us as we go in and out of the house—this morning there were even photographers on the roof of the house next to us, waiting to catch us if we went out onto our roof. L.'s lawyer, Mr. Strauss, and Mummy's lawyer, Mr. Kaufman, go back and forth at each other, and Mr. Strauss said yesterday that the press has gotten so out of hand perhaps we should call (get this!) a press conference. I thought only politicians did that. Wait wait, L. keeps saying, it will soon die down, but it doesn't, it doesn't—just keeps getting worse and I feel awful. It's as if my Lady Moon's turned into the Wicked Queen, if only Leopold would stop going on and on about her so that she can turn back again into herself, oh! Lady Moon, my Lady Moon.

Mr. Strauss says it's splashed all over the newspapers that my mother is selling the pear-shaped diamond engagement ring given to her by my father. She is forced to do this by my cutting her off without any money. Oh Mummy, don't, please don't.

L. finally thinks it's a good idea to give the press conference. It's to be held in the room where his scores are stored. He's preparing a statement which we'll hand out to all the reporters

at the press conference and that will be that, L. says. There is
to be no answering of questions at all at all, no matter what.
We will just enter the room, give each reporter a sheet of paper
with the statement on it, and leave. What's the statement going
to say? I ask L. I'm working on it now, he says.

I've seen the statement. It's not long at all. It says that we
are going to start a foundation. This foundation is to be called

the Gloria Stokowska and Leopold Stokowski Foundation, and guess what? I'm to be the secretary of this foundation which will be a full-time job because our foundation will help a lot of people. L. says it's important to get the idea across that everybody must have a job and this includes especially my mother. There should be a picture of me taken behind a typewriter—that I don't know how to type isn't the point, he says. Who are the people the foundation will help? I ask. We'll discuss that later, L. said, Mr. Strauss is working out—he gestured around vaguely—the details. It's a nightmare, but all this must be the right thing to do, because L. says so. I hope I die before this so-called press conference, but if I don't at least he'll be by my side in the lion's den.

But he wasn't. At the last minute, just as we were to go down to the room where Mr. Strauss had gathered the reporters, Leopold said I'd better go down alone, that if he went it might look like he'd influenced me. My hands got like ice and I started trembling and said I couldn't I couldn't, but he said it was the only way to make the reporters stop hounding us once and for all. Pray to Divine Mother, he said, as he handed me a stack of the statements and like a zombie I went on down the steps and into a room jammed with reporters and photographers. It was small, this room, and as I walked in they surrounded me, seizing the prepared statement I handed out to each one as fast as I could, but it didn't satisfy them at all, not one bit, and questions kept coming at me from everywhere all at once. I could hardly make out what they were until one woman shouted close to my ear— I'm Inez Robb and at your age I was working to support my mother, what do you have to say to that? To that to that to that? Oh God, oh God, would that I could say something to that, make her understand, if I could only make all of them understand—but how could I when I really didn't understand myself?

Stand over there, they kept shouting at me, and I found myself by a window in front of white curtains, puzzled as to why they were so dirty. It passed through my mind, this room's only used as a storeroom and before this moment I've only seen it once, but what had that to do with anything anyway, and I tried praying to Divine Mother, but she wasn't anywhere around so I shifted on to Leopold—I'm his wife, aren't I? He loves me, he loves me, he's waiting for me upstairs. . . . But where's my mother? And how did it all happen? And why am I in this strange room with dirty organdy curtains and paint peeling off the walls, unable to speak because L. said I mustn't—I mustn't no matter what, he had said that, yes, he had.

I kept looking around in the crowd for Mr. Strauss. But then I remembered, just as I'd started down, right after L. had said Pray to Divine Mother, he'd said Mr. Strauss would leave the room once I'd gotten there, that it was best I see the reporters completely alone without Mr. Strauss present so that they couldn't say I'd been influenced by the lawyer. There was a table by the window where L. had spread out sheets of music when he had gone down earlier to set the stage, so to speak, for the press conference. I sat down and put my hand on top of the pages. Over my body, slowly, mercifully, paralysis came, and I froze in fear as would a rabbit, my face settling into a grimace. Only my fingers could move as I spread them out over the notes of music Leopold had written on the page, finding, as my fingers touched the ink, comfort as the blind might from Braille. I held to this, to Leopold upstairs, waiting for me . . . soon, soon it would be over and I could leave the circus tent, run up the stairs, back into his arms, but until then I would have to get through this as best I could.

> *Lady Moon, Lady Moon, where are you roving?*
> *Over the sea.*
> *Lady Moon, Lady Moon, whom are you loving?*
> *All that love me!*

Innisfree, Greenwich, Connecticut, 1949

Our house on John Street is next to the road, but we have planted trees and fenced it so that, although painted barn red, it fades into the trees, giving us privacy from all who pass. We are snug as could be in our four-room house that looks out to laurel bushes and stones alongside a brook that meanders by on into the forest. On one floor is the living room, small, as is the kitchen, with a staircase ladder leading to bedroom and bath above. There are no other rooms, and L. has built, close by, a simple studio of glass bricks, heated with portable plug-in electric heaters, to contain his scores. Also close by is a toolshed, now converted into the studio where I work. L. is happy living in the beautiful nature, and as I am he, of course I am happy too. To say happy is perhaps misleading, for what I feel these days, each and every day, since I knew I was pregnant, can only be described as bliss and contentment. Centered . . . at peace with myself and all that has been and all that will be. For surely I shall never be bereft again or forget how I feel now, surely goodness and mercy shall follow me all the days of my life and I will dwell in the house of the Lord forever.

How I love what happens to my body as my belly swells, slowly, oh! so slowly, slow as moon swell, as day merges into night. And as time passes I find myself working in my studio less and less, for everything else seems unimportant to me now— without doing anything I am doing the most important thing in the world. How simple it is, this final answer.

Each day we rise early, breakfast on oatmeal, the John McCann kind, cooked in a double boiler, big cups of café au lait, before L. goes to his glass-brick house to work. I lie and dream, some-times falling back asleep, overcome these days by an overwhelm-

ing desire to drowse, and I give in to the luxury of this without a qualm, falling into hot chocolate like a marshmallow melting and turning loose—yes, this is happiness. On awakening it's time to prepare our lunch, which I bring from the kitchen to eat in the living room on the coffee table, now put to use as our dining table, set with best linen and cutlery. After this, a siesta with L., later I'll read from my special pile of books on the subject of Expectant Motherhood or Natural Childbirth, or drowse some more, looking forward to sunset time when I'll rouse myself to knock on the door of the glass-brick room where L. is working, time for our daily stroll down the road and through the meadow. How ravishing the scent of new-mown hay, as we pick the buttercups and Queen Anne's lace to put in vases around our house, for we are never flowerless. Dinner, and afterwards, every evening, I read aloud. We just finished *The Master of Ballantrae* and tonight start *War and Peace*. In fairy tales it's often said—be careful what you wish for, you might get it . . . how little they know, these tellers of tales!

So many plans to make—what to name the baby? It will be a girl and will look exactly like me, L. is certain, so of course I'm not even thinking it's a boy, although secretly I want it to be. I would feel so proud giving Leopold a son—his only son. But I keep this to myself and we make lists of girls' names, always coming back to Maria or Marya, spelled and pronounced in the Polish way, which I prefer. Imagine! Soon there will be a new person in the world—Maria Stokowska. A new person who will be Leopold and Gloria in equal measure, merged as in Leopold's and surely then he will trust me, tell me that most treasured and secret truth about himself that I thought I knew but do not, that secret no one else in the whole world knows . . . he will, he will! won't he? Until then, my faith does not waver even for a moment, for as his hand touches my belly, the baby turns within me, feet kicking, belief is restored and I wait in joy, for surely now his trust in me shall come to be, as our baby shall come to be. Yes, the time is soon at hand.

There are other plans to think on: more space is needed, a larger house in the country, also a place in New York. Yes, the city! At first, L. didn't want any permanent ties there—too far from the beautiful nature—but the demands of his work now make it necessary. He's conducting more and more in New York and will be conducting in Europe and all over the United States, and even though I will, of course, go with him, we'll need, with a family, firm bases to return to. Although I don't tell him, I'm really glad that perhaps we'll be in New York more. Carol's so far away, and L. doesn't encourage friends around—rightly so, of course, for they only intrude on our happiness, and all we want is to be alone together. Still, when he's away at rehearsals (I'd never breathe this to another soul) it gets sort of lonely, sometimes. Other plans are also afoot, travel is much on his mind as he looks forward to being able to accept, after the baby's born, invitations that flood in from orchestras all over the world, requesting him to be their guest conductor. Of course the baby and I will travel with him, and he's never said so, but he feels tied down sometimes, I know, having had to turn down so many engagements to be with me while I'm pregnant. He misses Europe, talks about it constantly, saying we'll be able to go there a lot now that the war is really behind us. I just listen and try not to let anything shake the circle of our happiness. I want nothing to change; as it is now, may it be forever so. I have everything I've ever dreamed about—a home surrounded by Leopold's love and soon our baby. Forever and ever in one place— that's what I want—it's not too much to ask, is it? So when this talk of travel all over the world looms over us, making me afraid, I say to myself, as Scarlett did—I'll think about it tomorrow— tomorrow at Tara.

A Letter from Sadja

August 23, 1950

Dear Gloria,

Having just heard the happy news, I want to write you at once and tell you how wonderful I think it is. How are you feeling? Is everything all right? I do hope so.

It must be lovely to have a baby son. What does he look like? What are you going to name him?

I hope you won't have to stay long in the hospital. But do take awfully good care, as I'm sure you will.

It is difficult to write this, Gloria, because we know each other so little. But I do want to tell you that what I say comes from the heart, sincerely. I know that you have made Daddy very happy, and this baby will of course make him even more

so. This would make me feel thankful to you even if I did not
know you. But as I do know you, something more is added.
I like you and want to wish you all happiness.

You are doubtless inundated with congratulations and good
wishes from many friends, and will be busy for a long time
recuperating and answering them. However, if you have a
spare moment, I would be awfully glad to hear from you about
how you are, and what the little one is like. And of course,
if there is ever any way in which I can be of help to you, you
need only ask.

I close with hopes that you will be up and strong soon,
and that your baby is well.

With love and best wishes to you,

Sadja

Oh yes! Inundated with joy. I sit up in this hospital bed with
the baby in a crib beside me and I keep looking and looking at
him, almost afraid that if I don't keep my eyes fastened on him
he'll disappear and it will all turn out to be a dream. It's as if
everyone in the whole world, even people I don't know, are so
happy L. has a son they have to express it in some way—flowers,
telegrams, letters keep arriving and arriving. There's no room
anymore for the flowers and the nurse keeps bringing them in
and taking them out again and still they keep arriving and arriving. Having a baby—giving birth—is not the way I expected
it to be. No—not at all. For one thing—it really does hurt. A
lot. I expected that, but believed what I'd read in Dr. Grantley
Dick Reed's book *Natural Childbirth* that "the pain is not unlike
a severe menstrual cramp" (ha, ha—some cramp!). Luckily we'd
driven from Innisfree to our new apartment at Gracie Square two
weeks before the baby was expected, just in case it came earlier,
and the very first night we were there I woke up at four a.m. in
a flood of water, called Doctor Finn, and he said to go immediately
to New York Hospital. We drove there through the quiet city
streets not saying anything, with L. holding my hand. I was

powerful, poised on the edge of something stupendous. He kept
on holding my hand as I lay in the hospital room waiting for the
labor to start, but after a few contractions everything would stop
and soon light came into the room from the sun over the East
River. Hours and hours went by, the contractions coming only
now and then, with doctors and nurses coming in and out—time
drifting along like this, with L. always beside me. I dozed off
to sleep, and when I woke up it was dark outside and a pain
went through my body quite suddenly and I cried out. There
was a lot of flurry and hurry and footsteps and L. walked beside
the bed as I was wheeled up to the delivery room. I'd told Doctor
Finn I didn't want any anesthetic but soon I was pleading for it,
the pain kept getting beyond me, beyond anything I had expected, beyond anything I had ever known, shot out of a cannon—
it was like that. A mask was put over my face and I started
hurling in space through a long dark tunnel, endlessly faster and

faster, stars and clacks of light kept flashing on and off on either side, and suddenly three people were hurling along through the tunnel with me. But who? They were familiar, but I could not place them, and we were going so fast in a flash they were left behind, and all at once coming towards me from the great distance—a figure, one of those doll toys that have a gourd-shaped body and can't stay put, as you tip it over it bounces back up again. It bobbed closer and closer—"Moosha Moo," it said, bowing and smiling as we rushed past each other. (Later I was to learn that in Chinese this means Welcome.) I hurled on, rushing into the light far far ahead at the end of the tunnel, dazzling it became as I got closer, so dazzling I knew it was the light of God I hurled towards—knew I was to enter into the center of God, knew that I was to know the secret of the universe. Propelled forwards, I hit the light, blinded for an instant as I crashed through, and as I did the answer came to me. It was so—simple— yes, so simple. And at the same time . . . there was something, something humorous—yes, tenderly humorous—about it . . . why hadn't I known before! I'll remember when I go back, this secret of the universe, hold fast to the answer. Oh yes! I'll remember . . . light flooded me and the sun and the glory of the son and I knew I had given birth to a boy and that it was the happiest moment of my life.

And this answer, so great and yet so simple? Do I remember? I keep thinking about it, but the more I do, the farther away it gets and whatever it was, or is—I can't for the life of me remember.

Day and Night

Our son is named Leopold Stanislas Stokowski III and we are ensconced, he and I, in the larger house we have moved to on Round Hill Road, still in Greenwich. L. expected us to go with

him on tour, but the baby's so little and I'm still not quite back
into my body again, a few months from now it will be easier for
us both to travel. So that is why for the moment the baby and
I are alone here in this house on the hill. Dodo sometimes comes
and stays with us and it's nice, the three of us (You and I together,
Love—Never mind the weather, Love), our world defined by the
baby, Stan. There are days when I paint or try to, but often my
mind is elsewhere, missing Leopold. Missing him and thinking
about things. Like Carol and Bill. They're divorced now for the
second time. She lives in a house in Santa Monica with Lucy,
her daughter—Aram's in school—and Bill lives in a house on
the beach at Malibu. She goes back and forth to pick up his
laundry and I think about her a lot, that drive back and forth
from one house to the other with piles of laundry in the backseat,
taking it back to her house to wash and returning it next day to
Bill, neat and crisp—for that's what she does. Then into my

mind comes what she said that night—remember?—in the railroad station in Reno—about living off of someone else's smile.
Do we measure our worth by the measure of the man who loves
us—hold fast, once we have found in his reflection the love we
seek, become desperate if we sense it slipping away, become
driven—do anything to hold on to it? Do we all live off someone
else's smile? Lately, there are moments when I touch another part
of myself, a center, hidden though it may be, it's there, a place
that has nothing to do with Leopold, or my mother, or for that
matter anyone at all. It only has to do with me. But I've only
recently become acquainted with it, will have to know it better
before I give faith to it, quite believe in it.

What I do believe in, have faith in, is the bed we share,
Leopold and I; there, in that night place, is love and freedom.
Joy. How close we are—yes, there, without question I possess
all of him. But I want more. In that other place, the world
outside our bed, he still holds back. But does he? Sometimes I
feel he doesn't, that it's his way, for he talks in essences, pronouncements, never elaborating on the subject at hand. Still—
what isn't said, I fill in, or try to, and in this way, quite often,
feel close to him, very close indeed, as if we are part of some
great thing, in a deep subterranean river that is our love and does
not need to be defined. I am secure then, sure that we have
merged by day as we have by night when no words are necessary,
would in fact intrude. However brief those moments are, the
time will come—it must!—when the strength of my love will
reach through to him and I will possess him by day as I do by
night. And as for the part of him I already have, well—I'd do
anything to keep that. And so it's true, I suppose, that I too live
off of someone else's smile.

It's lonely sometimes here when he's away, and yesterday it
was a treat to go to Betsy Close's for lunch. She's a friend of L.'s
since the war, when she organized a concert in Paris in 1939 for

the American Aid Society. She started talking about the United
Nations and what an uproar the Greenwich community got into,
opposed to the U.N. building here—What do you think about
it? she said. I looked nonplussed and she smiled in a most friendly
way, Haven't you a mind of your own? Yes I do, I said quickly,
Leopold's mind! Yes, can you believe it, that's what I said. And
I meant it. It was only later I got to thinking about it, about
Leopold and this mind of his which has become my mind (the
better to please him with, my dear). But after I'd said that, it
didn't occur to me that there was anything to question, it was
more like a—a—boast on my part. Yes, definitely a boast. I sat
there enjoying the cheese soufflé, quite pleased with myself,
listening to Betsy as she gave me her views on the U.N. situation.
It was really neat having a lunch like this, and it did cross my
mind that I wished we saw more people, went out more often,
for we live, in many ways, a most isolated life, we two. Going
to the village movie as it changes weekly is our big outing. Many
evenings we read aloud, and I kept thinking now of *Vanity Fair*,
last night when I'd come to the last page—"Ah! *Vanitas Vani-*
tatum!"—and Leopold had interrupted me. Indeed! he had said,
nodding sagely, *Vanitas Vanitatum!* He waved his hand, indi-
cating that I should continue, and on I went—"Ah! *Vanitas*
Vanitatum! which of us is happy in this world? Which of us has
his desire? or, having it, is satisfied?—come, children, let us
shut up the box and the puppets, for our play is played out.
. . . Finis," I read and closed the book. L. had put his head back
to mull it over. Ah! yes—Vanity Fair! Clearly he took a dim
view of it, but it was those puppets I was mulling over. Vanity
Fair! he mused, Vanity Fair! which brought him to the Princess
Evangeline and her Georgian Prince and their silly society friends.

But that's not what I mean when I sometimes wish we saw
more people, that's not what I have in mind at all—it's contact
with other humans, and now there is Stan to consider. He'll have
to have friends when he's growing up, won't he? That's not silly

society, but as Leopold went on and on I kept nodding my head yes, yes, yes, while somewhere within me, right up from the center, something stirred, rather like a kitten who's been sleeping and wakes up oh! so slowly, opens its eyes, and turns over . . . or was it a tiger?

Hotels

It was a long tour, weeks and weeks. Hotel rooms aren't home. Stan cried a lot, at night more than during the day. Just when we'd settle into one hotel, the concert was over and it would be time to pack up and move on. Now we're home, but only for a week before we start packing again. There's endless packing and unpacking, and just when I thought I couldn't, couldn't pack up again so soon, and about to say something, I found out I'm pregnant again. It's close after Stan's birth, but I'm so happy— now I'll have to stay in one place, maybe he'll stay with me, tour less? But he can't, of course, his concerts are booked a year ahead, still he's trying to rearrange things so that even though he'll be away most of the time while I'm pregnant, he'll be with me when the baby's born in January. He's as thrilled as I am. This time, he says, it will be Maria.

L. wants to build a bomb shelter on our land. He draws sketches of it. Shipshape as can be, with shelves for lots of cans— tuna, tomato soup, and so on, you get the picture. He's quite an architect. I think it's a foolish idea, but I keep quiet and just make a suggestion here and there, like, How about putting the bunk beds here instead of there?—things like that. What, I'd like to ask him, what if the bomb does explode and we're in our shelter, what's to prevent desperate people who don't have a shelter coming and taking ours? That is, if there are any people left around and about, desperate or otherwise. Anyway—who wants to live in a world where a bomb shelter is called home?

. . .

Leopoldo was against it, but while I'm waiting for the baby I want to be in the city at Gracie Square instead of in the country. Now, even though he's away, I feel closer to things, less isolated. He wants me to meet him in Europe next month where he'll be conducting the Royal Philharmonic, go on with him to Milan, etc., etc. Let me wait and see how I feel, I said, see if the doctor thinks it's all right to travel. Maybe I *should* go? Take Stan with me? It exhausts me, this thought—the trying to make a hotel room into a home room. And it never works. I love it here by the river with the baby.

And Dodo—she's here with us in her own apartment. It's part of ours, but separate, for as you enter our hallway there's a door on the left which leads into another area, complete with room and bath, with a narrow staircase leading to two rooms, one of which has been converted to a kitchen. All is sufficient unto itself, and it's as if she lives close by in her own little house next door, just as I dreamed it would be when I made those drawings long ago—the house the three of us would live in someday when I grew up, the Little Countess, Big Elephant, and me, so that no one would ever have power to separate us from our Caravan again.

And now it's all come true—except for the Little Countess, of course—she's still living at the Hotel Fourteen, nothing's changed there, except I did persuade her, finally, to move out of her one room looking out onto the elevator shaft. How dark it was in that room which was our Caravan, but we were happy there. She's moved now, at my insistence, across the hall to a suite of rooms where you can tell when it's day by the sunlight coming through windows that look out onto city streets, with people walking and cars moving, instead of dim silence. Yes, they're rooms filled with sunlight. Still—it's not the same. I guess some things you shouldn't try to change, and I've made myself stop pestering her with my wishing, wishing she'd spend more money on herself (now that I have it to give to her), but it's not in her nature. She saves it all, invests in the stock market, and walks around the corner to Schrafft's or Caruso's every late afternoon for her one meal of the day and picks up the newspapers on her way home, just like she always did. She doesn't buy clothes or anything, and the old tweedy orange knit sweater is still a favorite. All her money is being saved to leave to her own flesh and blood when she's in her grave . . . those fatal words are still spoken, and they make me wince as they did long ago.

Dodo, on the other hand, enjoys life more. She has a picture, framed and hanging, on the wall just as you enter her apartment—it's a poem about an old woman by the wayside wandering, but now she wanders no more, because she has a home—you get the gist. Above the poem is a drawing of a woman trudging along a road in Ireland (it must be Ireland because of the stone cottages and thatched roofs)—she has a pack on her back with all her worldly possessions, and the carrying of them makes her stoop over, leaning on her cane as she goes down the byway which stretches way far far away, disappearing into the final distance of a trembly inky line.

So I have accomplished much—Dodo has a home, and Naney a room with sunlight. Now if I could only please them in other ways everything would be perfect. Well, one way I do please them, both of them, is—Stan. His birth is heralded as a great and real achievement, and rightly so! We often visit Dodo in her house next door, the baby and I, sitting in her kitchen while I feed him and she makes tea. We chat away about nothing at all as the kettle comes to a boil and the clock tick-tocks, back and forth, on the wall. It's peaceful, like it's been there forever and always will be.

Other times Dodo does small things about the house, maybe goes to the agency if we need a replacement in our staff to interview applicants before I finally meet and decide, things like that, and it is through her that Nora Mulkerins came to us. She'd just come off the plane from Galway and is like a maiden in a Gaelic fairy tale. She's lovely as can be and helps me with the baby, she can cook and sew and there is no end to her gifts. People come and go—but I have a feeling Nora and I will be together for a long long time.

The only—well, how can I put it? fly in the ointment? sand in the oyster? mosquito buzzing around?—is the awful Smokey. Remember? The very same as in Junction City, Kansas. Only now that he's ancient, he's truly impossible. And he doesn't even take to the baby, imagine! In a perpetual snarl is he, and has to be locked in another room every time we visit. Dodo says, Dogs can't hurt you the way people do, and it gets to me in the same way that it does when Naney says, . . . when your Naney's in her grave, darling mine! (Sometimes I even feel she loves Smokey more than she loves me.) Then there are the marches he and Dodo take around and around the terraces every morning, quite military these marches, as if important matters are to be attended to, a destination to be reached.

It's funny, but you know, Dodo and Naney never see each other anymore, no, they are never in touch. After all they went through together, you'd think—oh, well, maybe that's why. We never talk about it either, Dodo and I, the Custody Trial, nor do we talk about her child who died in Ireland after she left her husband. I found out only recently that she had once not only been married but had a son!!! Yes, when she was sixteen she was married to Ernest Ball, who composed "When Irish Eyes Are Smiling" and "My Wonderful One" (Bill Saroyan's favorite song). What stunned me was that I couldn't imagine her having a life before she was—there—with me. But all children are that way, I guess, because it's only later you get a sense of time past, in time present, going on into time future. She has a portrait miniature of her son dressed in a pale blue sailor suit the same blue color as his eyes, and a hat with a blue pompon. All she's revealed is that she left Ernest Ball in sudden flight from a disastrous marriage, leaving their son with her sisters-in-law who loved him so, but they let him go out in the damp, without leggings, to show off his new suit and he caught a chill. Five he was when he died . . . and tears fill her eyes and I put my arms around her, craving to know more, but keeping quiet so as not to upset her any more than she already is.

You can see why I don't want to uproot us again just as we're settling into a real home. But then I remember the times when L. and I are apart, the ache with the missing of him. Maybe I should go—alone, without Stan, just to be with him for a few weeks? But the hotels, the going in and out, the endless corridors to elevators—right back where I was once upon a time long ago. Only now it's different, or it should be, because I'm the mother. Only sometimes it's not—different.

Forget I said that. It's not true anyway. I was only in a shaky mood because L. had just left. Letters from him come every day, and even though they are brief as Western Union telegrams or bulletins from Valhalla, they all say he loves me and I'm all set with passage on the *Queen Elizabeth*. Well into my fourth month and the doctor says it's safe to travel, so I'm all packed and set to go.

Peonies and Roses, 1951

At the last minute, daring though it was, I decided to fly over instead of going by ship as planned. Daring on my part because since the plane crash we were in, L.'s vowed we must never set foot in the air again. It's odd, because at the time he wasn't bothered by it and only now, years after, the possible dangers seep through to him. Anyway, I'm not one bit afraid of flying, so, not wanting to upset him, I asked Dodo to phone him in London once I was on the plane, leave word at the last minute that I'd be there in a few hours. From the airport I went straight to the Connaught Hotel, up to our room. The first thing I saw as I walked in was a vase of big fat white peonies and a letter.

Darling

I am so happy you came. The moment the rehearsal finishes I will rush to you.

If you will ring the bell the waitress will bring your breakfast. Have a good rest.

Very very soon
Leopoldo

Oh! it was lovely, everything. And I rang the bell and started unpacking. Almost immediately a personage from *The Merry Wives of Windsor* entered, wearing black with white apron and cap, starchy and jolly as could be. Tea with milk, please, toast and marmalade, I said, and soon there I was sitting in front of an open window having breakfast in the sunlight. All at once from the street below came the sound of a barrel organ, that tinny sound that tugs, you might say, at your heart strings. There's something, a *je ne sais quoi* about it—and now here it was rolling out "Roses of Picardy," bringing tears to my eyes (oh, well, we all have our little foibles). After breakfast I took a bath, a long soak in a rose-scented tub, and put on my best nightgown. Another Merry Wife came to remove the breakfast table, and when she left I pulled the curtains and stretched out in bed and thought about very very soon . . . my hair has grown long, long enough to sit on, and I brushed it out on the pillow, turned over and fell into deep slumber, and only woke up because his arms were around me . . . how close we were in that darkened room so long ago with sunlight filtering through the green silk curtains—why couldn't that have been enough?

The audience went wild as always at the concert. I'm so proud to be his wife. To think that in all the world it's me he's chosen. Oh, I'm so happy, happy I came here. He's different here, more open and giving to people, less suspicious—the truth is he really would like to live in Europe all the time. After the concert we had supper in our rooms at the Connaught, lobster thermidor in a silvered chafing dish, there were lilacs in a bowl on the table, pêche sorbet, and crystal goblets for the Château d'Yquem. To-morrow, he said quite formally, extending an invitation, to-morrow will you come with me to Bournemouth by the sea? There's someone there I want you to meet. Oh! yes, I said, yes, please—who? who am I going to meet? Tomorrow, he said, I'll tell you tomorrow—when we're on the train.

Someone to meet someone to meet, that's what he'd said—someone to meet. But when we got on the train he was silent, either looking out the window or examining the score he'd brought along in a briefcase filled with papers and other things. I waited, not wanting to push him or speak too soon, knowing that in his own time he'd tell me who this someone to meet was. Well, he would, wouldn't he? He'd said so last night. But his own time stretched on and on as the train chugged on and on and I got an awful headache. Out loud I said, I have an awful headache. But he bent closer over the score and made another notation on the music as if he hadn't heard. There was a bouquet of red roses wrapped in a cone of shiny white patenty paper on the seat beside him in our compartment, to be presented to the someone to meet. I kept looking at it, and the more I looked at it, the more jittery I became about the whole thing. Not only about this excursion, but about my place in the scheme of things, because for me the so-called scheme of things was only one thing—Him. And now there was this Someone to Meet person hovering around. I tapped on the window to catch his attention. Leopoldo—look at me, please, will you? And he did, but it was from elsewhere that the look came, you know—that place in him I can't get at. Please, tell me who we're going to meet. He put the score aside—long silence, long long long, but finally he did speak, gazing out at the cows clumped here and there in the meadows as we chugged past. The person we're going to see is she who took care of me as a child after my mother died, she lives in Bournemouth now, in a nursing home. Yes, by the sea by the sea, I said, willing him to turn towards me, but he kept staring out the window. Tight shut. What a fool to believe I was close to him, possessed him even in small measure, when I did not know until this moment that this person so dear to him was alive somewhere in the world. I wanted to jump off the train, show him that I too knew how to push away, shut tight. What's her name? I said. But he didn't answer as we chugged on and on past the cows. Does she know about me? I said. Yes, I have told her. . . . I walked out into the passage outside our compartment. A woman carrying a baby was coming towards me. The baby was screaming and flaying its infant arms as the woman squeezed past me— Baby, what's your name? I whispered—but it swayed on, down the passageway, in the woman's arms and disappeared out of sight into the next car. . . .

I can't go with you, I said, I'll wait here in the station until you get back. As you wish, he said coldly. But then he turned back, hesitated, She'll be so disappointed, she's been looking forward—(Looking forward, looking forward, I wanted to shout— and what do you think I've been doing, looking backward?! Of course that's just what I was doing, although I only know that now.) I closed my eyes and shook my head and tried to think of nothing at all, at all, and when I opened them he had gone. Maybe he was never going to come back. I walked around the station, jumpy, electrical plug pushed into the wrong current, itching for a train to pull up so that I could go back to London on my own—leave him before he left me—*that* would get through to him. But the station was quiet, the tracks deserted except for a stupid cat sitting between the rails, methodically washing its face in the sunlight with its irritating paws. Quite suddenly I was exhausted and I sat down on a bench to wait—maybe he really wasn't going to come back? and I started trembling, but there he was, standing in front of me, without the red roses. What a short visit it had been and now I wasn't scared at all, anger had come back and a presentation scene ran through my head: wheelchair in the solarium, placed facing the ocean, nurses hovering around, to catch a glimpse of *him*, an autograph or two maybe—"It's for my little girl, please"—she with lap robe and lacy knitted shawl, arms stretched out as he bounds towards her with the red roses, instead she's looking past him for the *me* she'd been told of. In the distance oh so faintly the sound of the sea, or is it a concertina on the beach droning out "I'll take you home again, Kathleen" (now I've gone too far)—yes, it was all clear as clear could be. Except her face—for a Dodo face kept coming to mind, still, that wasn't right either, and a Leopold face settled itself onto the hunched body of the person in the wheelchair and wouldn't go away. But it was too grotesque. . . .

Still, this Leopold face shadowed me on the silent ride back to London as it did for a long time after. It's only now, hundreds of years later, that I wish I'd behaved differently. Perhaps it was a test, that day long ago, a test he devised to see if I was worthy of his trust? And had I passed it—I would have reached through to him. But I was a different person from the one I am now, therefore it's fruitless, this wish of mine, for it couldn't have happened any other way than the way it did. Isn't that true? Things happen as they do, even though later they would have happened in another way. However, I do now and again wish it had been otherwise, and yes, the person I am today would have handled it differently. For the *she* I felt so threatened by would have been someone I'd very much want to meet, someone I'd very much want to know, because, of course, it wasn't his nurse (I know now)—it was his mother.

And my mother—what of her? I never hear from her, but I know that she and Aunt Thelma are seeing Naney Napoleon again. Just like that, as if nothing ever happened. How could that be, after all the terrible things that had come to pass, after Naney had said all those things in court about my mother? Well, the Little Countess always did say "Blood is thicker than water," and there they all are, back together again, happy as clams. Some clambake! I wonder if they talk about it—the Custody Trial—

or is it never mentioned, pushed aside as they talk of this and that, yes, just as though it never happened? Naney's perfume these days is Blue Diamond, and there's a big bottle of it unopened on her dresser. Just like Shalimar, Naney says, as she sniffs proudly at the sealed bottle. It looks like a diamond, this bottle, sort of, and is a bluey sort of color. It's a present from my mother, who has gone into the perfume business with Maurice Chalom. Naney Morgan gets tight-lipped if I bring his name up. Her penciled eyebrows curve up into an arc of disapproval, suggesting unspeakable things, things too dastardly to mention, not only regarding Maurice but—other things as well. However, I don't press her for news, don't want her to think I'm interested, that it matters to me. Less and less I see of her, although she comes sometimes to L.'s concerts at Carnegie Hall where we sit, two strangers side by side, in the box looking towards the stage, listening. It's never been the same between us since that time I broke down on the floor at the Hotel Fourteen when Naney offhandedly mentioned that it would never do to marry Winter Smith—No! For me to be Mrs. Smith did not suit her at all at all—being in love had nothing to do with marriage! Her words stick to me like the worm under the leaf and I try to forget, but just as I do, she'll say something cynical—it's hopeless, hopeless, to try and explain anything to her. Still, it's through her I can hear news about my mother, whom I want to know about but don't want to know about, if you know what I mean. Mummy . . . pushed down, far down inside me, and although I know she and the Queen Jonquil are living in a house somewhere in Beverly Hills, I don't know what street it's on, and even if I did, I don't know if I'd ever bring myself to mail the letters I write to her now and then. These letters don't get very far anyway— too much to say and not enough words. There's a certain monotony to them as well, each one ends up with Mummy at the top of the page and then the long sit as I wonder how to proceed because my head gets jammed up, clogged, and it ends up with nothing written on the letter except Mummy at the top, and then a stretch of white going on down to the bottom of the page, and if you turn it over, there it is blank on the other side too.

I'm on the *Queen Elizabeth* on my way back home—L. was frantic when I took the plane to London, made me promise I'd never fly again, ever. So of course I won't. It's nice on the ship and I spend a lot of time drifting along and sleeping, all the flotsam and jetsam of my unintegrated self moored, anchored fast to the center of me. For there is a center—it's only when I'm not pregnant I tend to forget. What I'd really like best of all (I'd never tell anyone this) is to be pregnant all the time, never not. Yes, really. Does that make any sense? It has something to do with feeling I'm doing the most important thing in the world without doing anything but just being. I don't know a soul on the boat except for a Good Evening and Good Night to Mr. and Mrs. Robert Johnson. He's the Princess Evangeline's brother and they have an early dinner every night at the table next to me in the Verandah Grill. I hadn't a clue who they were until the second night when they introduced themselves. I'd like to talk to them but can't think of how to start up a conversation. The high points are the radiograms from L., sometimes two in a day. This morning the baby kicked for the first time. I was lying in bed reading and all at once, sure as could be, the book almost got knocked out of my hands. Looking down I could see the skin of my belly pushed up by the little foot I carried within me. Right now I don't miss L. so much—well, I do, but I'm practicing getting used to it. There are months and months ahead before his tour is over, before he'll be—there's a knock on the door. It's the steward with another radiogram.

LOVE YOU FOREVER

LEOPOLDO

Yes, months and months before he'll be home again with Stan and me, but it's going to be all right because he and I—oh! yes—he and I are love and forever.

My Star

Well, he does write a lot. Cables too—but phone calls are complicated, he's moving around so much. All his letters are in a box on the night table by our bed, but they're not all that different from the cables. He's not what you'd call a wordy writer, and I keep reading them over and over trying to read between the lines, letters from Venice, San Sebastián, Loyola, Begona, Santiago, Montserrat, Madrid, Lisboa, Paris, Lucerne—well, I could go on and on. Stan's first birthday in August came and went, and weeks ago I finished rereading the complete works of Jane Austen, and now it's November and soon, soon, yes, by Thanksgiving, the long wait will be over and Leopoldo will be home. Since I got back from London we've been living in Greenwich during the heat of summer and it's been different this time, living alone here with Stan, very. I'm pregnant, all-powerful; nothing, not even planetary wars, could shake the orbit of my star.

All week preparing! Stan and I, as we polish tables with lemony wax, driving to Purdy's roadside market for vegetables, honey from the hives, fill bowls with apples, pile logs high in fireplaces ready to be lit. The long wait soon will be over . . . very very soon. Soon I will be driving to meet him through this most beautiful of autumns, soon—soon he will be home.

It was night still when I started driving into the city to meet him at the apartment. Not a car on the road until I reached the Merritt Parkway. Then suddenly it was light and cars appeared in front and behind and I was caught in commuters' traffic moving slow, then fast, then slow again, until I thought I'd go mad. But when I finally got there it wasn't because of the traffic that I missed him, it was because he'd given me the wrong time—

arrived from the ship much earlier—and when he'd arrived at the apartment and I wasn't there he'd left left left . . . and there he was when I got back to Greenwich, playing piggyback with Stan, bouncing him up and down, and I'd missed it all, missed his seeing Stan for the first time after all these many months. As for seeing me—he was distant, angry that I hadn't been there to meet him at the boat, almost as if I'd done it on purpose. But, anyway—very soon after, we made love and everything was put right again.

But not for long. A week later there he was charting out the tours that would flow on into the next year when this year's tours were over and after that on into infinity. Well, he would be here in January when the baby was born, and right now that's really all I care about.

Excerpts

It's eleven days over my due date. L.'s gone. He'd planned his schedule most carefully, allowing one week so he could be with us when and after the baby was born, but the time came and went and nothing happened, so he couldn't wait any longer. After Cleveland, where he is now, he's going on to Minneapolis and then on somewhere else and he won't be back for weeks and weeks. Please wait just a few days more, I kept saying, until the baby's born. Castor oil maybe? But the doctor said no, wait. As for L., he didn't say yes or no, and up to the last minute I thought maybe he wouldn't go. It must be my fault, but trying to reach him is like trying to break through a brick wall. (What exactly would I find if I did get through?) It's been that way since he got back from the last tour, and I try and try to please him, but it doesn't make a dent, and the more I try, the more distant he gets, except by night—no brick wall there, but day comes and there it is again, brick on brick, and there I am again, trying to get through. We spent an evening with Gian-Carlo Menotti and Sam Barber and they started talking about travel (no kidding) and places L. had been to—India and so on. May I ask you, Sam said to L., did you travel alone or with someone? Oh, alone, L. answered. Ah, yes! Sam said. Alone but free! Thanks a lot, Sam—but I kept quiet as usual. Alone but free! Maybe he's right.

I found one of those few-lines-a-day five-year diaries, which I bought, really because of its burnished claret-color leather, sensuous to touch. But I started writing in it and got in the habit of keeping this up every day. Lately I've taken to turning back the pages reading, leafing around here and there, reading without sequence back over our years together, hoping to find clues, discover maybe what has brought me to this place where I feel alone but far from free.

September 12   Mood all day of feeling that all is over between L. and me—forever. The impervious spirit I can't reach past. An almost crying edge of reaction to it. But I can and will control it. I will not be destroyed. I will go my way alone.

April 23   The *only* thing a woman truly wants and needs to be fulfilled is to be so secure in her man that when she closes the door that is the world.

February 5   To get driver's license. The long waiting in line, the dreariness. Happy serene evening with L. Think I have the answer.

February 14   Cold better. In bed with waves of life flooding me. The urge powerful and strong to live, to enjoy, to be. L. returns and I am happy. All serene. Feeling better. The fire and I dry my hair in its warmth as L. touches it.

February 20   Judy gives me birthday party. I feel like a true birthday child. The cake with soft sugar flowers on it. Lots of presents, among them a little ivory box with flowers painted on it. There were ice cream animal shapes in a nest of spun sugar with the cake and I wore the blue blouse with Brussels lace, made a wish as I blew out the candles. "Ah! Child, be careful what you wish for—it might come true."

June 2   Work all day at studio. Complete loss of time. Later to party. Horrible people. P.M. breaks a table. R.D. comes later—his obtuseness. The beauty alone in the studio, the horror of the people. Long for L.

March 4   Scene with Dodo. I must simply realize that she does not comprehend and never will. I have done all I could and still she is not satisfied and this leaves me deeply sad.

April 5   L. arrives. A great feeling of peace and a new cycle beginning. The fact that he will be here for a long period fills me with joy.

April 6   Great happiness with L. Early movie and studio dinner. I think he is pleased too at this new beginning.

April 7   Great pride and joy in going with L. and Stan to *Snow White*. Then Orsini. The feeling of circle and warmth flowing.

April 29   Moment at studio. Must realize that the L. inside of the G. can only meet on certain planes. Must keep it light with the deep stream of unsaid things giving it substance and truth.

January 10   Feel the only way L. and I can meet is on the physical plane. And, after all, this is something to cherish and build on.

January 11   Serene time with L. at studio. Must work more and discipline myself more.

April 9   L. and I take Stan to puppet show. Feeling of claustrophobia and noise. L.'s tension. We leave. I walk in the rain. Later as he makes love to me—the shadows on the ceiling from the fire—Paris, remember?

May 5   Terrible pressure from L. Man overheard talking to woman sitting next to me at hamburger counter: "I've always wanted to recapture again the child mood of supper at 5:30 eating bread and butter and rhubarb—the sun streaming through the window—but never have." Yes, it's what I call the Hour Between, day ending, night not yet begun. Tried doing needlepoint to tide over from end into beginning, but it's boring boring. Feel the power of L.'s personality trying to invade me.

August 7   Convinced that the power of longing attracts. That if one wants something enough and long enough—it will *Be*. Attracted by the electric current.

September 13   L. has closed his heart to me and I cannot reach him. Friendly yet nervous tension as I steel myself for his departure. Mixed feelings—relief—deep sadness—loneliness—coping alone again. Need time to myself to dry the feathers of a wounded bird. The air odd like false summer, strange El Greco sky.

May 27   Dodo's birthday party. Stan thrilled by it. Feel disoriented—with few roots. Alone in shallow water at the time the tide is at low ebb. Miss L. Feel quiet.

June 1   A letter this morning from L. that made me warm and deeply happy. I feel his love enfolding me. Later the moment working at the studio—the pigeons on the roof, voluptuous sound drawing me into it, soothing and beckoning.

June 6   Pregnant! Settling into bliss once more—oh how I wish he were here—but reached him in Paris. He sounded so happy. All is well and always will be. Soon he'll be *home*.

August 19   Strange illness during the day, borderline hovering between the world of vitality and the shadowy netherworld of unknowns. Dr. C. says stay in bed. Have terrible fear might miscarry, but knowing L. gets home tomorrow makes me hold on.

August 20   Have never felt so strongly the physical limitations of being a woman. We are bound by functional cycles. The fact of femininity pounds in every nerve and becomes the *whole*. Dr. C. comes. Later taken bleeding by ambulance to St. Luke's.

August 21   Miscarriage. Devastated. Dr. C. says often women get pregnant quickly after a miscarriage. I keep praying.

August 22   Home from hospital. L. in country closing house. The beauty of the day and the garden gay with flowers outside St. Luke's. Nerves very near surface. Glad to be home again.

And then I come to this entry written when I was pregnant once more—this time with Chris.

December 3   Terrible scene with L. He's accepted concert dates so near the time the baby's expected. Walked in snow streets. Wild thought about trying to reach Auntie Gladys asking her to be with me when the baby's born if L.'s not here. But she'd think I was insane—haven't been in touch with her since Old Westbury Capital.

December 26   Serene day with L. before he leaves. He'll be back in time for the baby—that is, if the baby arrives on time. Feel that slowly we can work towards a new life together with greater understanding and happiness. Can it be? Great happiness last night.

April 9 Serene day again and peace of mind, sense of well-being everywhere even though L. is gone. Worked well all day at studio.

I stop reading the back excerpts and come to the entry of today, the words I've just written—

January 29 Letter this morning from L. a little tentacle reaching me. I will never be capable of giving again as I did to him, and, because of this, I will never be free of my longing to reach him. Reread his letters to me when we first met. Shattered.

Later: He called to say he's coming back, told the press he's canceling his concert "for personal reasons" (the baby's birth). Sweetheart, I'll be with you soon. That's what he said.

The Son and the Glory of the Sun

The day he got back and the day after, nothing happened. He was in that other place, distracted, and made it very clear that although he had canceled the Cleveland concert—as he put it to the public—for "personal reasons," there would be no canceling of the Minneapolis concert for any reason personal or otherwise. Castor oil? I said again to the doctor, for the baby was now thirteen days late. If labor doesn't start tomorrow, he said—all right. That morning at 5:10 I woke up, no mistaking it—this was it, and we got to the hospital and I was taken right to the delivery room.

The pains came close together and had been strong almost from the beginning. But this time I was on top of them, because

I'd been there before—yes, and as I speeded on through the tunnel I knew what was ahead, knew that this time when I came back, I would remember. On and on, hurtling past lights, past the three people I knew but didn't know, and there as before coming towards me—Moosha Mco! and, as I crashed into the sun a cry exploded from the light surrounding me and through this blaze the crying followed me as I came back again, back into that room with a wall above me and whiteness all around me and I saw a circle—a wafer of light which was the moon, but no, it was a clock, a big clock hanging on the wall, with hands pointing to 8:01, precisely—and I knew that I had returned, and that I was not alone for my son had been born! and the glory of the sun and the son and the gold had returned with me. I held him between my breasts—Oh! he was beautiful, Don't leave me ever, please don't, no matter what. His eyes are brown and in them I saw myself. Someday I'll tell him—I will be able to won't I? He mustn't leave me before I can tell him—we'll be close, always as close to each other as we are now. . . . Christopher!

Four days we'll all have together before he has to leave for Minneapolis, just time to take us home from hospital, four days— that's a lot really, and Chris and I weren't alone when he came into the world—when we came down from the delivery room, Leopold was there waiting for us as I had wished. But it doesn't seem that important now. For although I am no longer carrying my child within me I look at him and I am contained, most powerful. We'll be fine, Chris and I, and so will Stan. I've turned a corner.

Pages from a Journal

Washington Christopher is five weeks old and here I am in a hotel again, this time the Raleigh, on a Saturday morning, while the children are at home in New York. I don't quite know why I came, because I didn't want to, but L. wanted me to and here I am. The concert is on Wednesday and then we go on to Toronto, after that Dallas, after that, somewhere, I forget. Last night we made love for the first time after the baby was born. Please God make it be by day as it is by night.

Later: At the last minute, packed, and checking out of the hotel on our way to Toronto, I told him I couldn't. He didn't like it—perhaps you'll meet me in Dallas? he said coldly. No, I want to get back to the baby, to Stan—I want to be home. He had nothing to say to this and as he got into one taxi, I got into another, and now here I am—home.

Florence But May has come and I'm not home. We're in Florence, arriving here via Paris, London before that. We're in Room 161 at the Grand Hotel and L. is happy as can be, and, because he's happy, I'm happy. He's different in Europe, he really is. Apparently the Vanity Fair that exists in America doesn't exist here, for we see people, go to their houses for dinner, lunch even with them in restaurants, and he enjoys these superficial outings, has a good time. Yesterday we went to Berenson's villa then on to Fiesole to meet friends for dinner. The premiere of Gian-Carlo's opera *Amahl and the Night Visitors* which Leopold conducted is a huge success. The Balanchine choreography, everything, was right from the first day of rehearsal, and L. was in such a good mood he even consented to newsreel cameras taking movies of us with Gian-Carlo in front of the opera house. After opening night there was a party given by Violet Trefusses at her Villa L'Ombrelliro. As we sat down for supper in the candlelit banquet hall, Gian-Carlo arrived. Pale with excitement he was held aloft by admirers and carried through the shimmering crowd, the jewels and flowers, to our table. There was much applause and laughter, fevered as we all were by success! triumphant. And L. didn't object, was in fact pleased, when Italian *Vogue* photographed me for the magazine one morning high on a steeple overlooking the Ponte Vecchio, swallows flying in dizzying circles, their cries all around us in the sky. But I was peaceful perched up there, forgetting about the camera, secure daydreaming about L., who would be waiting for me very very soon in the warm cool of our room shuttered against the sun for the hours of siesta. By our bed is a vase holding a most enormous rose, a peach rose, big as the moon. It is from the garden of a thirteenth-century villa belonging to the Seldon-Goths. We went there one day for lunch and when I saw it, drenched in rain, I was drawn into it, speechless. Mrs. Seldon-Goth snapped the branch right off from the bush, right then and there, and presented it to me. And it's there now by the bed in our room—waiting—and I think about that as I sit looking down at the people so tiny and far below. . . . Yes, he's another person when we're in Europe. But there are times, as in the garden when I saw the rose, that I die with the missing of the children.

While he was at rehearsal I sneaked away sometimes to wander the city alone, spend hours at the Uffizi, the Botticelli Room. One day stopped to get a sandwich lunch at the Arno Bar, a surprise to see Tommy Shippers there, alone at a table without Gian-Carlo. We smiled at each other without speaking—two conspirators who had taken a day off. After, I drove across the river to the cemetery on the hill to put flowers on M.B.'s mother's grave. It was untended, vines covering the tombstone. It upset me, thinking of her, Lilly Braggiotti, so loved by her family, but it is put right now, the vines are torn away and shall not choke her again.

Rome Staying at the Hassler. Quite by chance I ran into Harry Cushing, who now lives in Rome—how eerily he resembles his mother, my sister, Cathleen. Tonight we go to Countess Attolico's house in via de San Giovanni a Porta Latina for dinner, and tomorrow Mrs. Luce is having a reception for us at the American Embassy. Yes, in Europe our dance card is more than filled with invitations from Vanity Fair. There wasn't even a moment to see Harry, other than a quick greeting, as we were on our way to the Countess Mercati's for tea. How loving L. is to me, perfect. There is no one in the world his equal. I'm supposed to leave tomorrow but now that I'm going I feel I should be staying. Already the mood of departure is between us as if I'd already left—he wants me to continue on the tour with him to Hamburg, maybe I should? As it is now Harry and Maria Carmela Attolico are taking me to the airport—L. still doesn't want me to fly but I'm going to anyway.

1953–1954

Circling around and around, in and out, torn down the middle, but the more I try to get through to L. the more he shuts me out. It's like he's pushing me, pushing me away, and the more he does the more I fight to get through to him and at the same time hold on to myself, but it's like trying to hold on to something I'm not really sure I have. For although I can't reach *him*, I do reach this place in myself, sometimes, and as I do, something happens, and I get *ambitious*—yes, that's the only way to describe it—ambitious for it, afraid I might lose it. Because to make L. happy and please him, which is all I've ever wanted to do, I have to put this center aside, do everything exactly according to his way. He's away so much and I've started to make a life, so that I'm not suspended, holding my breath while he's gone, unable to breathe again until he comes back. But he resents this—Don't let Vanity Fair fool you! he warns me. I couldn't say this to anyone except you, but he's so damn impervious! so— you know. We were in Mexico once and there was talk of a movie being made there, the life of Jesus, and L. was going to do the music, lots of talk back and forth about casting and who was going to play the part of Jesus. You should, I said to L. (dead serious). He pondered this, giving it careful consideration before nodding—Yes, yes, I will consider it. (And he meant it, he was as dead serious as I was.)

In some ways I wish I hadn't discovered this part of myself, this part I'm ambitious for. Perhaps I wouldn't have if L. had let me get closer to him. Then I wouldn't have by necessity found what was within myself behind this locked door. Because when I felt I was—him, I was fulfilled, happy, and sought naught else. But then something seeped in and I started questioning, not only him but myself . . . started questioning the part of himself he gave me by day, for it was not as it was by night when we make love in that place where no boundaries exist between us. There would come moments when by day I felt on the edge of possessing him, but these moments are lost to me now, they come less and less, and as they do, something dies inside of me. . . . What does come from him is grand and courteous pronouncements, sarcastic but at least mercifully short, almost like he's jealous, although certainly there's no reason for him to be. One thing he does approve of is my work. Right from the beginning, he believed in my talent, took pride in my paintings. Last week Byron Janis came to the house to see L. before they start rehearsal and L. took him on a tour of the house to show him my paintings which hang in every room. L. was excited for me when I had my first show at the Schaeffer Gallery. And in many ways it's because of him that I have come to this point in my work. Yes, he always believed in it. But when it comes to my trying to find out who I really am—he turns away, doesn't understand, doesn't even want to try. It's almost like I'm trying to take something away from him, when my only intent is to give to him. I have so much inside me to give, and it hits and bangs against the brick wall of him and I'm hurt, exhausted with the trying. Yet there are some days, always after a night of love, when I wake believing again, hoping and believing it's all going to be all right, be like it was in the beginning when I thought he trusted me, be like it was in the days before the discovery that he didn't. I know where he failed, but where did I? Because somewhere I know it's all my fault. I asked him and he says the fault is with him. That's the first time he's ever admitted he might not be Perfect. The

children are so little, and it torments me, the atmosphere when he is here as he levitates up onto this throne high on Mount Olympus, far far away from us all. Only sometimes with the children, sometimes a brick comes loose and they get through to him because they are children and he's not suspicious of them, trusts them. I wonder if he will when they grow up. But although he doesn't really trust me, he still wants to possess me body and soul and he does, he does—up until now, that is—and even when he doesn't, somewhere deep inside of me he still does and always will. And so it goes around and around in a circle.

Well, I finally got through to him! at least for the moment. Can't think why I hadn't thought of it before—I cut my hair!!! It was the most amazing feeling sitting there as Mr. Michel's scissors went snip snip snip and it kept falling all around me, until there it was, all in a heap, on the floor. Mr. Michel's assistant was going to sweep it up, but I said, Put it in a bag, please, I'll keep it for old time's sake (ha, ha). Then I walked out onto Fifth Avenue feeling alone but free free free and not one bit scared. Heads turned as I sped along and I felt very sure of myself. Two days later L. got back from Kansas City and I wish I had a snapshot to send you—how he looked when he saw me. He almost had apoplexy, but when he said, It's like taking a beautiful jewel and throwing it into the sea, it really got to me and I knew I'd done a fatal thing. It had taken me six years to grow and he really did love it, my hair, and now it's gone. I went and got the bag it was in and took it right down to the East River outside our house and threw it in. It was a mistake to cut it off, a big mistake, and I wish with all my heart I hadn't done it.

Two Letters

Dear Cousin Eleanor,

It was the most magical evening—*La Forza del Destino*—and I'm still in a spin rather the way Cinderella must have felt after the ball. I'd always heard about opening night at the Metropolitan Opera but had no idea how incredibly glamorous it really is! When we first arrived I must admit I almost fainted when I stood there with you, Cousin Sonny, and Gian-Carlo being photographed by the reporters. There must have been a million of them! I don't know how you do it. But it's fun to see the picture in today's *New York Times* and to have a souvenir of an evening I'll never forget. I look sort of stiff, I think, in the picture (and I was! scared stiff) but can't wait to show it to Leopoldo when he gets back tomorrow from

Urbana. He hates being photographed for anything but his
work and we always avoid it but I hope he'll like this picture.
Anyway he'll see how we all looked and how beautiful you
were in that blue peau de soie and satin dress with the diamond
jewels. Wasn't Milanov superb! I couldn't help thinking
during her final aria, "Pace, pace . . . ," that maybe, here in
the Vanderbilt box, I might be sitting in the very same chair
my father had sat in watching this very same opera but with
another Leonora, spellbound as we were by Verdi's music—
well, I'm going on and on when all I really wanted to say is
thank you for inviting me to a lovely, lovely enchanted evening.

With love to you and Cousin Sonny,

Gloria

P.S. Of course I accept to be on your Committee for the March
of Dimes Benefit Ball—in all the excitement we were interrupted
when you were talking about it.

Dearest Oona,

We just got your cable. What great news! Please give the
baby a kiss from me and of course all our love goes to you
and Charlie. I may go to Europe in April with Leopold who's
conducting at La Scala in Milan (the first concert of the tour),
but we have a week free after and if it works out for you and
Charlie, maybe we could go to Vevey for two days on our
way to Paris? Let me know how this might work out for you,
although I'm still not sure yet if I'll go with him. It's hard to
leave the children. L.'s away so much, but there's nothing to
be done about that and I find myself flirting more and more
with what he calls Vanity Fair. And, of course, he's right.
Still, frivolous though it may be it makes me feel warm to be
in the outside world of people, feel part of the landscape of
this incredible city. And again—frivolous though it may be—
I'm having a lot of fun!

Please write me all your news soon. I'm so happy for you,

Oona, having a baby is the best in the world. I used to want to be pregnant all the time but things happen, things change and now I'm not so sure. Anyway, hope we see each other soon. Leopoldo joins me in sending you and Charlie tons of love.

Gloria

April in New York

The most amazing thing happened!!! Just as I was about to sail with L. on the *Queen Elizabeth* I came down with a cold— for days we'd been embroiled in one silent fight after another (they're the worst) until I said I wasn't going, which made L. settle himself behind that brick wall that puts me bereft of reason each time, although by now I know it so well you'd think it wouldn't, but it does. I was steeling myself for the departure, because part of me wanted to go with him and the other part . . . Well, anyway, the day we were to sail was our wedding anniversary—nine years ago to the day. But I steeled my heart and held on to myself, and as I did a call came from the busy busy Rosie Gaynor who was busy busy with her April in Paris ball, organizing and so on, saying Audrey Hepburn was sick and would I do them a big favor and fill in by being in the pageant at the ball?—something about Gilbert Miller playing Benjamin Franklin and me taking over Audrey's part as John Paul Jones. My nose was stuffed and eyes runny plus I knew L. would have a fit—if I was well enough to get myself rigged up in costume for Vanity Fair I could jolly well make it to the ship so I could traipse all over Europe with him. (Well, he had a point.) I never have a ball at a ball, but I got really caught up in the idea of this, nothing could have stopped me, because I had a strange feeling about it, something I shouldn't miss. So I drank pitcher after pitcher of water with squeezes of lemon juice and the next day when L. left (without saying good-bye) I left for a rehearsal at the Waldorf. Audrey's costume fitted to a tee and my head cleared all at once, suddenly! and the cold just went—like that—scared right out of me. I really was petrified as Gilbert Miller and I marched up, making our entrance from far away at the end of the ballroom, through the crowded tables, until there we were, spotlighted on the dance floor, parading towards the stage. As we approached, Mr. Miller said to me, quite casually, Have you ever thought of going on the stage? Yes, I said quickly. Yes, yes, I have. There's a play, he said, a play you'd be right for, by Molnár, called *The Swan*. By then we were on the steps almost up onto the stage—If you're really interested call me at the office, maybe try it out in stock this summer. I still can't believe it, or believe he's serious. He's probably forgotten by now and I'm certainly not going to make a fool of myself by calling him. But anyway, I'll never forget that it did happen, and I just couldn't wait to write it all down.

Waited and waited thinking maybe he'd call me—but of course he didn't. Couldn't sleep over it. Then a few days ago I was walking on Fifth Avenue past a phone booth and thought, Suppose he has forgotten, that's the worst that could happen, and I took out a nickel and called his office. No! he hadn't forgotten! not at all—and yesterday I had a meeting with him at his office and met George Banyai, his business manager, who's going to organize the production and see who'll be interested in booking it in a theatre this summer. It's late in the season, but there are some openings still in August. There are other plays you might consider, George said—*Sabrina Fair* or *The Lady's Not for Burning*, also T. S. Eliot's *The Cocktail Party*—there's a good part for you in that. But no, I stay by what Gilbert thought of for me, and *The Swan* it is to be. Of course I'm scared to death, but Dick Bender, who's going to direct the production, is going to start working with me on it right away. He's Gilbert's stage manager, and by the time we start rehearsing with the cast I'll know the play by heart and the blocking of it. I really can't believe all this is happening. I wish Carol wasn't so far away so

I could talk to her. I keep wondering what's happening and if she is really all right. Does she still see so much of Bill, or has she met someone else? I hope so but feel she hasn't, otherwise I'd know about it.

1954

July 18 I find myself almost wishing that he wasn't arriving tomorrow, wishing this because he will break into my life—for I have a life and it is *The Swan*. I have been unable to paint, unable to write, consumed by a sense of purpose which will come into being August 16, the day the play opens in Pennsylvania. Already my lines are part of me, already the play is blocked, and yesterday I started rehearsing with Peter Donat, who will play the part of the Tutor. The others in the cast I have met, but we will not work together until we meet in rehearsal a week before the play opens. Margaret Bannerman is to be my mother—she is known as Bunny and has been in the English theatre, as has Halliwell Hobbs who will play Father Hyacinth. The other parts are yet to be cast. As salary I am to take the eighty-five-dollar Actors' Equity minimum with a percentage of the gross at the end of each week. So it's all set, nothing can stop it now. Gilbert Miller is in Europe for the summer but seems most interested in all that's going on. I hear from George Banyai that he loves this play and has wanted to revive it ever since the original production when Eva Le Gallienne played Princess Alexandra, which is now to be my part. I sense in his tone that maybe, maybe—if I'm a success, this could become a Gilbert Miller production. Yes, tomorrow Leopold will be home. The children have grown in the three months he's been gone, but when I told them he'll be home tomorrow, tomorrow is only a word and it will only have reality when they see him. But I know what tomorrow means—it means protecting myself so that he will not take me from the precious concentration to which I dedicate myself. I want to be touched by nothing and no one but my work.

July 19   His arrival was calm, most calm. The mood of Europe still upon him. I find it hard to be calm. He has no interest at all in *The Swan*, does not believe in it. He's so forceful I borderline panic as if he's going to take the play away from me, do something so it will all vanish, before it has come to be. Even with the children I get afraid—it's like he's competing with me for them. Or is fear distorting my senses? After dinner we went to a movie, *The Wild One*. Marlon Brando's in it and he's quite something, makes you feel that you and only you can reach through to his inarticulate sensitivity. I was strangely affected by it . . . "Go, go . . . go!" symbol of our time. L. didn't think much of him or any of it, just didn't get it, and we walked home without talking—two strangers on an empty street in a hazy New York summer night. But later, in the dark, he came to me and all was as before, as it was when we first met. All else forgotten and we were no longer strangers.

July 20   But at daybreak—it was not forgotten. I must leave this atmosphere as soon as I can. I cannot work. I am stifled. Just now reading a story to Stan on the bed, he breaks into our mood, starts pulling him into a game of roughhouse. Fine, but let me finish the story, OK? But he doesn't answer and it's not, it's not OK at all.

The *New York Times* has asked Albert Hirschfeld to do a drawing of me for the Sunday theatre section. He came to the house and looked and looked at me in a most perceptive manner as he did a few squiggles, here and there, on a pad, which I was hoping to see but didn't. I'll have to wait, I guess, until I see it in the paper.

Later: Then over tea L. and I started talking, quite calmly, about such as we who want to be dedicated and have no place for love in the sense I wanted it. I apologized for all the years I didn't understand. I do now and I want what he does—but for myself. We will get along fine.

July 29   Alone drove to Mountainhome. On the seat next to me *Life* magazine with Gordon Parks's picture of me in the Worth costume for the play. Suspended, waiting till rehearsals start.

August 10   The Naomi Cottages where I'm staying are near to the Pocono Playhouse, my cottage cozy as could be, complete with fireplace and a kitchen (not much in use as we have most meals in the actors' dining room next to the theatre). Although it is summer the leaves are already tinged with autumn and the scent of change is in the air. As I went on the stage for the first time the light was warm and I was less afraid. The theatre is very much like a family, a family that holds together with undercurrents, passions, fights, and makeups, very much like families in the real life, but here in this make-believe family it is safe, perhaps because it is temporary and we are bound together only for as long as the play lasts and because of this, there is less chance of being hurt. Maybe. When you already know the end of something you can't lose it. But then the play closes —And what will poor robin do then, poor thing? There should be the next one to look forward to, but I have this feeling hovering over me that when *The Swan* is over, even if I am a success in it, my life will be over forever and I'll never work again. So I must make the most of this moment—now—the center of myself concentrated, dedicated. From now on this shall be put first.

August 11   Yes, we are all a family—a unit. It is as if we have taken the veil. We stand together in the trust of our craft. I have so much to learn, so far to go. Please, God, make me worthy.

August 12   Peter Donat and I drove to Buck Hill Falls. He took my hand as we crossed a brook and we sat on a bridge talking as it got dark. He's my romance in the play and I get caught up in this as a reality, a need almost to make the fantasy real. Later I cooked dinner and his warmth and sweetness touched me. L. hasn't said anything about coming to see me in the play. I'm glad. I really am. As if he did—he'd take it away from me. But

as I say this, pain shoots through me—a year ago this thought would have been inconceivable!

August 13   Inspired by P.D.'s beauty, wanting nothing from it, and yet I find myself at moments—expecting. But it's all part of the play and the scenes we have together, using reality to create fantasy, or is it vice versa?

August 15   Dress rehearsal. The edge of breaking this morning. Then I go searching for Peter and seeing him and the world we have created together in the play has reality, quiets me, restores. Later D.B. says, I want you to give a real actressy performance. I'll do my best, my best my best.

August 16   *Opening Night:* The knock on the door—"Half-hour, Miss Vanderbilt"—the waiting to get onstage—agony, tense in wrist and ankles . . . and then—caught up in light, feeling the audience with me—and the love coming to me in applause, applause, applause—and Peter, just before we take places for our curtain calls, the look of love he gives me, the warmth of the cast, the flowers spilling out of my dressing room. And the party after. What a family we are—jubilant, celebrating Christmas!

August 17   We're a hit! a hit! a hit! Sitting on my bed next morning and the knock on the door. Dick B. with candy, trembling with excitement—"They are ready for you!" Fulfilled—I have not failed him.

August 18   Matinee today and the warm thrilling response. The people who came back afterwards. The deep happiness and satisfaction. A warmth I've never known before from so many. Dick B.'s triumph and my joy. It is what I longed for.

August 19 Deluged with things I don't know how to handle. Need an agent, but got put off after Stephen Draper hot-footed it up here with a contract all filled out ready for Gloria Vanderbilt Stokowski to sign (Stokowski indeed!). George Banyai says, Wait, wait, wait until you meet an agent you have rapport with. He suggests Kay Brown or Gloria Safier. Meet them both, he says, and then decide—remember, signing up with an agent is like a marriage.

August 20   Cora Witherspoon came backstage after performance last night. Acting—is like a pitcher pouring water, she said, and then she went on telling me the riveting news that she and my father had once had a romance!—How he would have loved tonight! she said, and as she did, it was as if he had sent her—a message and a benediction. The lost feeling at night later as if it had never happened and the call to Leopold to see if he existed.

August 22   After performance drove all night to be with the children on Stan's birthday. L. was cold, impossible to reach. No interest at all in seeing the play. But I willed myself to tune him out and the time with Stan and Chris made me think it's worth anything to make them feel we'll all be together, that nothing will change.

August 23   Drive to the Cape to rehearse before opening at Richard Aldrich's Falmouth Playhouse. Must concentrate on my work more completely so that I channel what I have to give. There is no room in the life I want for the kind of love I once longed for.

August 27   Long talk with Hobby over part. Feel on the edge of expressing what I want. Moments of the old need again, longing for love and wanting to give to L. But all of this must be put into my work.
Later: Drive to the beach with Peter and after we got to see Marlon Brando in *Waterfront*. Tremendously moved and inspired by him. The concentration, emotion that struggles to articulate in words but instead projects from depth of soul.

August 28   Building a fantasy life around M.B. Suddenly P.D. seems limited in range and his lack of fire—exasperating. I must concentrate and give all to my work. I must be worthy.

August 29 Edward Chodorov comes back after performance. Asks me to be the lead in the touring company of his play *Oh, Men! Oh, Women!* Pleased to be asked, but there's gossip that since our success Gilbert Miller is seriously thinking about touring *The Swan* before bringing it to Broadway. Dick Bender leaves us all tomorrow on his way to London to stage-manage Graham Greene's play *The Living Room* before it comes to New York with Barbara Bel Geddes. It's as if Daddy's leaving us, the beginning of the end—for soon it will be over and we will be saying goodbye. I'll be home soon, I tell the children—then L. gets on the phone, cold and distant.

August 30   Hurricane warnings. Tonight's performance canceled. We gather in my cottage with pink candles, for all the lights are out. Rain pours, and the wind! You know, Marlon Brando stayed in this cottage when he was here with *Candida*, someone says. I think about that. . . . Really? I said. Yes, right here in this same cottage. Later I was unable to sleep as the rain fell on the roof in the dark night, making me think, as it always does, of Winter Smith and the rain as it fell on the roof of the cottage at Old Westbury Capital as he held me close and we loved each other in a dark night long ago. . . .

August 31   It gets dark earlier now that summer's coming to an end and the beach was in shadow, quite suddenly, as Peter and I sat talking about the play and how soon that will be over too, soon we are to part, all of us who have been so close these past weeks. But I want none of it to change. If Gilbert does tour the play I want us all to be together, no new members of the family. Soon, in a few days, Peter tells me, his girlfriend, Martine Bartlett, is coming here to be with him and see our last performances—our first and last invasion.

September 1   No lights, no performance. Suddenly lights go on and we go on in half-hour. Bad performance, nothing clicking.

September 2   Bad matinee. Good evening performance. Everything suddenly moving. Judy comes to see the play—her warmth. Hear Aunt Gertrude's daughter, my cousin Barbara, also in the audience, but she didn't come back to see me. Martine B. arrives. Feel nothing. I work better when not involved. I must work harder. Give more.

September 4   Play closes. On the drive back to New York Bunny Bannerman had a most frightful hangover, we had to make numerous stops along the way for milkshakes and Baby Ruths and got caught up in late-day traffic. It was hot and the

Baby Ruths kept melting in their wrappings. There is something touching about her, only tenderness and comfort should surround her always and lots of Baby Ruths and milkshakes. The farewells, the hugs and kisses, good-bye good-bye, and oh, will we ever ever work again?

September 6   On the drive back from Falmouth to Gracie Square I couldn't get my mother out of my head. I kept thinking about her although up until then I hadn't, at least I don't think I had—except the day after the opening night I did wonder (but only for a second) if she'd heard about it—about my success in the play. *That* would impress her. Or would it? Well, I was thin, that's for sure, thin as thin could be. Asked Dick Bender if I looked thin onstage. Thin? he said. Thin! Why you couldn't be thinner! So there, Mama! That'll show you. But show her what? Show her I was thin, I guess. As for the Little Countess and Big Elephant—thin was naught to them, and the only thing that would ever impress them really would be for me to wed His Richness the Emperor of Timbuktu and do nothing for the rest of my life. I can't make them understand the feeling I have, a feeling that if the pain and chaos inside me break free, if I can give form and permanence to them, some kind of—order, yes, that's it, order—I will (there is no other way to say this) put the things that happened long ago—Right! It's behind all that I do—far back as wanting to be an actress when I was fourteen, but when I talked to Aunt Gertrude about it I couldn't make her understand, and I certainly can't make Leopold understand now, about acting, can't make him understand that in each part I play maybe I'll find pieces of myself. And it's only the beginning, because I'm just starting to find out who I really am. I thought in Leopold I had found myself, but it doesn't work. I keep holding on hoping tomorrow it will, but now it's only in my work that I feel safe, and the play that has absorbed me these past months is part of this, drives me on thirsting for more. But there are times when the great love Leopold and I had for each other comes over me still, and I am pulled back to it, so that what I call the honest I of silent place contracts into a tight star, short-circuited once again because I don't believe in myself yet. It is only when I concentrate my energy towards some great thing that I trust myself. Leopoldo was this great thing, or so I believed, and—nothing could have prevented my leaving Pat-Pasquale to be with him—nothing! After that fatal meeting I dedicated myself to him and in the doing I merged with him, became him. But when I came to know that he had not let me into the final place of his heart, I knew that this great thing I had come to believe in wasn't real, knew that it wasn't true and that I too must close myself to him, find my way alone. I used to think I would die before I reached thirty (it seemed so impossibly far away, somewhere in infinity), so I'd have to hurry hurry. But now I am thirty! And I feel I'm going to live forever and ever. And the force of this knowledge starts fighting against the force of Leopold's will, as if we are in some deadly competition I am compelled to win, for now that some great thing is not him, it is my work.

Later: After I wrote in my journal today I read the entry for the exact same day a year ago—September 6—and it said: I pray L. and I are together for a long long time.

Marlon Brando keeps coming into my thoughts—yes, I think about him a lot—the way he is in *Waterfront*. Is he really like that, or is he an actor playing a part?

I'll never let you go, Leopold said when I got back. And because he says it—I believe it. But the raging in my soul doesn't accept it, something will happen, it must, or I'll explode and die and there will be nothing left of me but my spirit, which will be forgotten because it has not yet come to be. And so I am back again right where I was before I did the play, before the world opened up and I saw the golden ring on a carousel high up in the sky. . . . It goes around and around as it glitters in and out of sight, and I go around and around after it, reaching up, trying to catch it.

Phone Calls

We started talking on the phone, Carol and I, the week after I got back after the play closed. I feel in limbo, bereft with missing the closeness we'd all had working together—Dick Bender, Bunny and Peter, Hobby, dear Hobby—all scattered now, our theatre family, with a new season beginning, and wondering just like me when we'll ever work again. Please come, Carol said, I need you. I need you too, I said. There's so much I don't understand. I feel that something I've always wanted is just within reach—but now that it's here, I'm not sure what it is. It makes no sense, does it? Maybe because I still believe Leopold is it. But how can it be when the wall of bricks has turned to glass and we now face each other each day straining to see what the other looks like, mouths open, our lips move but no sound is heard, no words take shape, no answers given? How can there be, when there are no questions? We inhabit a strange and alien land—or are we enemies in a dark sea, for even in the nights when we make love we are silent in the seizure of drowning as we fight each to possess the soul of the other? But even if I win, even if I did possess his soul, he would be the victor—for I would have lost mine. And who is *he*? For it has come to this—I now no longer recognize my enemy. Yes! All has changed, nothing is the same—or was it always so? I'm so deep in it I no longer know, all I know is that when I wake it's with foreboding—something is going to happen, something terrible—it has to. But at the same time in another part of me I know it will set me free—free to find out who I am and where I'm going. I've met someone, Carol said—Kenneth Tynan. Who's he? I said. Well, you'll hear of him, darling, he's a theatre critic in London, quite brilliant, and he's coming soon to work in New York. He wants me to go to Spain with him, only he's married, and then there's Bill (there's always Bill). Today's Friday, I said. I'll be with you tomorrow.

Mermaids

Sweetest Angel Carol,

It was life-giving to see you, talk to you, be with you those hours we talked on and on, me about L. and you about Bill and Ken Tynan—I keep thinking about what you said, how you believe there is the one for the one in the world, and I used to believe that when I met L., but now I'm not so sure, still in some absurd way I get into a fantasy that if some incredible person loved me I would have the strength to break away from L., his power no longer claim me because another power greater than his would take possession of my soul. And even knowing, in my head, moving away from one power only to be absorbed by another isn't what I want, that what I really want is not to be absorbed by anybody but to be myself . . . still it doesn't stop me. Pain and confusion that I still want something I know doesn't exist—because I know in my heart that I'm never going to find it except in my work. But Carol, that's not really what I want to say to you. That day we drove to Malibu, to Bill's, so you could pick up his laundry— darling, you must leave there, you must leave your car and the driving back and forth to clean his house and cook for him. You have divorced him for the second time, you are *not* married to him anymore—it's *over*—you must leave—you *must*. And I'll help you. You can stay with me in New York—at my studio. You can write there, finish the book you've started, the theatre is there too—I'll find an agent for us both, you've always wanted to act again ever since you were in that Princeton production of Bill's play *Across the Board on Tomorrow Morning*—something will happen so that you will make a life

on your own. You must do this, otherwise you are going to
end up half dead and if you do—so will I. I'll never forget
Lucy that day we were at Bill's when we went swimming in
the ocean, how she clung to me as the waves hit against us,
calling me her "mermaid." I feel she's on the edge of
shattering, she has the delicacy of glass—and so do you and it
must not happen. It will *not*. Please, darling, I'll do anything
to get through to you. You must listen to me. Bill is your
nemesis and destruction if you stay there. He's mad, he really
is and he'll destroy you if you let him. But he has me to
contend with and I won't let it happen. Darling, we're about
to land. I'll call you soon as I can but I wanted to put this on
paper to you so you have to read it over and over again, *please*.
And about Ken T.—come to N.Y. first, settle in the studio,
then meet him in Spain knowing you have a place, a home,
to come back to and a *life*—for that's what it's going to be,
I promise you—

I love you
Gloria

The Girl Next Door

After the meeting with Gloria Safier I'm starting to have
doubts and keep wondering if I'm doing the right thing. Something tells me I'm not—but she knows the theatre and I don't.
We met at Michael's Pub and I liked her right away, but that's
not really why I said yes! so fast when she said she'd like to be
my agent. I said it because I'm desperate to get things moving
and be working again. Now there's no need to meet Kay Brown,
the other agent George Banyai suggested might be right for me.
I just wish G. Safier had seen me in *The Swan*, but she didn't,
and maybe that's why she's so against my touring in it. The very
day after I met her George called to say that Gilbert was all set
to commence production plans and we'd tour before coming to

Broadway. Even Jean Dalrymple wants to do a production here in New York at City Center with our original cast. Don't do it, G. Safier said, you don't want to be a Princess, you want to be the girl next door. Do I? Maybe she's right, maybe that is what I want to be. But I'm not all that sure. What does that mean anyway—June Allyson? But, as I keep telling myself, she knows all about the theatre and I know nothing, absolutely nothing, so she must be right. Wait, don't do *The Swan*, wait wait, she keeps saying, I'll get something better for you. But the days go by, and although she does call me every single day because she knows I'm desperate, desperate to work, so far they're just pep-talk calls, saying hold on and wait wait wait wait because she's working on it. And because I'm not working, the scenes L. and I go through almost every day now are more terrible than they have ever been, but it's the children that tear me apart. Last week he said, You will stay with or without, it matters not, I'll never give you a divorce. And that *is* the law, no divorce without mutual consent. But I've heard that before, and then the next day he'll go off on tour and I'll get a letter from him a few days later just like nothing ever happened because, of course, we made love the night before he left.

Well, the usual daily call came from G. Safier but this time she had news! Otto Preminger is going to direct a television special, a trilogy of Noel Coward plays: *Red Peppers, Shadow Play*, and *Brief Encounter*. Ginger Rogers, Trevor Howard, and Gig Young are to star, and he's interested in me for the part of Sybil in *Shadow Play*. I donned my October tweeds and put on my new maroon flat-heeled Delmans and off G. and I went to his suite at the St. Regis Hotel for the interview. They chatted around a bit while I listened and after a while he beckoned G. Safier to follow him into another room, leaving me to contemplate the Vertès reproductions on the walls. All the blond girls looked like Carol and all the dark-haired girls looked like me. Then they returned and it was time to go. As soon as we got out into the hall and started towards the elevator G. said, You got the part. I hugged her and wanted to scream with joy but I controlled myself. But, she said, he said, "She's got to be sexy," so I told him, "She's sexy, she's sexy." Oh yes! I said, I *am* sexy, as sexy as sexy can be, tell him to just wait, I'll be the sexiest girl next door you ever did see! And I will I will I will and I'm alive again because rehearsals start next week.

The Mirror

Late this afternoon when I got back from rehearsal L. was as usual sitting behind his desk in the library, dictating letters to Miss Swenson. When he's home that's what he does most of the day, dictates letters in answer to the vast network of correspondence that he receives. There must be millions and trillions of letters, here or there, in files, or drawers, or wastebaskets, all over the world, with that soaring signature of his I love so well, for he not only answers every letter he receives, he also dictates spur-of-the-moment letters to people he doesn't know, complimenting them about this or that. One of his favorite opening phrases is "In my opinion"—before going on to give it in that Western Union manner, a way of commenting on himself which fits into the overall picture he presents to the outside world. As for the inside world—nothing has changed. I stood in the hall listening and remembered a letter he had dictated soon after we were married, a letter to Wallace Stevens because of a poem of his I had read, a poem I admired, how thrilled I had been when, by return post, a letter had come from Wallace Stevens himself. How important it had made me feel, how important I had felt the day L. had dictated the letter all because of me. But now as I heard his voice as he measured out the words, oh so slowly, but without hesitation, the sound filled me with despair.

. . .

There was this bird, long ago, caught in the elevator shaft at my Grandmother Vanderbilt's house on Fifth Avenue. Big Elephant had taken me there to visit, but I don't remember much about it except the sound of this bird which had somehow gotten into the elevator shaft and couldn't get out. It kept flapping flapping in the dark, the sound of its wings came to us as it crashed back and forth against the narrow walls, and although the elevator was far down the hall of the vast house, its screeching came to us as we sat in the living room with my grandmother. On and on it came to us, beseeching for help, terrible to hear. But suddenly, just like that, it stopped, and my Grandmother said, Oh, they must have found a way to set the bird free. When Big Elephant and I left soon after, as we walked down the marble hall towards the elevator, two men were there ahead of us, hovering around, but as we came near they turned away, covering something with a towel. Don't look, lovey, Big Elephant said, moving faster, tugging at my hand, don't look. But I did and it was the bird, all bloody and smashed, one wing on its body, the other held up in the other man's hand, its neck broken, the beak open, oh! so open, set forever into a soundless screech. Yes, if I don't get free, I'll die.

I lean my body full against the cold glass, palms open, for this wall of glass is made of ice and my body melts through it to him. Only it doesn't and I press harder, fists tight, and with foot kick, kick against the wall. He stands there looking at me, but something is wrong, and it comes to me that perhaps tears have distorted my vision, but then I come to see that it is not a brick wall, nor is it a wall of ice I batter against. It is a mirror I stand behind, a two-way mirror so that I see him as he stands there, a pillar of ice, but on the side he stands the mirror is reversed and it is his own image that is reflected back to him. It is not that he does not want to listen—it is that he cannot, for he was set and frozen in himself long long ago, long before he met me, nothing for him has changed, it is I who have. I scream, throwing myself against the frozen glass, my body scorching through, the shards of mirror killing me in front of his eyes, but instead we stand face to face quite silent, separated by this mirrored wall of ice, no longer flat but curving closer, so slowly it moves, but soon it will surround me and I start choking, unable to breathe, and although I can still see him through the mirror as he stands on the other side, he sees only himself, but I keep pounding on the glass which is now curved all around me, still trying to reach him, unable to get out get out get out. . . .

The Bridge

The phone can ring and your whole life can change. It was Gloria Safier saying Jule Styne had called her—Frank Sinatra was in New York and wanted to meet me. Was I interested? It jolted me. Yes, it did, because even with L. away so much this past year and even though I had made a little life for myself when he was away, a life of which he was not the center—still he *was*. And as G. said this, I wanted to have it unsaid—wanted to run to him, pound through to him, *will* him to look at me, listen to me—see me. Are you interested? she kept saying. Are you are you? Stop! I wanted to scream. But I didn't.

I'd met him once before—backstage, remember?—the summer L. and I were married, at the Hollywood Bowl after L.'s opening-night concert. But that didn't count. It didn't count because he didn't exist for me, no one did then. I was veiled, and others existed in my thoughts only as people permitted to stand in Leopold's presence. Now it was different—in an instant everything had changed, and all I could think of was whether I was thin enough, thin enough to meet him. Maybe if I had a week, even a few days to go on a diet. . . . But I haven't—it's tonight.

. . .

And it's almost dawn now of that night and I haven't slept. It's like being on a roller coaster, unable to make it stop, unable to jump off even if I wanted to. Somewhere, still, I know that Leopold loves me, truly does . . . we are together tied, yes, body and soul—that no matter what happens we always will be. But he, that most suspicious of men, is always—at the fatal moment, finally—afraid to trust, and that is why I abandon hope, lose faith that he believed in the innocence and truth of my love. But have I? For somewhere hidden I know that he does believe, and this is the place I keep trying to reach in day as I do in darkness when we touch without words, when words would invade—be unthinkable. Why can that not be enough? Then other moments come to me (so many): how articulate he is in his belief in my painting, the strength he gives me—how will it be when he is no longer there? But then—back again, circling to the other times I've tried to get through to him, make him understand the changes happening inside of me—times when he only hears what he wants to hear. He can't listen—it's hard for him . . . ah yes! Vanity Fair—all too true, but that's not what I mean and so we are pulled asunder as, more and more, hopeless I turn away, outward towards a world that waits for me (but does it?), a world where I would be free to try the things I *must* . . . and to be free at last of this longing to possess him, never again to strain trying to break through the impenetrable wall of him—wouldn't that be the final freedom? I wonder if Frank's asleep? Soon he'll call, soon I'll see him again. This meeting comes to me as some kind of mirage, an answer to questions I have no name for. The room's filled with that unearthly half-light—as if it were twilight, only it's not, it's dawn—and I lie here going over what's happened since the phone rang . . .

It was all arranged through the intermediaries, G. and Jule, that we were to meet at 7:30—but where? Not here, I said, not here, no, I don't want him to meet me here. And I told G.

quickly that I'd be at Fern Gimbel's cocktail party and he could meet me there. Now I hadn't intended to go to this gathering, but it fitted right into the meeting. Yes, everything was fitting into place, speeding along on its inevitable course. And so I went, shaking inside, trembly after dieting all day, planning to arrive late, instead getting there early, much too early, moving around the crowded room holding my breath through eternities until I couldn't stand it another second and I put my coat on and went down to the lobby. As the elevator door opened, way in the distance the door on Park Avenue opened and a man entered, a man who walked past the doorman towards me without hesitation, down the long hall we walked towards each other, quickly, then faster and faster and there we were face to face. Although he had not waved, it was as if he had, from far away, waved in secret signal. It was what I had been waiting for . . . Now it's dawn, no mistaking it, as strips of light pattern themselves across the river in palest apricot fading into aqua on up into the sky, and soon it will be day.

I'm seeing him again tonight, and all day, even though I got no sleep, instead of being tired I feel high, like I'm taking deep drafts of some kind of rare oxygen that connects not with another *person* but with an unknown place in myself. This place is strong, a fortress even, yes! Because when I'm inside that place I have the courage to be free. Ah, but is it mine? Last night, there we were in one of those long limousines, black, too black—you know the kind, more hearse than car—Joan Blondell on the seat beside me, and facing us on jump seats, padded and ample as fireside armchairs, sat Frank and a silent, listening sort of person called Jimmy Cannon. Who are these people and why am I here? But that only flashed across my brain, an image of sudden light, as we drove on past the dark trees through Central Park—it was gone in an instant, and there we were again, four shadowy people with shadowy lights from the passing cars now and again gently washing over us. Later we had supper together—Jimmy Cannon

ever listening, Joan Blondell talking talking. It was then he turned to me and said that he'd thought about me, wanted to see me again, ever since that night he'd watched me in the audience at the concert, how I'd looked at Leopold as he conducted, my eyes never leaving him. I winced, for I remember it well. But I had pushed it out of my mind, as I must do now.

There is a moment of peril . . . the flash of Leopold's face as it came to me when we first looked upon each other and my eyes became—his. If I could see him *now*, go back to that instant, I would not leave. I'd understand and so would he—all erased, back as it was. God, help me.

Frank is to be here in New York for three weeks. Then he goes to Australia. Three weeks is the time given to me. In this time I must move, move fast. Soon it will be Christmas, Leopold will be back, this is my last chance. If I am to do this I mustn't think beyond it, and though I can't imagine a long tomorrow with F. and me in it, I have to try to believe this is what I've been searching for—the great thing that will lead to my own life. I cling to my children and keep telling myself it's easier for them, easier for them if L. and I separate now when they are so little, if it has to be—better now than later. But *is* it? I'm hurling towards something, half-conscious, thinking less and less, pushed along by instinct and feeling, blood drives me, masters me, pushes me along. I am strong because a person of power loves me—no longer will I be trapped in this death struggle L. and I are in. I could never do this without someone powerful behind me, and in three weeks when he's gone, by then it won't matter, won't matter if I never see him again. He is the bridge, the bridge to set me free.

Epilogue

Now, today, in this moment—thirty years later—I remember one time Leopold and I were in Ascona. We were sitting under a grape arbor in the late-afternoon sunlight, lingering over one of those long lunches we used to enjoy, and he'd said, Forgive me for my shortcomings. It was a surprise then, and it is a surprise now, as I remember it so many years later. It was so unlike him to say that. . . . In some funny way, now that he is dead, I feel sorry that he was unable to break out of himself. I think that he may even have tried once or twice, but he just couldn't, and there was no set of circumstances that could ever make that right. Yet it is also true that I would have died if we hadn't gotten married, I wanted him so badly, I loved him so much, and nothing in the world could have prevented our coming together— just as nothing in the world could have prevented our parting as we did. Things happen because it is impossible for them to happen in any other way, and it astonishes me that once again the love I had for him has come back to me as it was in the beginning. . . . With time, bitterness and pain gently slipped away, and a mysterious loving light shines strongly through the crystal of memory. Because as I have come to understand myself—I have also come to understand him.

My mother too I have come to understand: she never really knew one single thing that ever happened to her, she always lived off someone else's smile. And although I still search for her, and part of me probably always will, it is an ache I have learned to live with, and we have found, she and I, a place of peace where we rest together: closer perhaps in death than we ever were in life. Aunt Gertrude is another matter—little has changed, and I find myself no nearer to her now than I was then, and she remains in this way fixed within me. My Grandmother Naney Morgan has been long gone, but it is only now that I can bring myself to visit her grave. "Ah, darling mine," I hear her saying, ". . . when I'm in my grave!" Perhaps when the warm weather comes I'll go, but when I do it will not be to say good-bye, it will be to greet her, for somewhere I have never stopped loving her as I did before all the terrible things happened—after all (as she would say), she is "my own flesh and blood." I do think she was beset by demons which unbalanced her and drove her so that she was compelled to transfer the power she had wanted for herself onto me. It was energy misplaced; had it been directed elsewhere, perhaps it would not have destroyed.

And last I come to Dodo—the saddest of all these sad things. When I was a child, she gave me the love of a mother, but when I grew up it was hard for her to do this; perhaps some mothers can love their young only when they are that. As the years passed, my life went in directions different from the ones she had in mind, and it ended badly and it broke my heart. In many ways it happened for the same reason that Leopold and I ended as we did: she never did tell me the truth. But then I never asked her to.

It's taken me a long time to get from the child I was once upon a time to the person I am today. Yet it is a paradox that the child I was long ago still lives within me—only now she is no longer afraid. No longer afraid, for I trust myself. If the Black Knight came into my life today, I would not need a White Knight to rescue me—I would rescue myself.

ILLUSTRATIONS

(All photographs not otherwise credited are from the author's private collection)